D0208726

106 MORTGAGE SECRETS ALL HOMEBUYERS MUST LEARN – But Lenders Don't Tell

GARY W. ELDRED

WILEY

John Wiley & Sons, Inc.

Copyright © 2003 by Gary W. Eldred. All rights reserved.

Published by John Wiley & Sons, Inc., Hoboken, New Jersey.
Published simultaneously in Canada.

No part of this publication may be reproduced, stored in a retrieval system, or transmitted in any form or by any means, electronic, mechanical, photocopying, recording, scanning, or otherwise, except as permitted under Section 107 or 108 of the 1976 United States Copyright Act, without either the prior written permission of the Publisher, or authorization through payment of the appropriate per-copy fee to the Copyright Clearance Center, Inc., 222 Rosewood Drive, Danvers, MA 01923, (978) 750-8400, fax (978) 750-4470, or on the web at www.copyright.com. Requests to the Publisher for permission should be addressed to the Permissions Department, John Wiley & Sons, Inc., 111 River Street, Hoboken, NJ 07030, (201) 748-6011, fax (201) 748-6008, e-mail: permcoordinator@wiley.com.

Limit of Liability/Disclaimer of Warranty: While the publisher and author have used their best efforts in preparing this book, they make no representations or warranties with respect to the accuracy or completeness of the contents of this book and specifically disclaim any implied warranties of merchantability or fitness for a particular purpose. No warranty may be created or extended by sales representatives or written sales materials. The advice and strategies contained herein may not be suitable for your situation. The publisher is not engaged in rendering professional services, and you should consult a professional where appropriate. Neither the publisher not author shall be liable for any loss of profit or any other commercial damages, including but not limited to special, incidental, consequential, or other damages.

For general information on our other products and services please contact our Customer Care Department within the United States at (800) 762-2974, outside the United States at (317) 572-3993 or fax (317) 572-4002.

Wiley also publishes its books in a variety of electronic formats. Some content that appears in print may not be available in electronic books. For more information about Wiley products, visit our web site at www.Wiley.com.

Library of Congress Cataloging-in-Publication Data:

Eldred, Gary W.
106 mortgage secrets all homebuyers must learn—but lenders don't tell / Gary W. Eldred.
p. cm.
Includes bibliographical references and index.
ISBN 0-471-26395-8 (pbk.)
1. Mortgage loans. 2. Mortgages. 3. Housing–Finance. I. Title: One hundred six mortgage secrets all homebuyers must learn—but lenders don't tell. II. Title.

HG2040.15 .E43 2003
332.7′22—dc21 2002191060

Printed in the United States of America

10 9 8 7 6 5 4 3

Contents

Introduction: Will You Pay Too Much for Too Little? **ix**

1 Affordability Depends on You—Not the Lender 1

SECRET **#1** Affordability depends on you. 4
SECRET **#2** How you choose your property and arrange financing will add (or subtract) tens (or even hundreds) of thousands of dollars to (from) your net worth. 6
SECRET **#3** Separate the emotional from the financial. 8
SECRET **#4** Align your self-talk with your priorities. 10
SECRET **#5** Don't focus on the kind of home you want now. Focus on the kind of home you want 5, 10, or 15 years from now. 16

2 Increase Your Borrowing Power 19

SECRET **#6** 10,000 lenders set their own standards. 19
SECRET **#7** You can make your qualifying ratios look better. 22
SECRET **#8** You can lift your qualifying income. 25
SECRET **#9** Reduce your disqualifying debt. 29
SECRET **#10** Use compensating factors to justify higher qualifying ratios. 31
SECRET **#11** Never fib to a lender. 33

SECRET #12 Can't qualify on your own? Enlist the help of a cosigner, co-borrower, or co-owner. 36
SECRET #13 Let tenants pay your mortgage. 38
SECRET #14 Don't change your loan status. 46

3 Slash Your Cost of Interest 47

SECRET #15 Most borrowers who want a long-term fixed-rate loan should choose 15 years, not 30. 48
SECRET #16 Lower interest rates mean big savings. 52
SECRET #17 Lower rates magnify borrowing power. 53
SECRET #18 ARMs can offer greater borrowing power, lower costs, with manageable risk. 55
SECRET #19 State and local housing finance agencies offer low-interest mortgage bond loans. 57
SECRET #20 Assume a low-interest-rate mortgage. 59
SECRET #21 "Assume" a nonassumable mortgage. 62
SECRET #22 Save $1,000s with a Mortgage Credit Certificate (MCC). 66
SECRET #23 Seek employer assistance, or seek an employer who gives assistance. 67
SECRET #24 Trade off points for a lower interest rate. 69
SECRET #25 Negotiate a temporary buydown with the sellers. 70
SECRET #26 New home builders offer mortgage incentives. 71
SECRET #27 How to borrow jumbo amounts without paying jumbo rates. 72
SECRET #28 Your after-tax cost of borrowing may not be as low as you've been told. 75

4 The Risks and Rewards of ARMs 79

SECRET #29 ARMs do not necessarily present more risk than fixed-rate loans. 79
SECRET #30 For the short-term ARMs usually prove best. 84

SECRET #31 ARMs for the long run: How to lower costs and alleviate risk. 87
SECRET #32 You can (sort of) forecast interest rates. 88
SECRET #33 Watch out for low teaser rates. 91
SECRET #34 Your start (teaser) rate isn't your contract rate. 93
SECRET #35 There's no one best index. 94
SECRET #36 Don't ignore the margin. 98
SECRET #37 All caps aren't created equal. 99
SECRET #38 That flashy convertible could prove to be a clunker. 100
SECRET #39 APRs tell you nothing about ARMs—and very little about fixed-rates. 101

5 Perfect Your Credit Profile 105

SECRET #40 Emphasize all five Cs of credit approval. 106
SECRET #41 Credit scores can shape your destiny. 111
SECRET #42 Your credit score doesn't necessarily represent your credit strength. 112
SECRET #43 You can discover your credit scores. 113
SECRET #44 You can improve your credit scores. 115
SECRET #45 Garbage in, garbage out (GIGO). 117
SECRET #46 Credit repair firms can't fix your credit or boost your credit scores. 121
SECRET #47 Credit counselors can scam you, too. 122
SECRET #48 Credit counselors and debt management firms do not improve your credit record or boost your credit score's. 123
SECRET #49 Bankruptcy (Chapter 7) doesn't ruin your credit. 124
SECRET #50 Your ex-spouse can ruin your credit (and other tales of double counting). 126

6 The Lowdown on Low Downs 129

SECRET #51 You can buy with little or nothing down. 129

SECRET **#52** No matter how much you earn, FHA may hold the key to your home financing. 130
SECRET **#53** Discover FHA's best-kept secret: The 203(k) program. 133
SECRET **#54** Too many vets pass up VA loans. 137
SECRET **#55** The USDA offers a prime choice for low- to moderate-income homebuyers. 138
SECRET **#56** Community lending goes mainstream. 139
SECRET **#57** Not-for-profit housing groups help people in need buy and finance homes. 142
SECRET **#58** Local governments assist with down payments. 144
SECRET **#59** Even Fannie and Freddie accept little- or nothing-down loans. 145
SECRET **#60** Cut the cost of PMI by learning where rates break. 146
SECRET **#61** Before you obtain a PMI little- or nothing-down loan, understand the high cost you'll be paying. 147
SECRET **#62** Reduce the high cost of low down payments with a second mortgage. 148
SECRET **#63** Use pledged collateral to eliminate PMI. 149
SECRET **#64** Search for sellers with low-equity assumables. 151
SECRET **#65** You can avoid PMI with a higher interest rate mortgage. 152

7 Win Big Savings with Seller Financing, Foreclosures, and REOs 153

SECRET **#66** Sellers can nearly always beat the banks at their own game, but you must do more than ask. 156
SECRET **#67** Ask the seller and lender to cooperate with a refi blend. 159
SECRET **#68** Bridge the assumable gap with a seller second. 160
SECRET **#69** Avoid the bang of a bursting balloon. 161
SECRET **#70** Buy on the installment plan. 162
SECRET **#71** Try it before you buy it. 165
SECRET **#72** Buy and lease simultaneously. 167
SECRET **#73** Beat high interest rates with wraparound financing. 170

SECRET **#74** Don't dillydally with due diligence. 171
SECRET **#75** Negotiate a preforeclosure workout. 174
SECRET **#76** Buy (carefully) at the foreclosure sale. 177
SECRET **#77** Locate a foreclosure pro. 178
SECRET **#78** HUD may hold the keys to your home or investment property. 179
SECRET **#79** VA offers deals to both veterans and nonveterans. 182
SECRET **#80** Let Fannie or Freddie treat you to below-market financing. 184
SECRET **#81** Buy and finance directly with a lender. 186

8 Beware: Fine Print "Gotchas" at Work 191

SECRET **#82** It's a jungle out there. 191
SECRET **#83** Tell your loan rep to take out the garbage. 194
SECRET **#84** Don't place much faith in the Good Faith Estimate. 195
SECRET **#85** What's the real cost of a no-cost mortgage? 198
SECRET **#86** Does your loan permit unlimited prepayment? 200
SECRET **#87** An assumable loan may offer much less than you've assumed. 203
SECRET **#88** Appraised value doesn't necessarily equal market value. 205
SECRET **#89** On occasion, lenders want appraisers to lowball their appraisals. 207
SECRET **#90** Appraisals don't forecast the future. 209

9 Achieve Your Lowest Rate 211

SECRET **#91** Refuse to yield to the yield-spread premium. 211
SECRET **#92** Red and yellow, black and white, do lenders treat them all alike? 214
SECRET **#93** Rate quotes: Fact or fiction? 215
SECRET **#94** What rate will you get at closing? 216
SECRET **#95** Achieve your best rate. 219

SECRET **#96** Industry pros and government agencies need your help. 222
SECRET **#97** How to (almost) vanquish tricks of the trade. 225

10 Manage Your Home and Home Financing for Maximum Return 231

SECRET **#98** Treat your home and your home financing as an investment. 232
SECRET **#99** Stay alert for opportunities to refinance. 239
SECRET **#100** Use refinancing to create other benefits. 242
SECRET **#101** Refinance and safely invest the proceeds. 244
SECRET **#102** Never buy biweekly baloney. 248
SECRET **#103** Cancel your PMI. Get a refund from FHA. 251
SECRET **#104** Negotiate out of escrow. 254
SECRET **#105** Just say no to home equity loans. 256
SECRET **#106** Trouble, trouble, what to do? 259

Conclusion: You Can Live on the House 263

Index 269

Introduction: Will You Pay Too Much for Too Little?

This past year, 10 million homebuyers, homeowners, and real estate investors financed or refinanced $2 trillion in mortgage loans. But, you know what? The record shows that the great majority of these borrowers failed to obtain the best terms and lowest costs that were available to them. In addition, more than 10 million other homeowners should have refinanced, but didn't. And perhaps, most troublesome of all, millions of renters kept piling up rent receipts when instead they should have been building home equity.

How Mortgage Secrets Can Help You Avoid These Blunders

To help you gain from *Mortgage Secrets,* let's first look at why so many borrowers (and potential borrowers) make mortgage blunders. To a large extent, it's because they don't intelligently understand their choices. They don't know how to shop for property financing. They feel intimidated by all of this talk about "qualified" and "not qualified." Relatively few consumers can figure out the math of mortgage finance, and this leaves them vulnerable. Even worse, the mortgage loan business attracts more than its share of incompetent, inexperienced, and dishonest loan reps. Just like real estate sales, when the mortgage business booms, job seekers who want to make a fast buck flock to mortgage companies. These opportunists care little about doing what's best for their customers. They're just interested in making that six-figure-a-year income that hustling loan reps pull in.

The computer revolution in mortgage lending (credit scoring, automated underwriting) can also add to the difficulties of borrowers. Although computer processing may streamline paperwork and often results in faster loan approvals (or rejections), it has turned too many loan reps and underwriters into high-paid computer clerks: Fill out the loan application, plug the data into the underwriting program, and voilà, the loan decision is made. If you want to keep your job, don't question the computer. Don't stick your neck out to argue that your judgment stands superior to the mathematical models created by experts in statistics.

Forewarned Is Forearmed

I don't mean to throw stones at all lenders and loan reps. Nor do I believe that most loan reps would cheat their mother out of her social security check. But *Mortgage Secrets* does emphasize: To get the best loan terms, interest rate, and loan product available, you can't go into battle unarmed.

You must equip yourself with knowledge. You must get familiar with the tricks of the trade. You must know the right questions to ask. You must learn that nearly all lenders specialize in certain types of loan products and rarely deal in others. If you unknowingly ask a non-FHA lender to describe the pros and cons of FHA loan programs, you should not rely on the answer you receive. Likewise, because few lenders deal in mortgage bond programs, mortgage credit certificates, FHA 203(k) loans, or low-down-payment jumbo loans, experience shows that you won't get solid, straight-shooting advice about these products from most loan reps.

Going Wrong with Referrals

You may think, "I know that the quality of loan reps differs enormously. That's why I depend on a referral from . . . you name it, real estate agent, friend at work, Cousin Barb, or whoever." Now ask yourself: Are any of these people experts in mortgage finance? Probably not. So, how would they know whether the loan rep that they're recommending can be counted on to match you up with your best financing option? They can't.

False Beliefs. I regularly travel the United States and Canada, and talk with realty agents, loan reps, homebuyers, property owners, and investors. I am repeatedly amazed that people who believe they know what they're talking about most certainly do not. Josh Billings, a nineteenth-century American humorist, is supposed to have remarked, "I fear not the things that I do not know; rather, I fear the things that I know that just aren't so."

Each of us carries around myths, half-truths, and faulty interpretations that we believe reflect reality, but it's this "knowing what isn't so" that gets us into trouble.

Several Illustrations. Here's a short sampling of standard advice that I frequently hear from supposed loan experts and often see in print (other mortgage books, articles in personal finance magazines, and so on). You may even believe some of these "rules" yourself, yet, none is true.

- Don't prepay your mortgage if your investments will earn a return that's greater than your mortgage interest rate.
- Bankruptcy ruins your credit.
- Don't buy a home unless you expect to be in it for at least four or five years.
- Fannie Mae/Freddie Mac (the largest suppliers of mortgage money in the United States) set their maximum qualifying ratios at 28 percent (front ratio) and 36 percent (back ratio).
- Never accept a mortgage with a prepayment penalty.
- Risk-averse borrowers should avoid adjustable rate mortgages (ARMs).
- Never use a land contract.
- A good negotiating tactic with sellers is, "You name the price; I'll name the terms."
- Always get preapproved for a mortgage before you begin to shop for a home (half-truth).
- Borrowers with low FICO credit scores are condemned to paying high interest rates.
- It's extremely unlikely that you'll find a fixed-rate mortgage that you can assume. (Absolutely false. During the past five years, lenders have issued millions of such loans.)
- Most borrowers should get a 30-year fixed-rate loan. (Fortunately, increasing borrowers realize the poor quality of this advice.)
- Interest rates must go up as we're now at (or near) historically low rates.
- If you don't put at least 20 percent down, you'll have to buy mortgage insurance.

- Talk with a lender. The lender will tell you how much house you can afford to buy, and the amount of the mortgage for which you will qualify (one-quarter truth).

As you will discover from *Mortgage Secrets,* savvy borrowers question all canards, myths, and partial truths. Most importantly, by learning to think for yourself, you will shield yourself against costly blunders. With *Mortgage Secrets,* you will see how to work out the best financing options available to you and then find the mortgage and realty pros who can help you execute your plan.

Why I Wrote *Mortgage Secrets*

As someone who has worked as a committed educator and author in real estate for over 20 years, I am dismayed that so much bad advice has become conventional wisdom. These errors occur partly because of the explosion in the number of financial planners (and the financial journalists who quote them). For the most part, these planners know next to nothing about mortgage finance and buying real estate. In addition, I have read closely every other mortgage book on the market. Although several are pretty good, all suffer some combination of the following deficiencies:

- Clichéd advice that fails to stand up to critical review.
- Biased advice that derives from the author's limited personal experience. The advice does not reflect a comprehensive range of mortgage products and types of borrowers, and geographic areas. Similarly, other books give short shrift to seller financing—a choice that offers great money-saving possibilities.
- Failure to place the mortgage finance/property purchase decision within the borrower's mid- to longer-term goal of wealth building. (In other words, the property purchase/financing decisions that you make today will dramatically affect your net worth 3, 5, 10, and 20 years from now.)
- Too little attention to "special case" situations, when in fact, more than 50 percent of potential borrowers represent some type of special case.

- Little or no mention of how many popular financing choices (30-year, fixed-rate, low down payments, FHA, VA) impose high costs on borrowers; yet, borrowers can often solve the problems these loans address through other lower-cost alternatives.
- Misguided advice about preapproval, and how to competitively shop mortgage lenders. (That is, dialing for rates is perfectly silly and is almost guaranteed to sucker you into a bad loan decision. Likewise, comparing APRs typically provides little useful information.)
- Inadequate warnings about widespread tricks of the trade and the practices of predatory lenders.
- Little or no information to help you deal effectively with financing essentials such as appraisal, title insurance, property taxes, property inspections, homeowners association fees, and other ancillary items; yet, each of the essentials may seriously impact your mortgage qualifying, property affordability, and costs of property ownership.

You can now see that home finance requires far more than reading trite narrative and simplistic rules. Fortunately, when you do go further and explore your true financing choices, follow through with some basic (eighth-grade math) mortgage calculations, and begin this excursion into mortgage land with an open mind (what I call possibility thinking), *Mortgage Secrets* guarantees rewards far greater than you might imagine. The right choices today can easily mean tens (and possibly hundreds) of thousands of dollars to you over a period of 5 to 20 years.

* * * * *

During the mid to late 1990s, I offered my Stop Renting Now!™ seminars throughout the country. Through these seminars I talked with and learned from thousands of people in all walks of life and in all types of financial situations. Now in the pages of *Mortgage Secrets,* I answer the concerns, issues, problems, and quandaries that I witnessed firsthand during those exciting, problem-solving times. In that respect, there does stand one cliché that I do believe: "A good teacher learns more than the students."

The mistakes and solutions that you read about in *Mortgage Secrets* didn't just spring from my mind. They evolved from the lessons I learned by listening to real people with real hopes, unfulfilled dreams, and, yes, sometimes difficult problems. Through *Mortgage Secrets,* I want to reach the people I haven't talked with personally. I want to prove to you that no one needs to pay too much for too little. With the knowledge shared here, you will set your foundation for a lifetime of profitable home purchase and home finance decisions. I wish you good fortune.

CHAPTER 1

Affordability Depends on You—Not the Lender

Most supposed experts in home buying and home finance give this advice: "Before you even begin to shop for a home, meet with a lender to get prequalified for a loan.[1] With prequalification, you'll learn exactly how much home you can afford, and you won't waste time looking at homes outside of your price range."

Superficially, this advice makes sense. Why try to order filet mignon on a hamburger budget? Nevertheless, realize that this advice did not develop to chiefly promote your needs; it secured its place in mortgage lore to primarily advance the interests of real estate agents and mortgage lenders.

Their Interests, Not Yours

Prior to the emphasis on prequalification (or preapproval), realty agents might spend days or even weeks squiring potential homebuyers around neighborhoods. These hopeful buyers finally make an offer the sellers accepted. The buyers would then go down to their local savings and loan to apply for their loan, only to discover that for one or more reasons (credit, income, high debts, and so on), they cannot get the loan they need to close the sale. Although disappointing for the buyers and sellers, the real estate sales agent has lost valuable time and income. Too many dead ends like this, and the agent winds up broke and out of the real estate business.

1. Some say "preapproved," but that advice, too, fails to address the critical points raised here.

The Agents' Solution: Prequalification (Preapproval)

To combat this problem, real estate agents began urging potential buyers to first get prequalified (preapproved) and then bring their prequal letter to the agent. This way, the agent can keep buyers within their range of affordability. Smart realty agents soon learned that buyers who don't bring in a prequal (preapproval) letter probably aren't serious buyers. Avoid these tire kickers, or risk wasting precious commission-generating time and effort.

Mortgage Lenders Gain, Too

Prequal also serves the interests of mortgage lenders. Loan reps and mortgage companies have always lamented their heavy reliance on realty agents for mortgage loan referrals. Offend the real estate agents, and your home loan business runs dry of customers. With prequal becoming the conventional wisdom, mortgage companies can use this ploy to make an end run around their dependence on referrals from realty agents. Lenders can now directly attract potential borrowers through their own advertising.

"Give us a call before you begin shopping for a home. We'll give you a prequalification (preapproval) letter in less than 10 minutes. You'll show agents and sellers that you're a qualified buyer, and you'll gain a competitive edge over other buyers." Lender advertisements that tout this message now run in newspapers throughout the country.

What's Wrong with Prequalifying?

In theory, prequalifying (preapproval) for a loan doesn't just promote the interests of lenders and realty agents. Looking at homes you can't afford (unless you're just curious about how the other half lives), wastes your time and psyches you up for a big letdown. But here's the rub: Home buying and home financing weigh far too heavily in your overall financial and lifestyle planning to be shortchanged by a 10-minute computer exercise.

In point of fact, no simple qualifying formula can even begin to accurately tell you "how much home you can afford," or more importantly, "how much home you should buy." Plugging your current credit and finances into a prequal or preapproval computer program pushes aside the real questions you should ask yourself. Such formulaic analyses ignore critical issues such as these:

1. What are your goals to build wealth?
2. How do your budget constraints differ (positively or negatively) from those imbedded in the prequal computer program?
3. Are your current spending, saving, and investing habits consistent with your life priorities?
4. How long do you plan to own the property?
5. What steps can you take to improve your credit record or credit scores?
6. What steps can you take to improve your qualifying ratios?
7. What percent of your wealth should you hold in your home equity?
8. What types of real estate financing (other than those offered by the lender you're talking with) might best promote your goals for cost savings or wealth building?
9. What types of real estate financing (other than those offered by the lender you're talking with) might best enhance your affordability?
10. What type of property (fixer-upper, foreclosure, duplex, fourplex, single-family house, condo, and so on) might best fit into your financial goals?
11. How much money could you save by coming up with a larger down payment?
12. Should you use a fixed-rate mortgage or an adjustable rate mortgage (ARM)? What are the true risks and opportunities of each? Which offers the best trade-off of risk and return (quickest buildup of home equity)?

Although a relative few highly professional loan reps will help you accurately address important financial and life-planning issues such as those enumerated above, the great majority will not. The great majority lack the time, the intellectual acumen, and the will to guide you to your best decision. Indeed, never forget that loan reps, like car sales reps, want you to buy the product(s) they are selling. Would you expect unbiased auto advice from the sales agent at the Buick dealer? No? Then why would you expect unbiased advice from the loan rep at the Old Faithful Mortgage Company?

With that said, we return to the theme of *Mortgage Secrets:* Foremost, take measure of yourself. Learn your choices. Arrange your property purchase and financing decisions to advance your overall life and financial goals. The great majority of borrowers err because they attempt to minimize the monthly payment rather than maximize their wealth.

Most mortgage lenders emphasize where you stand financially today, but your focus must extend over a longer horizon. Most lenders emphasize your ability and willingness to pay your mortgage as evinced only by their approval formula. You must not accept this narrow view. You must decide for yourself if you should buy more (or less) property than the standard formulas suggest, and correspondingly, if you should borrow more (or less) than this lender's guidelines recommend.

SECRET # **1**

Affordability depends on you.

The folks who urge you to get prequalified for a loan rarely mention that potential borrowers may choose from dozens (actually hundreds) of loan products. Each of these products may vary with respect to interest rate, down payment, credit standards, monthly payment amounts, mortgage insurance premiums, qualifying ratios, closing costs, eligible types of properties, occupancy standards, and many other terms and conditions. Any of these differences can affect your loan affordability or approval.

A Sampling of Loan Programs and Techniques for Financing Real Estate

Just look at the 60 financing programs and affordability techniques listed in Figure 1.1. Although it's not complete by a long shot, a brief reading does illustrate my point: No loan rep (or anyone else) can tell you exactly how much loan you can afford unless they worked through all of these possibilities (singularly or in combination).

- FHA 203(b) mortgages
- FHA 203(k) mortgages
- FHA nonqual assumables
- FHA assumable w/qualifying
- HUD/FHA foreclosures
- VA mortgages
- VA assumable w/qualifying
- VA nonqual assumables
- FHA Title 1 home improvement loans
- ARMs
- Community reinvestment loans
- Co-ownership
- Compensating factors
- Fannie Mae Community Home-Buyers programs
- Fannie 97
- Fannie Mae affordable mortgage programs
- Freddie Mac central city mortgage programs
- Fannie Mae Start-up Mortgage
- ARM hybrids
- State VA mortgage programs
- Habitat homes
- Owner will carry (OWC)
- Second mortgages
- Real estate owned (REOs)
- Not-for-profit grant money
- Government grant money
- Employer-assisted mortgage plans
- ARM assumptions
- Lease-purchase agreements
- Interest rate buydowns
- Wraparounds
- Sweat equity
- Shared equity
- Interest rate buy-ups
- State mortgage bond programs
- Private mortgage insurance (PMI)
- New home builder finance plans
- Create value/fixer-uppers
- County down-payment assistance
- City down-payment assistance
- Energy-efficient mortgages
- Self-contracting
- Pledged collateral
- Blanket mortgages
- Cosigners
- Co-borrowers
- Shared housing/housemates
- Financial fitness exercises
- Accessory apartments
- Mortgage credit certificates (MCCs)
- Lease options
- Gift letters
- Homebuyer seminars, fairs, classes
- Homebuyer counseling centers
- Rural Development Administratio (formerly FmHA)
- Buy a duplex, triplex, or other income property
- Graduated payment mortgages
- Contract-for-deed
- Tenant-in-common (TICs)
- Balloon mortgages

Figure 1.1 Selected Sources and Techniques of Property Finance

Even after asking about all of these mortgage types, you wouldn't get a definitive answer. Take seller financing (OWC), for example, in which sellers determine their own qualifying standards and loan terms. Should one seller turn you down, another one might say yes to your proposal. Sadly, I've talked with far too many hopeful homebuyers who had been turned away from purchasing property by a loan rep's unthinking computer program. Absent knowledge about their full range of possibilities, these potential homebuyers needlessly accepted the loan rep's verdict of "unqualified."

Possibility Thinking

As you read through *Mortgage Secrets* and discover the ins and outs of home financing, keep asking yourself, "Would this idea work for me (us)?" In today's world of home finance, nearly everyone who wants to own a home, refinance a home, or even buy an investment property can come up with a finance plan that works for them. Knowing your options, though, doesn't just apply to the goal of affordability. For most people, building home equity wealth, saving money (slashing the costs of financing), and finding the best property for their personal needs also rank high among their life and financial goals.

SECRET # 2

How you choose your property and arrange financing will add (or subtract) tens (or even hundreds) of thousands of dollars to (from) your net worth.

If you're like most people, you probably prefer to live in a single-family house, condo, or coop in a good neighborhood. But would you be willing to live in, say, a fourplex for five years if it would boost your wealth by $100,000 or more?

How Rentals Boost Affordability and Wealth Building

When you visit a lender to get prequalified, most loan reps assume that you're buying a house or condo. Likewise, most borrowers don't question this assumption. The loan rep might tell you that based on your income, you could borrow $200,000. If you've got $50,000 for a down payment, you should look at houses in the $250,000 price range.[2]

In contrast to this common scenario, consider how much more you could afford to borrow if you bought a nice fourplex, lived in one unit, and rented out the other three. Because your rental income from three units will greatly expand your borrowing power, you could now buy a property worth, say, $600,000 (instead of $250,000).[3]

If each of these potential buys appreciates at 4 percent per year and the mortgage balance on each falls to 92.5 percent of the original balance, here's how your equity would build with each property:

Five-Year Equity Buildup

	Single-family house	*Fourplex*
Purchase price	$250,000	$600,000
Amount financed	200,000	550,000
Appreciated value @ 4 percent p.a.	305,000	732,000
Mortgage balance year five	185,000	508,750
Equity	120,000	223,250
Original down payment	50,000	50,000
Investment gain	70,000	173,250

As you can see, this part home–part rental property not only expands your affordability, it also boosts your net worth by $173,250 (vs. $70,000 for the house). In a world where people once again recognize that stocks offer highly volatile returns (and losses), homebuyers should consider the wealth-building power of their properties.

2. Don't concern yourself at this time with the specific dollar amounts used in this or other examples. Focus on the idea or technique. I realize that your finances and the property prices in your area may run much higher or lower than those here and throughout *Mortgage Secrets*.

3. *Mortgage Secrets* discusses the exact numbers in Chapter 2.

Other Wealth-Building Ideas

In later chapters, we'll go through other detailed examples that further show how your property purchase and financing decisions will materially impact your net worth 5 to 20 years in the future. These other examples will include mortgage prepayments, short-term mortgages, fix-up properties, bargain-priced properties, and low-interest-rate financing.

Surprisingly, relatively few homebuyers (or -owners) make these kinds of comparisons. Most people simply figure that their home will appreciate, and eventually they'll make a fair amount of money. No doubt, history proves them correct; however, history also shows that those buyers who include such estimates and calculations in their home purchase and financing comparisons can achieve much larger investment gains.

SECRET # 3

Separate the emotional from the financial.

You've probably heard it said before. Buying and financing a home triggers many emotional reactions: fear, pride, anxiety, hope, and even greed, to name just a few. You've probably felt at least several of these emotions yourself. The trick, though, is to identify, clarify, and separate all of these emotions from your financial goals and motives. For example, did you quickly dismiss the idea of buying a fourplex?

Personal versus Financial

If you dismissed the idea of purchasing and living in a fourplex, was it a gut emotional reaction? Was it a gut emotional decision, such as "I don't want to call an apartment building home—even if I am the owner"? Or did you look at the money that you could make and then consciously decide that even with an extra profit of $100,000, it's not worth it to you?

Subtle Distinction

Admittedly, I'm asking you to see a subtle distinction. What I'm saying is that emotional decision makers quickly jump to a decision based on what they like or dislike. They fail to fully understand that sometimes one must endure a little pain or discomfort to reap large rewards down the road. Or alternatively, they fail to appreciate that short-term impulsive pleasures often create unwise long-term costs (as with the highly popular, yet widely abused and wealth-destroying home equity loans).

Application to Home Purchase and Financing

For example, how many renters drive new or nearly new cars and then are precluded from buying a home or need expensive low– (or no–) down payment financing to make a purchase? How many people reflexively turn down bargain-priced fixer-uppers because they don't want to bother with making the repairs? How many buyers refuse to consider an ARM because they fear an interest rate increase? How many renters choose to remain renters because buying would give them a longer commute or locate them in a neighborhood inferior to the one where they are currently living?

I know from experience that all too often, emotional reactions to potential choices cause us to prematurely dismiss our possibilities without a full hearing on their benefits and costs. Just recently, I erred along these lines.

Emotional Rejection

In this case, I was evaluating an investment property (a single-family house). One strong attraction was the fact the owner was offering to carry back all of the financing on the property with just 5 percent down. The property was located in a neighborhood of professionals, and it suffered no problems of disrepair or deferred maintenance; however, these advantages aside, a couple of features in the house provoked a strong negative emotional reaction. As a result, I irrationally hesitated to make an offer. Rather than weigh all advantages and disadvantages, I focused only on what I didn't like.

That was a big mistake. The person who looked at the property immediately after I left bought it on the spot. My failure to quickly and rationally size up the opportunity cost me an excellent property that was offered with terrific financing.

Learn from My Mistake and the Mistakes of Others

Fully separate the financial from the emotional—only then will you be able to judge fairly whether the potential decision exposes you to more cost than benefit or more benefit than cost. As humans, we seem to be hardwired with emotional response; yet, when it comes to our financial future and personal well-being, we can't let those emotional reactions control us. We've got to persistently push to weigh and consider—identify what we like and don't like, what we want and don't want, and then attach a dollar price tag. Don't merely think here and now. Think of the full implications over time.

Throughout *Mortgage Secrets,* you'll read about dozens of property purchase and financing techniques. Each of these will offer trade-offs of advantages and disadvantages. And undoubtedly, some will require effort, inconvenience, or discomfort that may not at first glance seem appealing to you. Please, though, leave the possibility on the table until you've at least picked it up and examined it closely. Often, the road less traveled does lead to Oz. Motivational speakers often recite the following apothegm: "Do now what most people won't do. In 10 years, you'll do what most people never can."

SECRET # **4**

Align your self-talk with your priorities.

Are you reading *Mortgage Secrets* to learn how to overcome or get around some financial roadblocks, such as shaky credit, low cash on hand, self-employment, affordability, and so on? Good! You're reading the right book. You'll find more creative financing ideas here than anywhere else. But in one sense, the topic of creative financing begs the real question: Why do you face these roadblocks? Are you truly managing your money as well as you could?

If you're like most Americans, you've probably got big room for improvement.

Self-Talk and Money Management

In his excellent book, *What to Say When You Talk to Yourself* (Pocket Books, 1987), Dr. Shad Helmstetter convincingly argues that we bring about many of our own difficulties (financial and otherwise) through self-talk. Do you know anyone who uses any of the following expressions:

- I can't remember names.
- I'm always running late.
- I can never get organized.
- I'm always short of money. I just don't know where it goes.
- No way could we ever save enough for a 20 percent down payment.
- No way could we ever afford a home in that area.
- Get qualified for a mortgage? Not with my credit.
- At the rate we're putting away money for retirement, I'll probably be working until I'm 75.[4]

According to Dr. Helmstetter, every one of these statements (and many others like them) programs us to create the outcome about which we're complaining. "The more you think about anything in a certain way," he writes, "the more you will believe that's the way it really is." And when you believe that's the way it really is, you do little or nothing to zero out the problem. What is the solution? Reprogram those self-talk tapes.

Reprogram Your Brain to Deliver a Positive Message

To reprogram your self-talk, first completely erase those old messages. Never again describe your behavior in self-defeating or self-demeaning ways. Give yourself a jolt each time you let negative and problem-reinforcing thoughts short-circuit your search for effective improvements.

As self-defeating self-talk disappears from your everyday life, replace it with goal-promoting self-talk. For example, you might start this process by asking and answering questions such as the following:

4. Or how about this one: "I just can't seem to lose weight."

- What are six ways that I can save more?
- What are six ways I can cut back on spending?
- What are four ways I can stop running up my credit card bills and start paying them down?
- What are four ways that I can work towards a $1 million net worth within 15 years?

When you ask questions that point to where you want to go, your mind opens to possibilities. With possibilities in view, you then can program your self-talk to reinforce the behavior that will lead you to your desired goal(s).

Does Self-Talk Really Work?

Absolutely! I rely on positive self-talk to help avoid all health problems; to maintain a vigorous program of diet, fitness, and exercise; to improve work productivity; and, yes, to save, invest, and spend much more wisely. But don't just take my word for it. Go to Amazon.com and search for Shad Helmstetter. The last time I looked, his book had racked up nearly 50 reviews with a near perfect five-star rating.

Self-talk not only steers people towards their life goals, but I might add that mental health professionals have effectively treated those who suffer depression by getting them to adopt a regimen of positive self-talk. Perhaps most important of all, putting self-talk principles into practice will give you a brighter, cheerier outlook on life. Now that's a priority truly worth pursuing.

Get Started Now

As a start, why not review your spending and saving? Where does your money go? Does your spending align with where you would like to be financially in 5, 10, and 20 years? Or look at it like this: At current rates of interest, each $100 you cut from your monthly spending can add $15,000 to your home finance borrowing power, and up to $50,000 (or more) to your longer-term net worth.

Do you recall the recent best-seller, *The Millionaire Next Door* (Thomas Stanley and William Danko; Longstreet, 1997)? These Joe Average millionaires laid the foundation for their wealth building with

Rent	$_____	Beer, wine, liquor	$_____
Electricity	$_____	Other vices	$_____
Gas	$_____	Health club	$_____
Cable TV	$_____	Magazines	$_____
Internet charges	$_____	Newspapers	$_____
On-line charges	$_____	Furniture	$_____
Telephone(s)	$_____	Appliances	$_____
Car payment #1	$_____	School expenses	$_____
Car payment #2	$_____	Health insurance	$_____
Gasoline	$_____	Weekend trips	$_____
Automobile insurance	$_____	Vacations	$_____
Groceries	$_____	Housekeepers	$_____
Child care	$_____	Personal care	$_____
Clothing	$_____	Credit card interest	$_____
Electronics	$_____	Other	$_____
Lunches	$_____	Other	$_____
Dining out	$_____	Other	$_____
Entertainment	$_____	Other	$_____
Tobacco	$_____	Total	$_____

Figure 1.2 Your Spending Profile

wise (frugal) spending and very low use of nonproductive debt (credit cards, home equity loans, new car loans, department store accounts). Now complete the blanks in Figure 1.2 and ask yourself whether your spending, borrowing, and saving demonstrate a happy outlook for mortgage qualifying, property investing, and lifetime accumulation of $1 million (current dollars) or more.

Suggested Improvements

Do your spending habits show fits of extravagance, excessive borrowing, too little saving, and a general mismatch with your priorities? If so, adopt one or more of the following suggestions:

1. *Never say "budget."* No one likes to budget. It sounds too much like work. Instead, think priorities. Think reward. The quality of your life enlarges as you allocate your money according to your highest values. If you truly want to own the perfect home, put your money where your heart is.

2. *Stop paying rent.* For most people who don't yet own their own homes, rent is the biggest money waster. Can you eliminate or reduce your rent payments? Can you switch to a lower-cost apartment? Can you houseshare? Can you find a house-sitting job for the next 3 to 12 months? Can you move back with your parents or stay rent free with relatives or friends? Bank your rent money for 6 to 12 months, and for the rest of your life, you'll never pay rent again.

3. *Cut your food bills in half.* Eliminate eating out. Brown-bag your lunches. Buy unbranded foods in bulk. Prepare your food in large quantities and then freeze portions in meal-sized servings. Forget those $2-to-$3 microwave lunches and dinners. Locate a remainder and closeout grocery such as Canned Foods, Big Lots, or Drug Emporium. Or maybe you can shop at the new food warehouses that have opened in most cities. Food prices in discount stores run 20 to 50 percent less than in big-name supermarkets. Collect and use as many coupons as you can find. When you find bargain-priced items that you use regularly, buy them by the case.

4. *Cut your credit cards in half.* Vanquish credit card addiction. Adopt a strict cash diet. You will spend far less when you count out real cash. Besides, credit card balances zap strength from your home-purchasing power. Even worse, by the time you've finished paying off your credit card balances at 18 percent interest, you pay back two (or more) dollars for every dollar you originally charged—and that's in after-tax take-home dollars. After you consider that you only take home 60 to 80 percent of what you earn, you have to earn more than just $2 just to pay back every dollar you finance on your credit cards.

5. *Don't put the car before the house.* If you own a car that's worth nearly as much as a down payment on a house, sell it. Get rid of those cash-draining car payments. If your car(s) is (are) mostly paid

for, there's a good part of the money you need to move up the homeownership ladder. If you are thinking about buying a more expensive car, stop! Until you can afford your perfect home, drive the least expensive, dependable car you can find. For too many Americans, their car is the enemy of their house.

6. *Eliminate costly vices.* How much money do you spend each year on cigarettes, beer, liquor, drinks at restaurants, clubs or bars, illegal drugs, or other harmful habits? Add them up. Unbelievably, these costly vices range upwards of $1,000 to $2,500 a year or more. By eliminating them, you can really boost your power to save money and your health.

7. *Buy clothes in thrift shops.* Even if you're an up-and-coming investment banker on Wall Street, don't spend hard-earned after-tax dollars on expensive new clothing. How about an $1,800 Armani suit for $695 or an Emporio Armani silk paisley tie priced at $40? Both of these (and many comparable bargains) were available at GENTLY Owned in Atlanta. And these fashion items were new, bought at closeout. For recycled clothing, savings can be much higher. In her newspaper column, *Dress for Less,* Candy Barrie writes, "I'm a big fan of these [consignment and thrift] shops for the fashion bargains you can find there. . . . Get on down and you'll discover we're not just talking about 20, 30, or 40 percent discounts. Sometimes you can get your clothes for 90 to 95 percent off retail. Some wealthy people don't give their expensive clothes away, so they place them in consignment and thrift shops."

   Want to save money? Follow Candy's advice: Locate all the recycled and closeout clothing stores in your area or a nearby big city. Whatever your tastes and price range, you'll find that you can slash your clothing costs by 50 percent or more.

8. *Put off buying new furniture and appliances.* As with cars and clothing, most renters spend too much too soon for furniture and appliances. Even worse, instead of paying cash, they finance their purchases. They chain themselves to several years of payments at high interest rates. (Or increasingly, they are hooked into those "no

payments, no interest for six months" types of promotions that make credit spending all too easy.) Do yourself a favor—stifle this temptation. Like cars and clothing, most furniture and appliances depreciate in value faster than they depreciate in condition. As a result, you can find great secondhand bargains. I have bought many beautiful older pieces of high-quality furniture at prices less than the cheap particleboard furniture that most lower-priced furniture stores carry. Although buying used appliances can be somewhat risky, you can reduce the chance of problems by finding those available with transferable extended warranties.

When you buy clothing, cars, furniture, or appliances, let someone else suffer the depreciation. Pay only for the usefulness of a product. The less money you waste on depreciating assets, the faster you build wealth through home buying, trade-up homes, and other investments. Read and practice the principles of *The Millionaire Next Door.* You will never need to worry about home affordability and mortgage qualifying.

SECRET # 5

Don't focus on the kind of home you want now. Focus on the kind of home you want 5, 10, or 15 years from now.

To end this chapter, I would like to revisit through personal example a point raised earlier. At age 21, I bought my first home. It was a large old house that had been converted into four apartment units, and the garage (carriage house) had been converted into a fifth unit—which is where I lived. It was owner financed with 10 percent down and a 5 percent interest rate land contract. At the time, my friends had fun kidding me about the "dump" and my "slumlording." (Actually, the property wasn't *that* bad.)

However, six years later, while still enrolled in my Ph.D. program at the University of Illinois, I owned (among other properties) a four-bedroom, two-bath, brick house that I had bought from one of my professors. Where were my earlier friends and contemporaries living? Most were still living in apartments and rental houses. None lived in (much less owned) a home anywhere near as nice as mine.

What's the Moral?

As home prices throughout the United States have skyrocketed during the past five years, home affordability for first-time buyers is again emerging as a major problem. Many first-time buyers (especially) don't believe that they ever will be able to own the kind of home they like in the location that they want, so they hesitate to buy. But by hesitating, they will only get further behind.

Renters: Make Ownership Your First Priority

Had I continued to rent back when I was age 21, I would never have been able to buy the house I bought at age 27. Your best chance today to get the home you would really like in, say, 5 or 10 years is to first become a property owner as quickly as you can and then weigh carefully the advantages of buying the type of property where you can make some quick money by building equity fast (rental income, fixer-upper, bargain-priced foreclosure).

Do not lament the fact that prices have gone through the roof (remember, no self-denying self-talk). Instead, create a financial plan that will put you on the fast track to the home you really want if you're one of the many for whom affordability does present serious difficulties.

Gain a Great Tax Break

You're probably familiar with the mortgage interest tax deduction, but that's not the tax break I'm referring to here. Since 1998, homeowners have been able to sell their homes every two years and pocket their profits tax free (up to $250,000 for singles and $500,000 for married couples). This tax break means that you could buy a bargain-priced fixer-upper, renovate as you live in it, and sell for a fat profit (the economy willing) in two years; then repeat as necessary or desired.[5]

---

5. For more on this technique, see my book, *Investing in Real Estate*, 4th ed. (Wiley, 2003).

Does this sound like something you would want to try? Probably not. But then again, would you like to earn $100,000 to $250,000 (more or less) in tax-free gains over the next six years?[6] Have you created some other financial plan that will get you to where you want to be? No? Then the question becomes one of drift or mastery. It's your choice.

Affordability: Now or Later?

When the prequal/preapproval folks tell you come on down and see exactly how much home you can afford to buy, they mean how much they will loan you to buy a home right now. Although that may be useful to know, it need not end the story. Apart from shaping up your finances and searching out other more affordable loan programs, keep at least some thoughts on the future. The financial strategy you elect today can pave the way to the perfect home you'd like tomorrow.

---

6. Between 1996 and 2002, a friend of mine from a wealthy family earned $3.5 million renovating and flipping homes in San Francisco, Carmel, and Lake Tahoe. You can follow this same strategy—though perhaps not at the same level of prices and profit.

CHAPTER 2

Increase Your Borrowing Power

Because you're not likely to pay cash for your home, you undoubtedly want to determine how much borrowing power you can safely muster. Fortunately, no simple answer exists.

Why "fortunately?" Because if only one simple standard applied, people turned down by one lender would also be tossed out by every other lender. As it is, more than 10,000 mortgage lenders call the good ole United States of America home, and every one of these lenders sets its own lending standards—within, of course, applicable laws and regulations. This fact gives you the Baskin-Robbins range of choices and creative alternatives. With a good knowledge of lenders and lending standards, you can stretch and bend your finances to borrow far more than you might think; or you can take the safe road and borrow much less than many lenders recommend. Either way, the choice is yours because choice is the American way.

SECRET # 6

10,000 lenders set their own standards.

Conventional wisdom holds that the all-powerful national mortgage companies, Fannie Mae and Freddie Mac, set underwriting standards for the mortgage lending industry. In fact, though, Fannie and Freddie buy only about one-half the mortgages issued throughout the country. A big number, yes, but nowhere near universal. In addition, the underwriting standards applied by Fannie and Freddie do not mirror each other. Loan requests rejected by Freddie may get approved by Fannie, and vice versa. Both Fannie and Freddie publish underwriting *guidelines,* not absolute requirements,[1] so lenders who sell their loans to Fannie and Freddie remain free to use some discretion and flexibility.

Portfolio Lenders

Lenders who don't sell their mortgages to Fannie, Freddie, or other players in the secondary mortgage market are called portfolio lenders. Portfolio lenders include many banks, savings institutions, credit unions, pension funds, and life insurance companies. Although Fannie/Freddie-affiliated lenders may exercise flexibility if they choose to, portfolio lenders can tailor any type of loan that can find a market.

These portfolio lenders frequently look to Fannie/Freddie lending practices and then develop differentiated loan products that will permit them to compete effectively for some types of borrowers—for example, credit impaired, no-documentation, low-documentation, jumbo amounts over $325,000, no mortgage insurance, balloon notes, high qualifying ratios, income properties, farm land, rehab and renovation loans. Sometimes, portfolio lenders will even structure a financing arrangement to meet the special needs of a specific borrower.

Government-Backed Loans

Government-backed loans include a broad variety of programs that often permit some homebuyers (and sometimes investors) to obtain loans that they could not get from either Fannie/Freddie or most portfolio lenders. Some of the more popular government loans include:

- *Federal Housing Administration (FHA).* The FHA specializes in low-down-payment, easier qualifying loans.
- *Department of Veterans Affairs (VA).* The VA offers easier qualifying, no-down-payment mortgages to eligible veterans.

---

1. Fannie and Freddie do set limits on the maximum amount of loan they will buy from their affiliated banks, savings institutions, and other mortgage lenders.

- *Rural Development Administration (USDA).* As part of the United States Department of Agriculture, this agency helps low- to moderate-income families buy homes with low down payments and low interests rates.
- *State mortgage bond programs.* It's typically easier to qualify for these programs because they offer low-down-payment, lower-interest rate loans, and are aimed at first-time buyers, which is defined as anyone who hasn't owned a home within the past three years.
- *Community development loans.* Many states and cities encourage homebuyers (and sometimes investors) to buy and fix up properties in designated neighborhoods. To achieve this goal, community redevelopment agencies frequently offer purchase and fix-up loans on quite favorable terms.

What All of This Means for You

With this quick trip through some common types of lenders and loan programs (more details in later chapters), I want to again drill into your consciousness that lenders differ, loan programs differ, and qualifying standards differ. No loan rep can ever tell you how much home (property) you can buy, or how much money you can borrow. When you speak with specific loan reps, each will tell you how much (if any) money their funding sources will loan you. Never again think of mortgage loans as peas in a pod. They're more like large baskets of mixed fruit with at least a few poisoned apples.

Just as important (and sometimes more so), you could get different answers from different loan reps who work for the same lender and are working with the same loan program. How well the loan rep packages your personal information, and how effectively the rep responds to underwriter (or computer) queries can make the difference between a yes and a no.

Keep these potential quality differences in mind as you read through *Mortgage Secrets.* The knowledge gained here will not just help you figure out the types of financing strategies that could work best for you. It also will give you the solid footing necessary to stand your ground and perceptively question (or challenge) what loan reps tell you. Mortgageland abounds with hunters looking for lame prey. Appear vulnerable, and you could get skinned.

SECRET # 7

You can make your qualifying ratios look better.

You *can* make your qualifying numbers look better. Except for some low-doc or no-doc loans, the great majority of lenders will assess your borrowing power through the use of two qualifying ratios: the housing cost (front) ratio, and the total debt (back) ratio. Both the housing cost ratio and the total debt ratio give lenders a way to measure whether your income looks like it's large enough to cover your mortgage payments, monthly debts, and other living expenses (see equations below). Run-of-the-mill loan reps will merely take your financial data and plug it into their qualifying formulas (or computer program). Savvy loan reps, though, will do a "first review" with you and then, if desirable, suggest ways that you can improve your financial profile.

Calculating the Ratios

With the advent of desktop or computer underwriting, many loan reps and loan underwriters no longer explicitly calculate qualifying ratios. In fact, some newer reps wouldn't know what to do with a ratio even if it begged for mercy. Nevertheless, qualifying ratios matter a great deal. Only now, the math is hidden in the computer underwriting program.

Make no mistake. If you do make the effort to understand and improve your qualifying ratios, you will raise the odds for loan approval and increase the amount the lender will loan to you. Strong ratios may also help you slice your interest rate and your mortgage insurance premiums.

Housing Cost (Front) Ratio

You can easily figure your housing cost ratio with this equation:

$$\text{Housing cost ratio} = \frac{(\text{P\&I})+(\text{T\&I})+(\text{MI})+(\text{HOA})}{\text{Monthly gross income}}$$

where: P&I represents principal and interest (the basic monthly mortgage payment)

T&I represents the amount you must pay monthly for property taxes and homeowners insurance.

MI represents the monthly mortgage insurance premium you may have to pay if you put less than 20 percent down.

HOA represents the monthly amount you may have to pay to a condominium or subdivision homeowners association.

To keep things simple, let's say that your household income equals $7,000 per month. You need a loan of $235,000 to buy the home you want. For this preliminary review, you want a 30-year fixed-rate loan at 7 percent interest. This loan will cost you $1,563 per month (235 × $6.65, see Table 2.1). Property taxes and homeowners insurance on this

Table 2.1 **Monthly Mortgage Payment for Each $1,000 Borrowed at a Variety of Interest Rates and Terms**

Qualifying Interest Rate	*15-Year*	*30-Year*	*40-Year*
4.0	$7.40	$4.77	$4.17
4.5	7.65	5.07	4.50
5.0	7.91	5.37	4.82
5.5	8.17	5.67	5.16
6.0	8.44	6.00	5.50
6.5	8.71	6.32	5.85
7.0	8.99	6.65	6.21
7.5	9.27	6.99	6.58
8.0	9.56	7.34	6.95
8.5	9.85	7.69	7.33
9.0	10.16	8.05	7.71
9.5	10.45	8.41	8.10
10.0	10.75	8.78	8.50
10.5	11.06	9.15	8.89
11.0	11.37	9.53	9.28
11.5	11.69	9.91	9.68
12.0	12.01	10.29	10.08
12.5	12.33	10.68	10.49

house will total $400 per month. No mortgage insurance applies, but you must pay the homeowners association $125 per month to maintain the community swimming pool, tennis courts, and clubhouse. Here's how to compute your housing cost ratio for this example:

$$\text{Housing cost ratio} = \frac{\$1{,}563 + 400 + 125}{\$7{,}000}$$

$$= \frac{\$2{,}088}{\$7{,}000}$$

$$= .298 \text{ or } 29.8\%$$

Because the lender with whom you are talking has set a guideline housing cost ratio of 28 percent, your numbers look as though they might work. So, we next turn to the total debt ratio.

Total Debt Ratio

The total debt ratio begins with your housing costs and then adds in monthly payments for all of your installment (such as auto loan) and revolving (credit cards, department store accounts, and so on) debt. At present, your BMW hits you for a payment of $650 a month; the Taurus adds another $280. Your outstanding credit card and department store account balances total $8,000 and require a minimum payment of 5 percent of the outstanding balance per month ($400). Here are the figures:

$$\text{Total debt ratio} = \frac{\text{Housing costs + installment debt + revolving debt}}{\text{Monthly gross income}}$$

$$= \frac{\$2{,}088 + 650 + 250 + 400}{\$7{,}000}$$

$$= \frac{\$3{,}388}{\$7{,}000}$$

$$= .484 \text{ or } 48.4\%$$

With this loan program, the lender would like to see a total debt ratio no greater than 36 percent. Whoops. Looks like you've blown through this ratio. But does this mean you won't get the loan—or will have to settle for a lesser amount? Not necessarily.

If your credit score (see Chapter 5) is high enough, your loan may still get approved. If that doesn't work, maybe you can increase your qualifying income, reduce your monthly debt, or provide compensating factors.

SECRET # **8**

You can lift your qualifying income.

In the previous example, we *assumed* that your income totaled $7,000 per month. In the real world, though, figuring your income presents a somewhat greater challenge (and opportunity). To calculate *qualifying* income—that specific income amount entered into the denominator of your qualifying ratios—lenders evaluate your full range of actual and potential income from all sources such as:

- Salary
- Hourly wages
- Overtime
- Bonuses
- Commissions
- Scheduled raises
- Alimony
- Welfare/ADC
- Pension
- Tax-free income
- Child support
- Social security income
- Unemployment insurance
- Self-employment
- Moonlighting/part-time job
- Tips
- Disability insurance
- Dividends
- Interest
- Consulting
- Rents
- Annuities

As you look through this list, you can see that for many borrowers, no precise income figure can be calculated. Consider the entries for overtime, bonuses, and commissions. Over a period of months or years, these amounts could vary significantly.

Or what about unemployment insurance payments? How could someone who's unemployed (or expects to become unemployed) ever hope to get qualified for a mortgage? Why would income from this source count? Well, I know a savvy loan rep who routinely gets unemployment insurance counted. His borrowers work during summer stock theater for very good wages; then during the off-season, they regularly collect unemployment. So, their qualifying income includes both their earnings from acting and their regular checks from the government.

Regularity, Stability, Continuity

Lenders will count any income that you can show as stable, regular, and continuing. Usually, a two-year history with a promising and realistic future is enough to satisfy a lender. On the other hand, what if during the past five years you've typically earned sales commissions of $4,000 a month, but during the past eight months that income has jumped to $6,000 a month? Here, the loan rep or underwriter must make a clear judgment call that you can influence by persuasive evidence that your more recent earnings should weigh in heavier than your past years.

Or consider alimony or child support. You may possess a court order that requires your ex-spouse to pay you $1,500 per month, but your spouse displays a casual indifference to honoring this order. Sometimes you get paid; sometimes you don't. So, what amount will the lender count? This is again a judgment call that you can influence according to how well you explain your ex's past irresponsibility, and provide assurances of future compliance.

Future Earnings

Sometimes you can persuade a lender to accept future earnings that may lack a past or a present. Imagine your spouse has just taken a new job in Topeka. You previously worked as a teacher, but for family reasons, took a leave of absence for the past two years. After the family gets settled in your new community, however, you plan to return to teaching full-time. Will the lender count your future earnings? With a good argument and evidence of intent, you can probably get at least part of this potential income included. In fact, Fannie/Freddie both offer dispensation for "trailing spouses."

Recent college graduates or recent graduates from professional schools such as nursing, law, medicine, business, or engineering can also secure mortgages without immediate past or present income or employment. A contract for a new job may work to establish your qualifying income.

When Current Income Doesn't Count

For the past 12 years, you worked as a master mechanic at the local Ford dealer. You earned $5,350 a month. Then, six months ago, you got hooked on Shaklee products. You quit your job at Ford, and became a Shaklee sales distributor. Business was slow at first, but during the past three months, you've cleared close to $25,000. Will this income qualify? Sorry, your newfound success would not impress most lenders. They would tell you to reapply after proving your sales skills for another 18 to 24 months.

Maximize Your Qualifying Income

To secure the loan approval and maximize borrowing power, present your income history, current earnings, and future prospects as optimistically as possible. You must anticipate and respond effectively to any negative signals that may cause the lender to doubt the amount, stability, or continuing nature of your income.

Overcome the Negatives

If your earnings were lower last year because you went back to school to secure the education necessary to obtain a raise or promotion, make sure the loan rep knows it. If you earned $60,000 last year, but as of September 1 of this year you've taken in only $40,000, show the lender that your big earnings season runs from September to December. Provide evidence that typically you earn 40 percent of your commissions during these three months, so you're actually on track to outpace last year's record.

If self-employment earnings complicate your income, prepare thorough explanations. For truly complex situations involving important amounts of money, enlist the aid of your accountant. Potential problems, for example, can include tax losses offset by positive cash flow, or strong business profits yet small wage or salary draws from the business (to minimize your personal income taxes). Most run-of-the-mill loan reps can't effectively understand these issues without guidance or persuasive input from you.

Without such input, most loan reps will figure your income too conservatively. They follow rules such as, "When in doubt, leave it out." Or, consider the following two different earnings patterns.

Earnings Patterns

Year	*Jack*	*Jill*
2001	$40,000	$50,000
2002	45,000	45,000
2003	50,000	40,000

Each of these earnings patterns shows average annual earnings of $45,000, and, respectively, most recent earnings of $50,000 and $40,000. Common logic might hold that lenders would use a consistent method to calculate qualifying income from each of these patterns. But no. Without persuasive evidence from each borrower, the lender would probably qualify Jack using the three-year average of $45,000; and to qualify Jill, the loan rep would use the most recent income of $40,000.[2] Why? Play it safe. Never give borrowers an even break—unless the borrower can show just cause.

Put Positives in Writing. Don't think that you can effectively make your case orally. Award-winning explanations can sway hearts and minds of loan reps only if put on paper. Lenders follow this rule: "If it's not in writing, it doesn't exist." Loan reps and underwriters need "protect your job" paperwork piled higher and deeper. Such paperwork doesn't just protect the frontline lending personnel. It also protects lenders against repurchase requirements that may be imposed on them by Fannie, Freddie, or the mortgager insurer (or guarantor).

Also, nearly all lenders today monitor loan quality and file data integrity through internal audits. Without the paperwork necessary to justify their loans, lenders could run into trouble with regulators, stockholders, or bank insurers such as the Federal Deposit Insurance Corporation (FDIC). If you want a lender to view your past, present, and future in-

2. Lenders would probably use income from the past two years and the year to date; however, this example illustrates the principle.

come more favorably than it would otherwise, write out and deliver your evidence—before the lender formally reviews your application.

SECRET # **9**

Reduce your disqualifying debt.

Any type of legally enforceable recurring debt obligations may count toward your total debt ratio; therefore, high monthly repayments can prevent you from obtaining loan approval. At a minimum, high debts will reduce the amount that you can borrow. From the following list, total your current required minimum monthly payments.

◆ Car #1	$_____	◆ Alimony	$_____
◆ Car #2	$_____	◆ Child support	$_____
◆ Car #3	$_____	◆ Merchant account #1	$_____
◆ Motorcycle	$_____	◆ Merchant account #2	$_____
◆ Jet ski	$_____	◆ Merchant account #3	$_____
◆ Power boat	$_____	◆ Judgments/liens	$_____
◆ Furniture	$_____	◆ Personal loans	$_____
◆ Student loan(s)	$_____	◆ Mortgage #1	$_____
◆ Appliance	$_____	◆ Mortgage #2	$_____
◆ Credit card #1	$_____	◆ Other	$_____
◆ Credit card #2	$_____	◆ Other	$_____
◆ Credit card #3	$_____	◆ Other	$_____
◆ Credit card #4	$_____	◆ Other	$_____
◆ Medical bills	$_____		

Total monthly debt repayments = $

What to Count, What to Leave Out

For purposes of calculating the total debt ratio, lenders usually divide your monthly payments into two types. These include installment debt, which includes self-liquidating debts such as autos, boats, medical bills, and student loans; and revolving (or open) accounts, which include Visa, MasterCard, American Express Optima, Home Depot, Texaco, and any other types of credit lines that remain open until you or your friendly creditor close them.

Not All Payments Count

Most lenders ignore payments for *installment* debts that are scheduled for payoff within 6 to 10 months from the date of your mortgage application; however, if the lease on your auto is set to expire shortly, you're out of luck. Those payments still count against you. The lender assumes (unless convinced otherwise) that you will continue to incur this expense when you lease a new car to replace the old one.

You do, however, get a break for qualifying when lenders look at your revolving debt. Even if you regularly pay hundreds of dollars more per month than your minimum payment(s) due, most lenders will only count your payment as 5 percent of your outstanding balances. Or when less than 5 percent, your actual minimum required payments—providing you inform the lender accordingly.

Prepare Well in Advance

As with proving your qualifying income, prepare your desired debt profile as soon as you can. Not only will this tactic lift your qualifying ratios, it *may* also boost your credit scores. Here are some tips:

- *Consolidate bills* One payment of $280 a month will hurt you less than four payments of $125; however, don't close three accounts and then run another up close to its credit limit. Credit scoring doesn't like high balances relative to card limits.
- *Pay down debt.* If your installment debt has only 11 or 12 months to go, prepay two or three payments. That pushes those debts off the table and out of sight—under the rules followed by most lenders.
- *Pay off debt.* If you can swing it, get rid of as much debt as you can.
- *Avoid new debt.* No matter how much you are tempted, take on no new debt prior to applying for a mortgage. Even if you can easily afford it, you're better off waiting until after you've been through closing.

These tips especially apply if your ratios are pushing against the lender's guideline total debt limits; your credit score falls below, say, 700; or you're requesting a low-down-payment loan (a loan-to-value ratio of greater than 80 percent). A pint-sized debt load can help offset the warts in your credit profile.

SECRET # 10

Use compensating factors to justify higher qualifying ratios.

No two families (or people) are alike. That's why many lenders will step outside of their approval guidelines when you give them prudent reasons to do so.

Compensating Factors Make the Difference

Gordon Steinback, an executive who works for the Mortgage Guarantee Insurance Corporation, says his firm "routinely approves borrowers who don't meet standard underwriting criteria." Yet, as Gordon points out, "regrettably, too many borrowers never get beyond the application stage. This happens because these borrowers don't meet the so-called 'standard' qualifying ratios and are needlessly screened out prematurely by [those] real estate agents or loan officers at the local level [who too quickly try to pigeonhole borrowers as simply qualified or unqualified]. Experience shows, however, that a large percentage of borrowers fall into a gray area. They could get approved for a loan if only someone would show them how."

Types of Compensating Factors

What types of compensating factors will lenders consider? Virtually anything positive that reasonably demonstrates you can make your monthly payments responsibly and control your finances. Here are a dozen examples:

- You've been making rent payments that equal or exceed the after-tax cost of your proposed mortgage payments.
- You have a good record of savings. You regularly spend less than you earn, and use credit sparingly.
- You are situated on the fast track in your career or employment. You have a good record of promotions and raises.
- For your age and occupation, you have a high net worth, such as cash value life insurance, 401(k) retirement funds, stocks, bonds, savings account, other real estate, and so on.
- You have put aside more than adequate cash reserves to handle unexpected financial setbacks.
- You or your spouse will generate extra income through part-time work, a second job, tips, bonuses, or overtime.
- You carry little or no monthly installment debt. This can work well when your housing cost ratio exceeds its guideline, but your total debt ratio falls within its limits.
- You've been through a homebuying counseling program that helps homebuyers develop a realistic budget. Fannie and Freddie lenders give special deals to first-time buyers who complete these programs. Many only last four hours, and they're well worth the time.
- You're making a down payment of 20 percent or larger.
- Your employer provides excellent benefits: auto, cash reimbursement for a home office, a superior health and dental insurance plan, large contributions to your retirement account, and so on.
- You earn an above average income. Budget-conscious people whose earnings exceed $4,000 or $5,000 a month often enjoy the financial flexibility to devote more money to housing than typical qualifying ratios indicate.
- Your nonhousing living expenses are lower than average. You would explain that you can afford a higher mortgage because: the home is energy efficient; you can walk to work or just drive a short commute; you have no costly vices (smoking, drinking); you spend conservatively by backpacking for vacations, driving a cream puff 1997 Ford Contour, and buying clothes at the outlet stores; you're handy with tools so you can perform your own household maintenance; or your food costs are low because your parents supply you

from their garden with all the fresh and home-canned vegetables you can eat.

Put Your Compensating Factors in Writing

After you've developed a list of reasons why you can afford the mortgage you want, don't just tell your loan officer. Put your reasons in writing. Get supporting letters from your employer, minister, landlord, clients, customers, or anyone else who can vouch for your good character, creditworthiness, job performance, or personal responsibility. Sometimes, too, it's a good idea to write out a family budget. Show your lender that your monthly income exceeds your monthly spending. (VA loans may actually require this step.) Then back up your budget with proof: financial records, cancelled checks, letters, and all of the compensating factors you can think of. With convincing written evidence, you'll be able to break through qualifying guidelines that deter or delay other ill-prepared borrowers.

SECRET # 11

Never fib to a lender.

To stretch their buying power, more than a few borrowers stretch the truth. "Everybody fibs a little," they say. "Besides, how's the lender going to find out?" Verifications, that's how.

Verify, Verify, Verify—Then Audit

Most surely, lenders will check your income and debts. They may also want proof of your divorce or separation agreement, where you're getting the money for your down payment, any gifts you claim to have received, bank and investment account balances, and virtually any other fact that is material to your loan application.

Verification of Income

To verify income, your lender may call or write your employer, inspect your pay stubs, ask to see copies of your tax returns, and/or request your permission (Form 4506) to contact the IRS directly.[3] In performing these checks, the lender will compare all numbers obtained through third-party sources with each other and with those provided on your loan application. Should the lender discover (nontrivial) discrepancies, it will delay or deny your loan.

So, don't inadvertently (or intentionally) err with the figures you provide. Carefully confirm their accuracy and agreement.

Verify Debts

To verify the amount of your debts, the lender will obtain credit reports from the three major credit repositories (see Chapter 5). In addition, the lender may ask you to provide your most recent monthly bank account statements. The lender may also run a separate check of public records to look for outstanding judgments or liens against you. Because discrepancies among debt balances are common, take care to provide evidence that the figures you show on your application reflect the truth.

For example, you may have paid off your car loan two or three months ago, but Experian still shows a balance of $1,400. If you can't get Experian to quickly correct its error, give the lender a copy of your auto title, lien satisfaction, and canceled check.

Other Verifications

As previously noted, you may want (or be asked) to provide numerous other types of verifications. To make sure you're not (improperly) borrowing funds for your down payment, lenders frequently require you to provide bank statements from the past three months. Also, if you're separated or divorced, previous joint debts with your (ex-) spouse will still show up on your credit report. Make sure you list these debts on your application. Likewise, should your divorce agreement saddle you with financial obligations, declare these, too. Even if they don't show up in your credit file, the lender will likely discover them by obtaining a copy of your executed divorce or separation agreement.

---

3. If you complete this form, clearly mark the years you want the lender to see; otherwise, you give some nosy underwriter permission to look at your full history of tax returns.

The Application Itself Contains Many Clues to Your Integrity

Most lenders will carefully review your loan application. They search for numerical discrepancies, missing information, gaps in dates, inconsistencies, and any whiffs that smell fishy. "Hmm," the lender muses, "You say you've been out of college only three years, but you show no debts for student loans on your application and you report cash savings of $25,000. Would you mind telling me how you managed that feat?"

Experienced loan reps and underwriters have examined hundreds of loan apps. Their eyebrows raise easily. If your life story evokes an air of mystery, don't leave the loan rep in the dark. Provide firm evidence that you're traveling the straight and narrow. Even innocent lapses in your application can spell trouble, if not satisfactorily explained.

An application with warts and lapses that is effectively explained will stand a better chance of approval than an application that's deceptively perplexing. The best lenders would rather solve borrower problems that relate to income or debt than run the risk of loaning money to someone they do not trust. In testimony before Congress, the great banker J. Pierpont Morgan was asked:

Q. "Is not credit based primarily on money or property?"
A. "No sir, the first thing is character."
Q. "Before money or property?"
A. "Before money or anything else. Money cannot buy credit. Because a man I do not trust could not get credit from me on all the bonds of Christendom."

Take J.P. Morgan's advice. Don't try to play games with the lender. Report all income and debts truthfully. Not only will such honesty result in greater borrowing power over the long run, it will keep you out of jail. Lying (or misrepresentation) on a mortgage application subjects you to thousands of dollars in fines, and up to two years in federal prison.

SECRET # **12**

Can't qualify on your own? Enlist the help of a cosigner, co-borrower, or co-owner.

Okay, you've revamped your financial profile (income, debts, credit) and still your borrowing power's too weak to get the property you want. Consider bringing in a cosigner, co-borrower, or co-owner. Here are some examples of how these techniques have helped first-time homebuyers—but they can also be adapted for use by investors.

Cosigners, Co-Borrowers, Co-Owners

"I'm not sure about this one," say loan officer Tiffany Lane to homebuyers Paul and Cindy Jackson. "Even counting both your incomes and 75 percent of the rents from the garage apartment, your qualifying ratios are still high and your credit is blemished with two 30-day late payments on your car loan during the past 12 months. I want to see you get your home, but I'd feel a lot more comfortable presenting your application to the loan committee if we could get one of your parents to cosign your mortgage."

A cosigner is someone who guarantees to make your mortgage payments should you fail to do so. A cosigner is usually a parent or other close relative. For borderline applications, getting a cosigner could tip the mortgage underwriters in your favor. Cosigners can't change a flat turndown into an enthusiastic yes, but in marginal cases where you look pretty good—but not quite good enough—a cosigner can give a lender the confidence necessary to approve your mortgage.

Co-Borrowing

But what if your buying power needs a rocket engine booster? You might look for a co-borrower. Whereas a cosigner only figures marginally in a loan approval, a co-borrower fully participates in the mortgage application process. If your qualifying ratios blow past the loan program's limits, adding in a co-borrower's income to your ratio calculations could bring them safely back into approval territory.

You would use a co-borrower when in the eyes of a lender, your *qualifying* income alone doesn't look like it will support the amount of mortgage you want to borrow; however, even with a co-borrower, if you can raise the money each month to make your loan payments—housemates, accessory apartments, second job, self-employment, tight budgeting, or whatever—that's perfectly all right. The lender won't care where the monthly payments come from, as long as you make them on time.

Co-Owners

At age 74, lifelong renter Mary Mills had ruled out the possibility of owning her own home. She believed she was too old and lacked adequate income. But one day she read a flyer distributed by Shaker Heights Realtor, Frank Berry. This flyer explained a technique that Frank calls "co-op buying." Frank says, "It was something I stumbled upon . . . . I stumbled on it by talking to people. I learned that with so many people unable to buy houses by themselves, some do it as a team. Relatives and nonrelatives alike sometimes go together to buy their homes."

Intrigued by this idea, Mary Mills called her daughter-in-law. Yes, she, too, wanted to become a homeowner, but didn't think she could afford it by herself. So together, they contacted Frank to see if he could help them. Well, Frank was the right person to call. Within several months, Mary and her daughter-in-law became first-time homeowners. By combining their incomes, they were able to buy and move into their own duplex.

Brenda Daniels and Family

Another of Frank Berry's clients was Brenda Daniels. She went in with her aunt, sister, and cousin to buy a two-family house in the Union-Miles section of Cleveland. Together they raised a three-percent down payment and all joined in the mortgage qualifying process. "These co-owner buyers aren't treated any differently from the traditional married couple or single buyer," reports Thomas Deighton of Security Federal Savings & Loan. Although as Thomas admits, co-owner purchases take longer to close because they require multiple applications, credit reports, and other documents for each buyer, and the lender must review all of them.

Realtor Frank Berry agrees that co-owner deals are more complex and require him to work harder. "But, I feel this is sort of a mission for me," says Frank, "to give them a home because they don't have it. Every buyer I've done this with had previously counted themselves out of home ownership. That's the amazing thing about it."

Equity Sharing

Although co-ownership usually works best when you buy with family or friends, some Realtors specialize in matching professional investors with homebuyers. This technique is called equity sharing. In exchange for part ownership of your home, tax shelter benefits, and appreciation potential, an investor will contribute a down payment, borrowing power, and sometimes part of your monthly payments. You and the investor negotiate the exact terms of your agreement.

During the 1980s, when interest rates and down payments were much higher than they are now, equity sharing was widely promoted as a good way to achieve home affordability—especially for first-time buyers in cities with high-priced housing. Today, with lower interest rates and so many new, easier qualifying loan programs, equity sharing has lost much of its reason for being.

In addition, in days gone by, many investors figured on home appreciation rates of at least 10 percent a year and heftier tax benefits than those currently available. With these conditions changed, homebuyers and investors have dropped their affection for equity sharing. Yet, it's still a technique to keep in mind. Buying a home or income property with an equity sharing investor sure beats renting or investing in stocks. As equity share Realtors point out, "Half a loaf is better than no loaf at all."

SECRET # 13

Let tenants pay your mortgage.

In my 1996 book, *Stop Renting Now!,* I urged first-time buyers to increase their borrowing power by "letting tenants pay your mortgage." I urged potential buyers to choose a two- to four-unit rental property and live in one unit for a few years until they built up some nice-sized equity.

Anyone who followed my advice would have made a very handsome profit—far better than stocks. "But that was then, and this is now," you say. True, yet the advice still holds strong profit potential.

"I'm trying to buy my first home, but without success," writes Lorrain Stark to nationally respected real estate columnist and investor Robert Bruss. "My problem is that I don't have enough income to qualify for a mortgage. [Do you think] I should buy a two- or three-unit rental property . . . to provide income to help pay the mortgage?"

Bob Bruss responds that he thinks it's an excellent idea. In fact, that's how he got started in real estate. "My first [home]," Bob answers, "was a triplex where I lived in one unit . . . . The rental income provided the money for my mortgage payments . . . . My triplex wasn't my dream house . . . [but] few of us can afford to buy our dream home when we start out. Eventually, though, we can build equity and then move up to the home we really like."

Should You Buy a Two- to Four-Family Home (or Larger)?

As I mentioned in Chapter 1 (*Mortgage Secret #5*), you may be tempted to reject the idea of buying a two- to four-family property (or larger). Your goal for home ownership may be to get yourself out of an apartment, not back into another one. What may be worse, it's unlikely that you would relish the headaches and hassles of managing tenants. But . . . before you throw out this possibility, take a hard look at the numbers.

Even if you can presently afford a single-family home you want (or close to it), give serious thought to how tall you want to stand financially three to eight years from now. After you realize the wealth-building advantages of combining rental income with home ownership, you may change your mind.

How to Finance a Two- to Four-Family (or Larger) Home

For starters, realize that virtually every home financing technique mentioned throughout *Mortgage Secrets* is available for two- to four-family, owner-occupied properties. You can buy with FHA, VA, conventional, private mortgage insurance, or any type of seller-assisted financing. In fact, seller-assisted financing for rental properties is generally more readily available than it is for single-family homes. In addition, you can find assumables; you can use a buydown, a second mortgage, an ARM, a graduated payment mortgage (GPM), even state bond money, and mortgage credit certificates (MCCs). Assumable buydowns, GPMs, and MCCs boost your affordability and are explained in later chapters. You can sometimes buy with five percent down or less. If you don't have all the up-front cash investment you need, bring in a co-owner as a partner.

Even when you can't figure out a borrowing strategy that will get you into a single-family home, you can certainly develop the financial techniques to buy a two- to four-unit property. In fact, depending on where you live, you may find it easier to finance a multiple-family home than a single-family house.

On the other hand, most *larger* multifamily properties and some *nonconforming* two- to four-unit properties can be more difficult to finance through a *typical* mortgage lending institution. If you locate one of these tough-to-finance properties, the fact that lenders shy away from it—or maybe require a 20 to 30 percent down payment—could work to your advantage.

Because the more difficult it is to finance a property through a financial institution, the greater the chance that the owner will offer seller-assisted financing. As long as you get the property inspected closely to ensure good physical condition and make sure it complies with zoning and building regulations, this type of multifamily investment property could easily open your door to your future perfect home.

Prices and Rents Vary by City and Neighborhood

If you live in Berkeley, Queens, or the District's Capitol Hill, a well-kept fourplex might cost you $550,000 or more. In Pittsburgh, Peoria, or Paducah, you can buy small multifamily investment properties for as little as $100,000. As to the relationship between rents and price, these, too, vary significantly by city and neighborhood. In Detroit, you can find rental properties selling for $75,000 that generate $1,000 a month in rent payments. In San Francisco, a four-family unit that generates $5,000 a month in rents might sell for $750,000.

Nonetheless, one fact is certain: No matter where you live, a two- or four-unit (or more) investment will give you the borrowing power to buy a higher-priced property. This multifamily unit can help you build wealth faster than the lower-priced single-family home you otherwise could afford.

Run through the Numbers: A Comparison

Imagine you're considering a single-family home priced around $100,000. You plan to put $10,000 down, and borrow $90,000 at 8.5 percent interest for 30 years. Your principal, interest, property taxes, and insurance (PITI) plus upkeep will run $950 a month.

As another possibility, you find a nice fourplex with four large two-bedroom units priced at $235,000. All four units are currently rented and bring in $2,750 a month. With help from your parents, you could put $15,000 down on this fourplex and finance $220,000 over 30 years at an interest rate of 9.0 percent. For this property, your PITI plus repairs and maintenance will cost $2,300 a month. You plan to hold whichever property you buy for a period of five years. How will these choices differ financially?

Equity Buildup. One big advantage of the fourplex over the single-family home is equity buildup. For any given rate of appreciation, the larger property will help you accumulate wealth faster.

Equity Buildup (4 Percent Annual Appreciation)

	Value in five years	*Mortgage balance*	*Equity*
Fourplex	$286,700	$210,915	$75,785
Single-family	122,000	85,951	36,049

Equity Buildup (6 Percent Annual Appreciation)

	Value in five years	*Mortgage balance*	*Equity*
Fourplex	$316,968	$210,915	$106,053
Single-family	134,880	85,951	48,929

These numbers again show that at the same rate of appreciation, you build wealth faster if you buy an income property. A $300,000 property that appreciates 25 percent over five years will give you $75,000 in appreciation. A $150,000 property that appreciates 25 percent over five years will give you only half that amount. Naturally, your results could turn out better or worse, and will depend not only on your property's rate of appreciation, but how well you can enhance its value. Still, the logic is straightforward: An income property can put you into a higher-priced property, and help you build your net worth more quickly.

Lower Monthly Costs. An income property can boost your power to build home equity in another way, too. Even though you may pay a higher price for a two- to four-family or larger property, your net monthly housing costs will probably end up lower. In the previous example, the four-unit property costs $2,300 a month for principal, interest, property taxes, insurance, and upkeep. If you forgo $700 a month from your building's rent collections of $2,750 a month because you move into one of the four units, the other three units will still yield gross rents of around $2,000 a month.

When you subtract that $2,000 of rental income from your outgo for mortgage payments and operating costs of $2,300 a month, you're personally spending only $300 each month. You save $650 a month as compared to the $950 a month you'd pay for that $100,000 single-family home you otherwise would have bought. Over a period of five years, these monthly savings would total close to $40,000. If you raised rents each year and banked your housing cost savings, you could probably accumulate more than $50,000 over five years. Add these savings to your equity buildup, and you would have pyramided your $15,000 down payment on the fourplex into as much as $125,000—and possibly more.

Share with Housemates

In some sky-high housing markets around the country, singles and couples might try Doreen Bierbrier's strategy. "My biggest accomplishment in Washington, D.C.," writes Doreen Bierbrier, "was buying a house and creating a management system for it that worked." Doreen describes her experiences in her book, *Living with Tenants: How to happily share your house with renters for profit and security* (McGraw-Hill, 1986).

"When I bought my first home," Doreen explains, "I was earning a modest salary . . . . I decided that the only way I could buy a house in a good neighborhood was to find one large enough to accommodate a couple of housemates who paid rent. If everything worked out, the rental income would cover more than half of my house payment and two-thirds of my utilities. Adding in tax advantage and appreciation, I figured buying a home would actually make me money. Even better, some time later when the house was paid off, I would own a valuable asset free and clear . . . . It's amazing how things fall into place [even when you think] you have no choice."

Generate Income with Your Single-Family Home

As Doreen points out, you can generate income from your home even if you choose to pass up a two- to four-family property in favor of a single-family house. Today, this technique is so popular that there are a half-dozen or more books on the market with titles such as *Homesharing and Other Lifestyle Options; Housemates: A Practical Guide for Living with Others;* and *The Complete Roommate Handbook.* The latest U.S. Census reports that 6.1 million homeowners now share their homes with non–family members.

This idea worked so profitably for Doreen Bierbrier that she quit her modestly paying job and, within a year and a half, bought three more houses that she organized as houseshare room rentals. In fact, Doreen bought her second home using a VA assumable mortgage and borrowed the down payment from her father. Unfortunately, today, most lenders won't permit housemate rents to count as qualifying income, so you may have to talk to a savvy mortgage broker who could find a willing lender.

John Walker, however, got around the qualifying income problem by asking his mom to come in as a co-borrower on his mortgage. That got him past the lender's scrutiny. After moving into his home, he found two housemates to pick up over half of his monthly mortgage payments. John's mother never paid anything.

Realtor Mary Rodriguez tells of one of her buyers who bought a house that was then rented by three women. Instead of evicting these tenants, the new buyer moved in with them. "He didn't even ask for the master bedroom," Rodriguez recalled.

Choose Your Home Carefully

If a houseshare could work as part of your financial strategy, make sure you buy a house that adapts itself well to roommate living. Privacy, security, location of entrances, noise, parking, as well as kitchen and bathroom access are critically important. Before you buy, pose as a potential tenant and meet with other homeowners who are advertising for housemates. Identify those house features that would appeal to you if you were to live as a roommate in someone else's home.

Also, size up the rental market to learn which home features and locations pull the highest demand and rental rates. In expensive cities, room rents often range between $400 and $800 a month. At today's lower interest rates, houseshare income can add $75,000 to $150,000 (or more) to your borrowing/buying power.

My Personal Experience

I've seen this housesharing strategy work well firsthand. During the time I taught at the University of Virginia, I spent many weekends in Washington, D.C. To avoid hotels when in D.C., I participated in a houseshare. The fellow who was buying the house collected enough from me, his girlfriend, and one other housemate to cover two-thirds of his mortgage. And this house was no slouch—a $300,000 (16 years later, now $850,000) Georgetown three-story home. Although skeptical at first, I actually found the experience fun.

Likewise, Doreen Bierbrier enjoyed the personal side of housesharing. "For me," Doreen explains, "the advantages of sharing my house with tenants have overwhelmingly outweighed the disadvantages. Having housemates [not only] made it possible for me to buy and maintain a house at a time when most people told me my salary was too low to consider buying. [But also] tenants have provided countless hours of companionship, laughter, and insights into everything from Republican fund-raising to Vietnamese cuisine—things I never would have discovered had I lived alone."

Accessory Apartments

Maybe you don't want to take in housemates, or buy a two- to four-family home, but you need more income to boost your borrowing power.

Then consider a midpoint solution. Buy a home with an accessory apartment. These units are commonly known as a granny flat, garage apartment, carriage house, studio, efficiency, in-law quarters, or basement suite. In Vancouver, British Columbia, for example, more than 100,000 homes include basement suites. They not only boost owner borrowing power, they also provide an essential supplement to the super-tight housing market in Vancouver.

Accessory rentals usually permit you to share your home without noticeable effect on your daily living. And they don't require the same level of management and upkeep that some multifamily properties require.

By adopting the accessory apartment happy medium, you can generate $350 to $750 a month in income. If you borrowed, say, $175,000 to buy a home with an accessory apartment that rents for $450 a month, your net out-of-pocket costs of home ownership would probably drop below $750 a month. If this idea to raise your borrowing power appeals to you, go out and look at some homes with accessory apartments. Counting this extra income, you'll be able to buy a larger house, or perhaps move into a more expensive neighborhood.

Create Your Own Accessory Apartment

If you can't find the home you want already equipped with a rental unit, you can always create your own. That's what freelance artist Andrea Pogue did.

Andrea bought a three-story fixer-upper and converted the lowest floor into an accessory apartment that she rented to two sisters for $550 a month. When Andrea fully realized the income potential of her house, she carried her idea one step further. After the tenant sisters moved out, Andrea moved herself up to the third floor of her house. She then renovated both lower floors into two private units and rented them for $750 a month each.

"I don't earn much," says Andrea, "and I doubt that I'll ever become another Andy Warhol and make a fortune. So it's great to have the security of rent checks coming in. I'm now receiving $1,500 a month. That's enough to pay my mortgage and cover part of my property taxes and homeowners insurance."

Zoning and Inspections

Before you buy a house with the intent to add an accessory apartment, investigate whether zoning or building regulations might restrict your rights to operate the property as you have planned. Likewise, just as some houses work much better than others for houseshare arrangements, so, too, do some properties lend themselves more or less readily to apartment conversions. As you inspect and evaluate houses, visualize whether they offer good opportunity for creating an accessory rental unit.

SECRET # 14

Don't change your loan status.

After you shape up your income and debt profile, and submit your mortgage application, don't change your loan status until after you've closed your loan. Too many hopeful borrowers believe that after their loan approval goes through, they're home free. Not true. The lender may continue to verify your employment (income) and monthly bills up to the time of settlement.

A job change or loss, a new car lease, or ordering new kitchen appliances on your Sears credit card could give the lender the right to revoke your approval, and yet charge you for various mortgage costs such as application fees, appraisals, surveys, title checks. Even changes that you consider positive, such as a new job with a raise in salary, could be viewed by the lender as job instability or uncertainty.

In some instances, the loan rep might ask you to revamp your finances to pay down debt, settle a disputed collection account, satisfy liens or judgments, or make some property repairs or improvements. To retain loan approval, you should honor these requests, if possible; however, if you are plagued by some past collections, liens, or judgments that remain unpaid, disclose that to the loan rep before you apply. Should you not want to pay these debts, you may need to find a more tolerant lender. Basically, though, make no financial changes that would materially change the information you've provided during the loan application process.

CHAPTER 3

Slash Your Cost of Interest

If you've read other books or articles on mortgages, you've probably heard the clichéd advice, "Shop 'til you drop. Call lenders and search for the best rates. A rate just one-half percent lower than the competition can mean thousands of dollars to you over the life of the mortgage."

What's Right and What's Wrong with This Advice?

First, what's right. No question, saving one-half percent on a mortgage interest rate can put thousands into your pocket. You most certainly should shop for your financing and compare interest rates and other costs (see Chapter 9); however, dialing for dollars to find the best rate on a 30-year fixed-rate mortgage (as most borrowers do) won't likely achieve this objective.

Rate Quotes

No loan rep can know the interest rate a lender will charge you until after you've submitted your application for a loan. Interest rates for 30-year fixed-rate mortgages will vary according to your credit score, qualifying ratios, amount of down payment, type of property, and other variables the loan reps won't learn until after they've got all of your financial data in front of them. In addition, mortgage rates can change daily. No loan rep can confirm the rate you will pay until the day you lock, or the day funding occurs.

These loan reps who do offer you a lowball rate quote are probably setting you up for bait and switch or other disreputable sales tactics (see Chapter 9); however, even given these deficiencies in the telephone rate quotes, the quotes themselves aren't the real problem. The real problem is that most borrowers err in their choice of financing. Borrowers mistakenly assume they should originate a new 30-year fixed-rate mortgage before they've fully explored their other financing alternatives.

Alternative Terms and Sources of Financing

Without a doubt, the most expensive loan product on the market is the 30-year fixed-rate mortgage popularly offered by mortgage companies, banks, and savings institutions.[1] Correspondingly, unless you've let more than a few bills slip by unpaid, or suffered some other qualifying difficulties such as no provable income because you've been working "off the books," rarely will shopping among lenders net you a one-half percent lower rate. Because of the competitive nature of mortgage markets, rates for grade A borrowers among major lenders seldom vary by more than one-eighth (at most one-fourth) percent.[2]

In stark contrast, if you truly want to save money in terms of interest rates, total long-term interest costs, and other fees of borrowing, you will avoid the standard 30-year fixed-rate loans offered by most lenders and search for alternative terms and sources of financing.

SECRET # 15

Most borrowers who want a long-term fixed-rate loan should choose 15 years, not 30.

For four decades, the 30-year fixed-rate mortgage has ranked as the most popular loan product because it permits borrowers to obtain larger

1. For purposes here, I'm ignoring the costly practices and loan programs of predatory lenders (see Chapter 8).

2. Borrowers with lower credit scores yet perfect payment records may find that shopping for rates will yield big savings. See *Mortgage Secret #41*.

loans and buy more expensive houses. With this advantage, the loan appears to please the interests of homebuyers, mortgage lenders, and real estate agents. More recently, though, increasing numbers of borrowers have begun to question the expense of this long-standing, near-automatic choice of loans.

The High Costs of 30-Year Loans

I would bet that until the past couple of years, not more than 1 out of 10 potential homebuyers carefully weighed the costs and benefits of 15-year as opposed to 30-year mortgages. In automatically thinking 30 years, they focused on affordability as the only determining feature. Don't make this mistake. If you're going to insist on a 30-year loan, at least make this choice in full view of the price it will cost you.

Total Interest Costs

You will pay an astonishingly higher amount of interest with the 30-year loan, relative to a 15-year loan. Your savings on the 15-year plan result from two sources: The 15-year loan typically will lower your interest rate by anywhere from .375 percent up to .6 percent as contrasted to the 30-year loan, and you pay interest for only half as long. Based on current rates, look at the interest cost comparisons in Table 3.1. As you can see from these figures, you will pay $153,242 more for the pleasure of taking twice as long to pay off your mortgage—a pretty hefty cost disadvantage.

Table 3.1 **Save Big with a 15-Year Loan**

The Differences between a 15-Year Loan and a 30-Year Mortgage

	15-Year	*30-Year*
Mortgage amount	$200,000.00	$200,000.00
Interest rate	5.9%	6.5%
Payment frequency	Monthly	Monthly
Monthly payment amount	$1,676.92	$1,264.13
Total interest paid	$101,846.91	$255,088.92
30-year cost premium		$153,242.01

Table 3.2 **Equity Buildup Due to Mortgage Paydown of $200,000: 15-Year vs. 30-Year**

	15-Year	*(Balance)*	30-Year	*(Balance)*
Original loan	$200,000	($200,000)	$200,000	($200,000)
	48,189	(151,829)	12,799	(187,201)
Total paydown @ 10 years	113,048	(86,952)	30,466	(169,534)
Total paydown @ 15 years	200,000	(-0-)	54,898	(145,102)

Equity Buildup

As *Mortgage Secrets* emphasized in Chapter 1, you should weigh the effect your financing will have on your future net worth. To help with that calculation, look at Table 3.2. Not including appreciation, the figures clearly show that the 15-year mortgage grows your home equity much faster. After 15 years, you've paid off the full $200,000, but with the 30-year loan, you still owe a whopping $145,102.

Alternative Use of $412 Per Month

If you're a savvy investor, you may say, "Hold on here." The cost and equity advantages illustrated in these tables ignore the extra $412 a month that you will have to pay to reap these interest-saving advantages. You may figure that you could invest $412 each month in your 401(k), and earn (over the long term) a rate of return of 10 or 12 percent a year. So, after 15 or 20 years, your pile of investment funds would weigh much more than the interest savings and equity buildup that the 15-year borrower will receive.

Under some circumstances, you're right. And we will go through some calculations along those lines in Chapter 10. For now, however, recognize that the 15-year benefits shown will result without risk. You can count on them. Any time you talk investments that promise yields of 10 percent, 12 percent, or higher, you could end up with much less or even lose principal. Money held as home equity offers far more security than cash held in stocks or bonds (see *Mortgage Secret #98*).

Equity Buildup with Appreciation

All other things being equal, lenders will qualify you to borrow more money if you use a 30-year loan; however, thinking in terms of net worth, let's see how the 15-year mortgage compares to the 30-year loan if the most you want to pay per month for principal and interest is $1,264. With that size of payment and a 15-year fixed-rate loan, you could borrow around $151,000. Nevertheless, as Table 3.3 shows, you still build equity faster with the 15-year home financing.

Table 3.3 **Equity Buildup Due to Mor tgage Paydown of $151,000: 15-Year vs. 30-Year**

	15-Year	*(Balance)*	30-Year	*(Balance)*
Original loan	$151,000	(151,000)	$200,000	(200,000)
Total paydown @ 5 years	35,502	(114,498)	12,799	(187,201)
Total paydown @ 10 years	65,578	(865,422)	30,466	(169,534)
Total paydown @ 15 years	151,000	(-0-)	54,898	(145,102)

Both loans require a payment of $1,264 per month.

Say that you would like to trade up homes in five years. With either type of mortgage, you would have placed $20,000 down. That means with the 15-year mortgage, you bought a home priced at $171,000; with the 30-year, a $220,000 property. Each property appreciates at 3 percent per year. Table 3.4 shows how your total equity would compute.

Table 3.4 **Total Equity Buildup (3% Appreciation) @ Five Years**

	15-Year	*30-Year*
Purchase price	$171,000	$220,000
Appreciated value @ 3% p.a.	198,531	255,420
Mortgage balance @ 5 years	114,498	187,201
Total equity	$84,033	$68,219

Or, what if we assume a 5 percent per year rate of appreciation (see Table 3.5):

Table 3.5 **Total Equity Buildup (5% Appreciation) @ Five Years**

	15-Year	*30-Year*
Purchase price	$171,000	$220,000
Appreciated value @ 5% p.a.	219,393	282,260
Mortgage balance @ 5 years	114,498	187,201
Total equity	$104,895	$95,059

Again, the figures show that even with a 5 percent per year appreciation rate, you would build equity quicker with the less expensive house and mortgage than the more expensive house and mortgage. In this example, you would need an 8 percent annual appreciation rate before the 30-year mortgage actually gave you a larger home equity after five years.

The common advice has always been to buy the most expensive house you can afford, and you will build wealth faster through leverage and appreciation. But this advice often fails. For most borrowers in most markets, the 15-year mortgage, even on a lower-priced home (holding payments the same), will give larger and safer returns.

Don't misunderstand. *Mortgage Secrets* does not specifically encourage you to obtain a 15-year fixed-rate mortgage, but do yourself a favor. Before you automatically decide on a 30-year mortgage, get a sharp loan rep to work through the numbers with you. From a wealth-building view, the 30-year fixed-rate loan on a higher-priced house proves superior only during periods of extraordinary high rates of appreciation.

SECRET # 16

Lower interest rates mean big savings.

You already know that lower interest rates save you money, but do you know how much? Look at Table 3.6. You can again see the striking difference in total interest costs between 15-year and 30-year loans. Also, recall that lenders typically charge about one-half percent less for 15-year rates. For example, if market rates were 7.5 percent (15-year) and

Table 3.6 **Total Interest Costs Per $100,000 @ Selected Interest Rates**

Rate (%)	*Monthly Payment ($)*	*15-Year (Total Interest, $)*	*Monthly Payment ($)*	*30-Year (Total Interest, $)*
4.0	740	33,128	477	71,864
4.5	765	37,628	507	82,376
5.0	791	42,326	537	93,248
5.5	817	47,060	568	104,372
6.0	844	51,884	600	115,820
6.5	871	56,798	632	127,520
7.0	899	61,784	665	139,508
7.5	927	66,860	699	151,712
8.0	956	72,008	734	164,132
8.5	985	77,246	769	176,804
9.0	1,014	82,556	805	189,656
9.5	1,044	87,956	840	202,544
10.0	1,075	93,428	878	215,900
12.0	1,200	116,018	1,028	270,296
14.0	1,332	139,706	1,185	326,564

All figures are rounded.

8.0 percent (30-year), the interest costs would be $66,860 and $164,132, respectively—a savings of nearly $100,000 for the 15-year mortgage (on a $100,000 loan).

Even if you compare rates solely within either the 15-year or 30-year categories, you can see how much an interest rate means in terms of both the monthly payment and total interest charged. It certainly does pay to search for financing that offers the lowest rate and cost.

SECRET # 17

Lower rates magnify borrowing power.

In Chapter 2, you learned that lenders look closely at your income and debt levels to determine how much they will lend you. High debts or low qualifying income can reduce your borrowing power. In addition, rising interest rates will slice your borrowing power as they increase your costs of borrowing. You can see these relationships in Table 3.7.

If, after looking at your income and bills, a lender says you can devote $900 a month to your mortgage payment (principal and interest), you could borrow $150,300 at 6 percent interest, but only $102,600 at 10 percent interest. The figures in Table 3.7 again reinforce this point: To increase borrowing power and slash interest costs, find lower rate financing. How do you do that? Here are six techniques that *Mortgage Secrets* will look at in the remainder of this chapter and several later chapters.

- Consider an adjustable rate mortgage (ARM).
- Call your state and local housing finance agencies about mortgage bond money.
- Search for a lower-rate mortgage assumption.
- Buy from a builder or developer who is offering discounted interest rates.
- Weigh the benefit of paying points.
- Ask the seller to pay for an interest rate buydown.

Table 3.7 **How Much Can You Borrow at Various Interest Rates and Monthly Payments?**

Monthly Payment (P&I, $)	*4% ($)*	*6% ($)*	*8% ($)*	*10% ($)*	*12% ($)*
400	83,800	66,800	54,500	45,600	38,900
600	125,800	100,200	81,700	68,400	58,300
750	157,200	125,200	102,200	85,500	72,900
900	188,700	150,300	122,600	102,600	87,500
1,000	209,600	166,900	136,200	114,000	97,200
1,250	262,100	208,600	170,300	142,500	121,500
1,500	319,100	250,400	204,400	171,000	148,800
2,000	425,466	333,783	272,465	227,943	198,350

Term = 30 years.

SECRET # **18**

ARMs can offer greater borrowing power, lower costs, with manageable risk.

Borrowers often use ARMs to help them qualify for a larger loan. During periods when long-term interest rates head up, lenders will dangle lower qualifying teaser rates (see Chapter 4) in front of borrowers to attract them to ARMs; however, ARMs may also save you substantial interest costs. Don't automatically reject an ARM because of the fear factor, "No way, would I take an ARM. Rates may head up. I want to sleep well, not toss and turn worrying about skyrocketing mortgage payments."

After closely weighing benefits, costs, and risks, many borrowers find that some types of ARMs clearly beat the 30-year fixed-rate mortgage. Be aware, too, that no preset cost-benefit relationship prevails. Sometimes ARMs look very attractive relative to 30-year, fixed-rate mortgages; sometimes their advantages narrow or disappear. Terms and rates can also vary significantly among lenders. Rather than sell to Fannie Mae or Freddie Mac, many lenders hold ARMs in-house. These *portfolio* lenders set their own rules and rates rather than follow the standards set by the secondary mortgage market. So, shopping for ARMs may turn up a super bargain. Consider the experience of the Klar family from several years back.

The Klars Save a Bundle

Through smart shopping for their one-year, adjustable-rate mortgage, Neil and Eileen Klar located an ARM with a start rate of 4.25 percent—well below the then-average initial ARM rate of 5.71 percent. During their first year, the Klars made payments on their $450,000 mortgage of around $2,200 a month. The fixed-rate mortgage they were offered at the time carried an interest rate of 8.875 percent, and would have required payments of $3,580 a month—a one-year out-of-pocket ARM savings of $16,560.

Even if the Klars had been hit with maximum annual increases in their ARM payments due to rising interest rates, it would have taken nine years for their total ARM payments to catch up with the fixed-rate payment they were alternatively offered. By that time, they may have moved on to another home. Or, with inflation then running at 2.5 percent a year, the chances looked good that at some point during those nine years, fixed rates again would fall substantially, and the Klars would refinance. Either way, they were nearly certain to come out ahead with their ARM.

As it turned out, the Klars figured right. By the time they did refinance several years later, their full savings, relative to their fixed-rate alternative, totaled $58,371.

The Buchleightners Used a Hybrid

Increasingly, many home buyers are choosing some type of hybrid ARM. These ARMs may be referred to as 3/1, 5/1, or 7/1 options. Walter and Sara Buchleightner found a competitively priced 3/1 ARM. Their $200,000 loan started with an interest rate of 6.37 percent and held steady for three years. After that, it adjusted once a year for its remaining 27-year term. By choosing a 3/1 hybrid, Walter and Sara cut their mortgage payment from $1,599 a month for the then-proposed 9 percent fixed-rate plan to $1,240 a month for the ARM they selected.

Explaining why they were attracted to an ARM, Walter says, "Paying $1,240 a month sounded so good. We looked at rentals here [in Stamford, Connecticut], and they were going for twice what a mortgage payment is. Our rate was also so good. I shopped the mortgage market and I had people quoting me a full point higher."

Would You Rather Do the Two Steps?

With most ARM hybrids, the mortgage interest rate is fixed for, say, three, five, or seven years and then adjusts annually for the remaining term of the mortgage. In contrast, a two-step (5/25, 7/23, 10/30) starts with a low interest rate; then after the initial fixed-rate period of, say, 3, 5, 7, or 10 years, the interest rate adjusts to market and holds constant for its remaining years. If the market for fixed rates stands higher at the time of adjustment, however, you could refinance into another lower cost ARM.

Which Type of ARM Is Best?

No hard and fast rules apply to ARMs. Adjustables come in all shapes, sizes, and combinations. There are as many models of ARMs as there are models of automobiles. They can change just as quickly, too.

People do say that if you're going to own a home for only a few years, you should select an ARM to benefit from its lower start rate. Although that advice is generally valid, it doesn't always hold true. On occasion, the mortgage market goes into an inverted yield curve. At these times, short-term rates (ARMs) can actually cost more than longer-term rates. We experienced that situation both in the early and late 1980s.

More commonly, though, ARMs do provide advantages. As the experiences of the Klars and Buchleightners show, if you shop the mortgage market, you may be able to discover a bargain-priced adjustable that lifts your buying power while saving you thousands of dollars in interest. Your most important task is to price and compare a variety of ARM models; then decide which plan can best stretch your buying power, save you money, and, through low annual and lifetime caps, minimize your future risk of payment shock. (*Mortgage Secrets* discusses the various detailed features of ARMs in Chapter 4.)

SECRET # 19

State and local housing finance agencies offer low-interest mortgage bond loans.

Congress has enacted legislation that permits states, counties, cities, and various government agencies to offer below-market mortgage financing. Under these programs, state and local governments sell tax-free bonds to investors to raise low-cost mortgage money. The government then takes this money and makes lower-interest-rate loans available to first-time homebuyers (usually defined as anyone who hasn't owned a home for at least three years, or possibly homebuyers who have recently divorced and now want to buy a home on their own).

To locate a bond program in your area, ask knowledgeable Realtors and mortgage lenders. Also, closely read mortgage loan and real estate ads. Look for terms such as "bond money" or "bond financing." This type of mortgage money might be referred to by the abbreviated letters of the issuing government agency, such as:

- GRFA (Georgia Residential Finance Agency)
- THDA (Tennessee Housing Development Agency)
- CHFA (California Housing Finance Agency)
- NJH & MFA (New Jersey Housing and Mortgage Finance Agency)
- MHDC (Missouri Housing Development Commission)
- MSHA (Maine State Housing Authority)

Of course, this list just samples bond finance programs. To investigate beyond asking Realtors and lenders, telephone the community finance, housing, or redevelopment agencies that have been set up by your state, county, or local governments. These are frequently the same types of government offices that offer down-payment assistance to first-time homebuyers (see Chapter 6).

Turndown Turns into Good Fortune

When Carol Ochs and her brother Jason decided to buy a home together, they visited Champion Federal Savings to find out how much house they could afford. Carol chose Champion Federal because she had kept a checking account there for six years. During this same period, she had paid off two car loans with no late payments. At the time Carol and Jason talked to the Champion loan officer, 30-year fixed-rate mortgages were around 9 percent. Because together they wanted to keep their PITI under $800 a month, the loan officer suggested that Carol and Jason look for homes priced around $85,000. Having visited some open houses, though, Carol and Jason didn't think they could find a home in the neighborhood they wanted at that price.

Their loan officer then suggested switching to an ARM, but Jason wasn't keen on that idea. "I just don't think I'd be comfortable with an interest rate that could jump up every year," Jason said.

"Well then," the loan officer replied, "it looks like you'll just have to wait for interest rates to come down."

"But waiting may not do us any good," Carol shot back. "If interest rates drop sharply, home prices may go up—in fact, prices are sure to go up even if rates stay where they are."

"Well, if you don't want an ARM, that's just the risk you'll have to take," the loan officer responded indifferently.

The Ochs Find Bond Money

Fortunately for this brother and sister, as well as Carol's three-year-old daughter, the Ochs didn't naïvely accept the Champion Federal loan officer's advice. They decided to talk to other lenders and Realtors. As a result, Carol and Jason learned of the Montgomery County Housing Opportunities Commission. This government agency was offering bond money mortgage financing at 7.1 percent, 30-year, fixed-rate. With this lower cost financing and an $800 a month payment, the Ochs could buy a home in the $100,000 to $110,000 price range—the right amount to get them into the neighborhood they wanted.

Stay Alert: Bond Money Comes and Goes

Governments do not offer unlimited amounts of bond money to finance home mortgages, so you must stay on the lookout for this type of home financing. Likewise, interest rates for these programs fluctuate. Bond money will often shave at least a one-half point off the current market interest rate. Some programs, especially those directed toward low- to moderate-income families, might cut their interest rate by 2 percentage points or more. Either way, you've boosted your home-buying power and slashed your interest costs. So check out the low-interest loan programs that your state and local housing finance agencies are offering now, or plan to offer in the future.

SECRET # 20

Assume a low-interest-rate mortgage.

If (when) market interest rates climb back up, you don't have to pay those higher rates. Instead, shop for a property with a low-interest-rate assumable loan. Imagine it's three years into the future and you want to buy a home, but market interest rates are again hovering around 9 percent. You fondly recall those bygone days when 30-year fixed-rate loans were at 6 percent. If you could only climb into a time machine.

Return to the Past with an Assumable Loan

When you assume a mortgage, you roll back the clock and take over the mortgage of the seller at the same rate the seller is paying—even if that rate sits well below current market rates. Years ago, nearly all sellers could transfer their low-rate mortgages to their buyers. By the early 1980s, however, most lenders had changed their mortgage contracts to include the notorious Paragraph No. 17 "due on sale" clause. This clause prohibits routine assumptions, and upon sale or long-term lease requires sellers to pay off their mortgage balance.

As a result, too many people today erroneously believe that *all* assumption possibilities have died. To further the problem, loan reps seldom tell borrowers about assumptions because such agreements take place directly between sellers and buyers. You cannot walk into a lender's office and say, "I'd like one of those low-rate, assumable mortgages that's going to save me tens of thousands of dollars." Before you can assume a real estate loan, you must locate a seller who has one.

What Sellers Can Offer Assumable Financing?

Generally, sellers who have financed their properties with FHA, VA, or most types of adjustable rate mortgages can offer an assumption to their buyers. Realtor Roger Rodell describes his experience with assumables during a past period of high mortgage rates. Roger said, "I'm promoting low-interest, assumable FHA/VA mortgages. True, buyers do have to qualify to assume these loans. And some of the lenders I deal with aren't too eager to push through loan assumptions for a few hundred dollars in transfer fees (compared to the several thousand dollars they earn for new loan originations). But the lower rates and monthly payments make qualifying easier, and the cash savings for buyers are tremendous. If a fairly priced home with a low-interest-rate assumable hits the market, I tell my buyers to go for it. Don't try to pull the sellers down. When there's a pile of $1,000 bills sitting in front of you, don't get greedy and demand an even better deal.

"I've worked out the numbers," Roger continued. "Over a period of five years on a $100,000 loan, as compared to a 9 percent new mortgage, a 7 percent assumable will save you $8,400 in interest. Over 10 years, the savings are nearly $17,000; over 25 years, you'll keep an extra $42,000. And those numbers don't include the $2,000 to $4,000 that an assumable might save you in points, origination fees, appraisal, and closing costs.

"Or here's another way to figure it," explained Roger. "Let's say your low-interest assumable saves you $135 a month over the amount you'd pay with new financing. If you bank those savings every month in an IRA or 401(k) plan that earns a return of just 6 percent a year, after 25 years your accumulated savings with interest will amount to $93,200. Now you can see why I refer to a good low-interest assumable as a pile of $1,000 bills."

Short-Term Strategies

In some situations, you might even gain by assuming a mortgage that carries a higher-than-market interest rate. Imagine current rates are at 6.5 percent, and you're negotiating with a seller whose assumable mortgage has a rate of 7.5 percent. Not worth assuming? Don't jump to that conclusion. Assumptions usually cost less in terms of time, effort, and cash-to-close than new mortgage originations; therefore, under short-term strategies such as the following, this 7.5 percent assumption could prove profitable.

- You plan to own the property for only a year or two.
- Inflation has dropped to almost zero, and rates are sure to fall further. You want to time your new mortgage to coincide with the market bottom that you foresee.
- You plan to improve the property to increase its value. You'd then like to get a new loan based on this higher value.
- Your borrower profile displays some warts. New financing at the lowest rates available could prove iffy. In contrast, qualifying for the assumption will probably not require the same exacting standards. One year or two of perfect payments could set you up to then qualify as an "A" borrower.

How to Find Assumables

Presently, millions of outstanding FHA/VA loans (fixed-rate and adjustable) permit assumptions. In addition, most conventional (Fannie/Freddie) and portfolio lenders will allow sellers to transfer their adjustable-rate loans to buyers. To find these loans requires you to ask and investigate. Sellers or their realty agents frequently don't know or don't publicize this fact. On the other hand, when interest rates shoot up, the search for assumables becomes intense. Savvy sellers and agents then tout their assumables to favorably differentiate their properties from others that require buyers to obtain more costly new financing.

Lower-Rate Assumable ARMs

Nearly all adjustable rate mortgages include lifetime rate caps. No matter how high market interest rates climb, ARM borrowers know that their loan rate will max out at 8, 9, 10, 12 percent or higher. Consequently, in periods of extraordinarily high current rates, you can find ARMs that are maxed out—or close to maxed out—yet still sit below the going rates for new 30-year, fixed-rate mortgages. In that case, you're sitting pretty. Your (assumable) ARM rate can't go up much, but it can go down.

SECRET # 21

"Assume" a nonassumable mortgage.

Nearly all non-FHA/VA long-term fixed-rate mortgages include the infamous Paragraph No. 17 (the "due on sale" clause). This clause reads (in part) as follows:

> ¶ 17. If all or any part of the [mortgaged] property or an interest therein is sold or transferred by the Borrower *without Lender's prior written consent . . . Lender may, at Lender's option, declare* all the sums secured by this Mortgage to be immediately *due and payable.*

Very few people understand the precise wording of this clause, but that wording carries significant implications.

What This Clause Does and Does Not Say

Notice that nothing in Paragraph No. 17 prevents owners from selling their properties to their buyers without paying off their mortgage. This clause only gives lenders the right to call the mortgage due and payable if such a transfer occurs without "Lender's prior written consent."

You Can Assume a "Nonassumable" Mortgage

Nothing prevents a buyer and seller from asking a lender to give its written consent. Why would the lender agree to accept your request? Here are several reasons:

- The sellers have fallen behind in their payments, and you agree to bring the mortgage current.
- The interest rate on the mortgage equals or exceeds the current market rate. Lenders hate "portfolio runoff" of their market or above-market-rate loans.
- You, the sellers, or both parties give the lender substantial amounts of other business such as loans, CDs, and savings and checking accounts.
- You or the sellers promise to move much of your banking business to the lender.

Will these or any other reasons you can think of persuade the lender to grant its consent? Sometimes yes, sometimes no, but it doesn't cost to ask. When the situation warrants, lenders do oblige.

Unfortunately, most people ask the wrong question and then get the wrong answer. When looking at a property, they query the seller or agent by asking, "Is the financing assumable?" If the mortgage includes a "due on sale" clause, the sellers or real estate agent will answer, "No, the mortgage is not assumable." Wrong answer. The correct answer is, "Yes, it's assumable with the lender's consent. If you would like to try to assume it, we can make an offer to the lender."

Buying Subject to: "Assuming" without Consent

Again notice that the wording of Paragraph No. 17 does not stop the owners from selling a mortgaged property to anyone they choose. Nor in such sales does it *require* the sellers or the buyers to pay off the loan. This clause merely gives the lender the right (or option) to call the loan due.

So, sometimes when buyers and sellers believe that a lender won't approve an assumption, they complete the sale anyway and never inform the lender that the property has a new owner. The buyer then continues to make the payments to the lender on the same terms and interest rate that applied to the sellers. Contrary to what some people say, this "subject to" technique is neither illegal, immoral, or fattening. It does not even violate the mortgage contract.

Risky Business for Buyers. This technique may rattle the nerves of both buyers and sellers, however. If the lender learns of the sale, it might mail the seller a nasty letter and demand a very large check. With the loan called due, someone would quickly need to come up with a cash payoff, a refinance, or a negotiated settlement with the lender. Weak borrowers who can't come up with the cash, credit, or negotiating power to satisfy the lender face foreclosure. The borrower will probably lose whatever cash they've already invested in the property, and suffer serious damage to their credit record. On the other hand, when buyers are financially strong enough to deal with this "call" potential, their risks of problems are low.

Risks to Sellers. Typically, under a lender-approved mortgage assumption, the lender qualifies the buyers of the property. When the buyers pass muster, the lender then issues a novation or release of liability to the sellers. The sellers are now off the hook. Whatever happens to that mortgage in the future does not concern them.

Not so with "subject to" unauthorized property transfers. In those cases, the sellers' credit and finances remain at risk for as long as the mortgage remains outstanding. If the buyers pay the mortgage late, the lender forwards scurrilous remarks about the sellers to the credit bureau. If the property goes into foreclosure, the lender will chase down the sellers for any money (deficiency) judgments the court awards it.

Is This Technique Worth the Risks? Yes, but only for knowledgeable, creditworthy, financially strong buyers. And only for sellers who can be assured they've adequately protected themselves against the buyers' default. I have used "subject to" financing on several occasions. In 1981, for example, market mortgage rates were at 16 percent. I bought a property "subject to" that carried a mortgage rate of 10 percent. Because this property was a "flipper," I quickly resold after just 18 months, but even during that short period this "subject to" mortgage arrangement saved me $17,000 in interest, points, and closing costs.

Amateurs Beware. Several current authors and real estate get-rich-quick gurus are now peddling this approach to the uninformed and inexperienced, except instead of saving money on interest, they're pushing it to the credit impaired as a means to buy property without laying prostrate before a lender. Here's my advice: Amateurs beware! Although this technique can prove appealing in some situations—short-term holding periods, high interest mortgage environment, credit impairment—don't fall for the con of the hucksters. "Subject to" financing holds big risks for sellers and buyers. Accept them only after you've consulted disinterested expert real estate counsel.

Will Lenders Really Call the Loan? The gurus say, "Don't worry. Here's a bag of tricks. Use these tricks, and the lender won't find out about the property transfer. Surely what the lender can't see won't hurt you. No problem. Just keep the lender in the dark."

Do these tricks work? Not likely for any extended period of time. After suffering through the tumultuous 1980s and early 1990s, lenders have become far more savvy. Within a year or two, at most, the lender will probably find the light switch.

"No worry," the gurus say. "Even if the lender discovers the transfer, chances are it won't call the loan due. Most lenders follow a 'don't ask, don't tell' policy. They're not going to advertise their waiver. As long as your mortgage checks keep flowing in on time and the property taxes and insurance get paid, your risks are small." On this point (for now at least), the gurus may be right because interest rates on most "subject to" mortgages today exceed current market rates. When rates spike up, though, I suspect lenders will send out the enforcers. Stay prepared.

SECRET # **22**

Save $1,000s with a Mortgage Credit Certificate (MCC).

The mortgage credit certificate (MCC) program can shave $1,000s off the cost of your home financing. This tax credit plan was created under United States tax legislation, and is now available in about 25 states. Although an MCC doesn't directly reduce your interest rate, it does help you qualify for a larger mortgage with lower payments by cutting thousands of dollars off your income tax bill.

State and local housing finance agencies sponsor MCC programs in cooperation with selected mortgage lenders. To promote the Massachusetts American Dream/MCC first-time buyer mortgage plan, one lender's ad says, "This special Mortgage Credit Certificate will lower your income taxes and increase your buying power." See Figure 3.1 for an example of how the Massachusetts Housing Finance Agency (MHFA) describes this program for an 8.875 percent, 30-year fixed-rate mortgage of $100,000.

Using the MHFA American Dream/MCC mortgage plan, you could qualify for a $100,000 mortgage with an income of just $30,900 a year; otherwise, to borrow this amount under a conventional 8.875 percent, fixed-rate mortgage, you'd need to earn around $42,000 a year. From a different perspective, with a standard 30-year fixed-rate mortgage at 8.875 percent, an annual income of $30,990 ($2,575 a month) would qualify you to borrow just $72,550. (This example applies a .28 housing cost ratio and a PITI of $721 a month—a $571 payment for principal and interest plus $150 a month for property taxes and homeowners insurance. Of course, the MHFA used 8.875 percent only for illustrative purposes. Market or below-market rates typically apply.)

Limiting Features of MCCs

As with many government programs, not everyone is eligible for an MCC. In most cities you would have to earn less than, say, $50,000 or $60,000 a year, and buy a home priced at less than, say, $160,000. (These figures are illustrative. Each sponsoring government agency sets its own limits.)

$100,000 Loan	Conventional	MCC/American Dream
8.875%	*Monthly Amounts*	
Principal and interest	$795.64	$795.64
Taxes and insurance (est.)	200.00	200.00
MCC value	0.00	–147.42
Net payment (PITI)	995.64	848.22
Housing cost ratio	.28	.33
Required income to qualify for mortgage	$3,500.00	$2,575.00

Figure 3.1 MHFA's MCC Program

In addition, similar to mortgage bond financing, MCCs come and go. "The clock is ticking for Chicago's mortgage credit certificate program, which encourages home ownership for working class people by slicing their tax bill to Uncle Sam," advised T.J. Becker in the *Chicago Tribune.* "The current program expires on New Year's Eve." Fortunately for Chicagoans, shortly after that MCC plan ended, Chicago started up a new one. But it, too, will run out. So if saving $1,000s and stretching your buying power appeals to you, act now. If available, don't wait for your area's MCC program to expire. If not available now but as a coming attraction, put your name on the list so you'll stand near the front of the line when these tax credits next become available.

SECRET # 23

Seek employer assistance, or seek an employer who gives assistance.

In John Grisham's best-selling novel, *The Firm* (Random House, 1991), senior law partner Royce McKnight uses employer-sponsored, low-interest-rate home financing to help recruit Mitch McDeere into the law firm . . .

> "As you know" [Royce tells Mitch], it is very important to us that you buy a home. It adds stability and prestige, and we're very concerned about these things, especially with our associates. The firm provides

a low-interest-rate mortgage loan, 30 years, fixed rate, non-assumable should you decide to sell in a few years. It's a one-shot deal, available for your first home. After that, you're on your own."

"What kind of interest rate?" [asks Mitch].

"As low as possible without running afoul with the IRS. Current market rate is around 10, 10.5. We should be able to get you a rate of 7 to 8 percent. We represent some banks, and they assist us. With the salary we're paying, you should have no trouble qualifying. In fact, the firm will sign on as a guarantor, if necessary."

"That's very generous, Mr. McKnight."

"It's important to us. Once you find a house . . . all you have to do is move in."

Could your employer use its influence with banks or other mortgage lenders to help you and other employees get below-market financing for your home? At Colgate-Palmolive, Robert Berg says, "We came up with a mortgage assistance plan that used the financial muscle of the company to help our employees get the best possible terms. Our program is a very cost-effective fringe benefit . . . it's tax-effective to employees, and much more desirable than just giving people a salary increase."

As part of Fannie Mae's efforts to make homebuying less costly, Fannie has developed an employer-assisted program it calls Magnet. In cooperation with Fannie Mae, participating employers offer their employees many types of homebuyer helper techniques which include lower interest rates, down-payment assistance, second mortgages, loan guarantees, closing cost assistance, and interest rate buydowns. Most employers know that homeowners make more stable employees. If your employer values your contribution to the firm, don't overlook this potential technique to boost your buying power. When bargaining for a new job, ask to receive mortgage assistance as part of your pay and benefits package. Keep in mind, however, your exit strategy. Find out what happens to the mortgage—or other home-buying assistance—if you get downsized or change jobs voluntarily. The employer could withdraw its contribution, or even declare the loan due, as is the practice with loans against an employer 401(k) plan.

SECRET # **24**

Trade off points for a lower interest rate.

Nearly all lenders trade off points (fees paid at the time the mortgage money is loaned) and interest rates. Say you're looking at the choices shown in Table 3.8.

Which of these choices will give you the lowest costs? It all depends on how long you keep your mortgage. If you keep your loan for more than three years (36 months), the 6.75 percent/3-point loan will save you the most money. Although you must pay an additional $3,000 at closing to get this lower rate, this loan will save you $85 a month over the 8.0 percent/0-points loan. In comparison to the 8.0 percent mortgage, you'll earn your $3,000 in points in just over 35 months ($3,000 ÷ $85 = 35.29). After that, it's all gain.

The previous figures illustrate a simple way to compare costs,[3] although the actual trade-offs you see will differ from these. This calculation is a good method to select the lowest loan *based upon your expected circumstances.* A trustworthy and competent loan rep will go over interest rate/points trade-offs with you to figure out which look best. A greedy loan rep will steer you into the interest rate/point combination that yields the largest sales commission. Don't ask your loan rep, "Which one is best?" Instead, ask him or her to show you the rate sheet that displays the full list

Table 3.8 **Illustration of Different Payback Calculations: Interest Rates/Points Trade-Offs**

	$100,000 Mortgage at 30 Years		
Interest Rate (%)	*Points/ Amount*	*Monthly Payment ($)*	*Months to Break Even*
1. 8.0	0/0	733	00
2. 7.75	1/$1,000	716	58 months
3. 7.5	1.5/$1,500	699	44 months
4. 7.25	2.0/$2,000	682	39 months
5. 6.75	3.0/$3,000	648	35 months

3. To calculate and compare precisely, you would figure in principal reduction and tax deductions. These complexities won't significantly change the results for most borrowers.

of trade-off choices—often as many as 10 or 12—then work through the numbers together. Only after a full explanation should you decide.

SECRET # 25

Negotiate a temporary buydown with the sellers.

"When I'm working with first-timers who want to lower costs and increase affordability," says Realtor Nathan Browne, "I ask the sellers to pay points to reduce my buyers' mortgage interest rate."

To illustrate this technique, say your lender quotes a fixed 8 percent interest rate for a 30-year loan. With a 3-2-1 buydown, your first year's interest rate would drop to 5 percent. For years two and three, your interest rate would move up to 6 percent and then to 7 percent. For the remaining 27 years of the mortgage, your monthly payments would remain at the originally quoted 8 percent interest rate.

On a $100,000 mortgage, here's what your approximate monthly payments (principal and interest) would look like with a 3-2-1 buydown from an original 8 percent interest rate.

Temporary Buydown	Monthly Payment
Year 1 @ 5%	$537
Year 2 @ 6%	598
Year 3 @ 7%	659
Years 4 through 30 @ 8%	724

Using a .28 housing cost ratio (ignoring property taxes and insurance), without this buydown, you'd need a gross income of around $2,750 a month to qualify for this loan. With the buydown, you could probably qualify for this $100,000 mortgage with a gross income of $2,025 to $2,375 a month, depending on which interest rate the lender would use to qualify you. Liberal lenders might use the 5 percent, $568 a month payment. More conservative lenders might not give you the full benefit of the buydown for purposes of qualifying. Instead, they might qualify with an interest rate of 6 or 7 percent. Either way, the temporary buydown significantly boosts your borrowing power.

How Much Do Temporary Buydowns Cost?

In the previous example, the 3-2-1 buydown would probably cost around $5,500. As a rough calculation, you can figure this cost by summing the total percentage points you're buying down (such as 3-2-1 equals a total of 6 points) and then multiply that percentage times the mortgage amount. Discount that dollar amount by 5 to 15 percent. (You would negotiate the exact cost of your buydown with the lender.)

Buydowns don't come cheap. Nevertheless, if affordability is your goal, a buydown can work wonders to reduce your monthly payments and help you qualify for a larger mortgage. To pay for the buydown, you could contribute some of the money, the sellers could pay part, and for low- to moderate-income homebuyers, government housing finance agencies, or even the lender itself (as part of a first-time homebuyer program), might pay part of the cost.

SECRET # 26

New home builders offer mortgage incentives.

To beat their competition, some new home builders and condo projects offer mortgage interest and down payment incentives. When the following builder promotions appeared, for example, their terms fell below the market by a wide margin.

- At Village Pokai Bay, "Fee Simple, Single Family Detached Homes priced from $183,900 are being offered with 5 percent down and financing designed for the first-time home buyer with payments starting at $924.53 per month."
- At the Napa Yacht Club, "You can move up to Napa for less. . . . For a limited time 7.625 percent, 30-year fixed-rate financing."
- In Nashville at Bentree, "New Homes Special financing at 6.87 percent . . . . Four new homes for you to choose from. . . ."

- In Kansas City, Brittany Bell New Homes says, "If you've been discouraged by rising interest rates . . . here's an opportunity for you! By special arrangement we can offer this incredibly low interest rate [5.0 percent] for a limited time on many new homes. . . . Don't miss out on this opportunity to get even More Home For Your Money!"
- In a variety of its 40 developments located throughout the Delaware Valley, Toll Brothers tells homebuyers, "The Quality Lasts Forever, But Our 7 Percent Mortgage Programs with 0 Points Won't."

Naturally, like all builder promotions, special finance packages ebb and flow, but you can generally find something good if you look for it. Or, if you don't find what you need, negotiate your own special financing. "If you're hunting for a new home," writes real estate consultant, Jim DeBoth, "negotiating a financing package should be at the top of your list of priorities along with amenities and home selection."

When you talk incentives with home builders, don't just focus on features such as decorator allowances, landscaping, carpet grades, and lighting fixtures. You can add these later yourself. Rather than ask for top-of-the-line appliances or a built-in security system, negotiate a 3-2-1 buydown, a six-month moratorium on monthly payments, or even sweat equity (see *Mortgage Secret #53*) to help offset your down payment. When it comes to fashioning your mortgage strategy, builder finance plans can rank even higher than home price, features, and amenities. Note, too, that mortgage incentives from builders gain importance and tend to multiply when mortgage market interest rates head up.

SECRET # 27

How to borrow jumbo amounts without paying jumbo rates.

Each year Fannie Mae/Freddie Mac set limits on the maximum-sized, single-family home mortgage that they will buy (now set at $322,700).

Elephant-sized amounts in excess of Fannie/Freddie limits are known as jumbo loans and usually carry an interest rate that's about one-half percent higher than Fannie/Freddie's best rate. When Fannie/Freddie's 30-year fixed rate wandered around 6.0 percent, lenders typically priced jumbos at 6.5 percent. (Shop closely, however. Recently I've seen jumbos priced at just .25 percent over the Fannie/Freddie rate.)

Save Interest with a Second Mortgage (or a Higher Down Payment)

If you wanted to borrow $350,000, that extra one-half percent for the jumbo loan would cost you $114 per month more ($2,212 as opposed to. $2,098).[4] Viewed a little differently, you're paying $1,888 per month to borrow the first $315,000, and $324 per month for the additional $35,000 to bring your total home mortgage up to $350,000. In terms of interest, for that extra $35,000, your effective charge is around 11 percent. If you limit your first mortgage to Fannie/Freddie's maximum, therefore, you could borrow the remainder ($35,000) as a second mortgage. As long as your interest rate on this loan equals 10 percent or less, you're saving money.

Alternatively, if you can come up with $35,000 more for your down payment, you would profit—unless the cash or investment source of this down payment was earning a very safe tax-free return of 11 percent or greater (not an easy feat in today's investment climate).[5] You also could pledge collateral to secure this $35,000 (see Chapter 6).

These examples illustrate tiered financing, which can often save you money. This same technique applies to loans with low down payments and mortgage insurance (also in Chapter 6). You need not understand how to make these calculations, but you must see the potential of the technique and then get a smart loan specialist to run the numbers.

---

4. These numbers are approximate. At the time of writing, Fannie has not yet released its maximum loan amounts for the coming year.

5. Unless you're investing in income properties, that is. See my books, *Investing in Real Estate*, 4th ed. (2003) and *Value Investing in Real Estate* (2002), both published by John Wiley & Sons.

Table 3.9 **Two to Four Units: Borrow Jumbo Amounts without Jumbo Interest Rates (2003)**

Units	*Lower 48 States (Loan Limit, $)*	*AK, HI, VI (Loan Limit, $)*
1	322,700	484,050
2	413,100	619,650
3	499,300	748,950
4	620,500	930,750

Buy a Two- to Four-Unit Income Property

When most loan reps quote Fannie/Freddie's maximum loan amount, they typically recite the figure that applies to houses and condominium units. Because most borrowers prefer this type of housing, loan reps forget to mention that these megaplayers in the mortgage market also give their lowest rate financing to borrowers who own and occupy two- to four-unit properties (see Table 3.9). In addition, Fannie/Freddie establish higher limits for Alaska, Hawaii, and the Virgin Islands.

FHA also permits higher loan amounts for one- to four-unit properties (see Table 3.10). Even though these amounts may exceed the maximum FHA single-family (and Fannie/Freddie) loan limit, most lenders do not assess a jumbo premium for these mortgages.

Although covered in Chapter 3, note here that jumbo loans not only charge higher interest, but also typically require 10 to 30 percent down. In contrast, ordinarily you can finance two- to four-unit properties for 10

Table 3.10 **Two to Four Units: FHA Loan Amounts (2003)**

Units	*Basic Limits*	*High Cost Areas*
1	$154,896	$280,749
2	198,288	359,397
3	239,664	434,391
4	297,840	539,835

Unlike Fannie/Freddie, FHA designates its maximum loan amounts county by county throughout the United States.

percent down or less. With faster equity buildup, higher property value for appreciation gains, a non-jumbo interest rate, and low down payment, two to four units do make strong economic sense. As I have urged before, more homebuyers (investors) should avail themselves of the profit opportunities these properties present.

SECRET # 28

Your after-tax cost of borrowing may not be as low as you've been told.

Real estate agents and loan reps frequently tell potential borrowers not to focus on the nominal rate of interest that lenders are charging. Instead, borrowers should consider only their after-tax costs. Good advice, but their specific figures usually err.

The Standard Line

The standard line goes something like this:

Borrower: "Wow, the loan on this house is going to cost us $1,350 a month. But we're only paying $850 for rent.

Realty Agent: "Oh, don't worry about that. Remember, in the early years nearly all of that payment goes to interest. And you can deduct interest off your tax return. If you're in the 30 percent tax bracket, your after-tax monthly cost will total around $950 (.7 × 1,350). Considering the great advantages of buying your own home—especially appreciation—owning will actually cost you less than rent."

Like most sales agents, I, too, strongly advocate home ownership, but get the numbers right. Don't fool yourself, or let others mislead you. As it turns out, agents and loan reps who recite this party line overstate the value of those interest tax deductions for most people. Unless your taxable income exceeds $114,650, you're not in the 30 percent tax bracket. For most moderate wage earners, effective income tax rates fall within the 15 to 27 percent range.

On the other hand, if you're among the fortunate many whose taxable household income exceeds $114,650 a year, your combined state and local marginal tax rates will push you above 30 percent; however, you face a different problem. Above $100,000 a year, the government thinks you're too rich to deserve the full benefit of the interest deduction. At that income level, the government starts slicing back the amount you can deduct.

How to Really Calculate the After-Tax Cost of Your Monthly Mortgage Payments

To accurately calculate your tax break, first estimate your total monthly payment:

Monthly payment + P + I + HOI + MI + Tx + HOA

where: P = principal

I = interest

HOI = homeowners insurance

MI = mortgage insurance

Tx = property taxes

HOA = homeowners association dues

In Chapter 2, you saw that monthly payments may include numerous items other than principal and interest, such as debt repayment. As a starting point, then, estimate the amount that you will pay monthly for every expense. Next, back out only the amounts for interest and property taxes.[6] For example, if your total monthly payment of $1,600 includes every expense item in the list, interest and property taxes might amount to only $1,200 per month, not $1,600 per month. This amount is all you can deduct (12 × $1,200 = $14,400 as opposed to $19,200).

After you estimate *your* future interest and property tax figures, pull out your most recent tax returns. Recompute your income taxes with

6. Here I just want to show why the tax break for monthly payments isn't nearly as large as you've probably been told. To actually perform this calculation, you would need specific figures for your home and home loan.

these amounts as deductions. But here's the catch: To deduct property taxes and interest, you must give up the standard deduction of $7,950 for married couples ($4,750 for individuals filing separately).

So, low- to moderate-income (nonitemizing) homebuyers who buy modestly priced houses (say, under $150,000) will experience a net gain of no more than $2,000 to $4,000—and possibly much less. Nonitemizing middle to upper-middle income earners may net a gain in deductions of around $3,000 to $6,000. If you already incur a number of other expenses you could deduct if you itemized, your gain will be greater. And if you earn over $150,000 (adjusted gross income), your mortgage interest will add nothing to your tax deductions, even if you already itemize.

Tax Deductions Exceed Tax Savings. The figures cited in the previous section for tax deductions do not translate directly into tax savings. To actually compute your tax savings, subtract these and other allowable deductions and exemptions from your adjusted gross income; then turn to the tax tables in the back of your 1040 booklet or professional tax guide. Figure your new tax liability, and compare it to the taxes you previously paid. How much difference did you find? If you're like most homebuyers, you'll find that the savings amount to much less than the tax savings estimates of most real estate agents and loan reps.

Let me again emphasize that nothing written here intends to discourage you from buying a home. On the contrary, *Mortgage Secrets* strongly advocates home ownership. History and demographic forecasts both fully support the idea that your home will prove to be your best investment. Nevertheless, before you buy or refinance, carefully calculate how much your proposed purchase or refinance will change your after-tax monthly cash flows. Beware of overestimating the tax benefit of mortgage interest deductions. For most homeowners, this deduction doesn't yield the amount of benefits that is widely promised. You will need to compute the actual savings, if any, that you can expect; then after you know your true monthly costs, ask, "Does this amount fit within my comfort zone? Does it leave me sufficient funds for saving and investing? Will I be able to financially manage those out-of-the-ordinary, yet always-to-be-expected budget-busting surprises?"

Absolutely, buy a home.[7] But don't assume large tax savings. More than likely, the actual amount will be less than you've been told.

Plan to Close in January or February. If you're not currently itemizing your income tax deductions, plan to close your financing in January or February. In that way, you can use the standard deduction for the preceding year, and you will maximize your mortgage points, interest, and property tax deductions for the year in which you buy.[8] If you close in June or July, you may not gain enough deductions to make itemizing worthwhile—or if so, just marginally. All of your potential home ownership deductions for that year will go to waste.

Understandably, you probably won't want to schedule your home buying simply to take advantage of tax law. But if convenient to do so, plan accordingly. As Robert Bruss, the nationally syndicated real estate expert and attorney points out, you often can get your best deal on a home between Thanksgiving and New Year's Day. Because relatively few buyers home-shop during the Christmas season, motivated sellers may eagerly accept your low-end offer.

---

7. See for example, *The 106 Common Mistakes Homebuyers Make (and How to Avoid Them)*, 3rd ed. (Wiley, 2002). The biggest mistake of all, #106, "Continuing to Rent."

8. Homebuyers may deduct all costs paid to the lender as compensation for the borrowed funds. In addition to interest, such amounts include origination fees and loan discount points, but not the appraisal, title insurance, or garbage fees.

CHAPTER 4

The Risks and Rewards of ARMs

Now's the time to put aside the many misconceptions about adjustable rate mortgages (ARMs) that plague potential borrowers, loan reps, realty agents, and those authors of popular books on mortgages who display a confused understanding and give faulty advice. These misconceptions can keep you from the information you need to make an intelligent and informed decision. As a result, you may bypass ARMs without a second look. Or worse, you may select an ARM for the wrong reasons.

SECRET # 29

ARMs do not necessarily present more risk than fixed-rate loans.

People often think of ARM risk as chance of loss. If interest rates head up, borrowers stand to lose a lot of money as their monthly payments skyrocket past the amounts that they would have paid with a 30-year fixed-rate mortgage. Alternatively, people view the ARM risk in terms of uncertainty; you never know whether you'll be able to afford the higher payments. So, you live in fear that potential rate hikes will wreck your budget—or even worse, force you into a quick sale of the property or even foreclosure. A closer look proves that these two risks are both exaggerated and misconstrued.

Risks As "Chance of Loss"

Although the monthly payment on your ARM could balloon past your fixed-rate monthly payments, if you follow the advice of *Mortgage Secret #31,* that will probably never happen. But for the sake of argument, let's assume that it does. Have you really suffered a loss? Not necessarily; to calculate "loss" in this sense, you would need to total all of your interest paid compared to the amount of interest you would have paid with a fixed-rate loan. Experience shows that throughout most of the past 25 years, those borrowers who have chosen ARMs have paid less total interest for the same amounts borrowed than their 30-year fixed-rate contemporaries.

Regret or Loss

Human nature has programmed us to feel emotional pain and regret when hindsight reveals that our decision turned out badly. But that's not the same thing as loss. That's life. Say you buy a new Buick in March for $19,000. You tell all your friends about the great deal you negotiated.

In April, General Motors announces a $3,000 rebate program, or zero percent financing for three years. Have you suffered a loss? No. At the time you bought, you (presumably) got the best deal available. But do you kick yourself for not waiting? Do you, after the fact, concoct stories about how you felt GM would soon come out with a rebate deal, but immediate gratification overwhelmed your perceptive talents?[1] Probably yes, if you're like most people.

Fixed-Rate Borrowers Should Suffer the Same Types of Regrets

What if you pass up a one-year ARM with a 4.0 percent start rate and a 5.5 percent contract rate, no points, in favor of a 7.0 percent, one-point, 30-year fixed-rate (a trade-off that was available several years back). Then, within the next 18 months, the 30-year fixed-rate falls to 6.0 percent. At the same time, the contract rate on the one-year ARM falls to

1. The perceptive talents necessary to forecast interest rates attach to very few mortals. But in *Mortgages Secret #32,* you will learn several clues to look for.

3.75 percent (T-bill index + 2.5 margin). You're now paying hundreds of dollars more per month than you would have paid with the ARM.[2] Do you feel the same high level of regret? Maybe not. Why?

Because when your ARM goes up, you're cash-out-of-pocket. In contrast, when interest rates fall, you've missed a chance to benefit immediately, but you suffer no explicit financial loss. The economic effect, however, remains the same: In both cases, ARM or fixed-rate, when the market moves against your present interest rate (down for fixed-rates, up for ARMs), your monthly payments may stand higher than they otherwise would have been had you only chosen differently at the time you originally obtained your mortgage.

Separate Emotions from Economics

Okay, I've said it before and will say it again: Work the numbers with a mortgage pro you can trust. Recognize that no matter which type of mortgage you choose, you can't know the true economic costs until after the fact; but you can forecast likely costs and benefits under a variety of reasonable (or even unreasonable) eventual outcomes. Only after weighing these calculations can you decide which choice looks best. Gut reactions such as, "We don't want the risk of an ARM" make no economic sense.

All mortgages present risk in an economic sense—either out-of-pocket or opportunity costs. Your mission, should you choose to accept it, is to vanquish the emotions and focus on the numbers. More often than not, you will discover that some type of ARM will save you money and help you qualify for a larger loan. Yet it's this latter advantage that can create a true risk.

Rate Increases and Wrecked Budgets

When in college, I bought a classic Jaguar XKE at a super bargain price. The car looked great, and (as hoped for) it impressed the coeds. Unfortunately, these (yes, emotional) benefits overwhelmed my rationality. The car ended up costing far too much to operate (repair, repair,

2. You could possibly refinance, but that could cost you several thousand dollars—a loss that you would not have incurred had you selected the ARM. Of course, the ARM borrower could also refinance into that new lower rate.

repair!) for my budget at the time. Had I held on to that car, it would sell today for 10 times what I had paid for it.

The Lesson for ARM Borrowers

What does this story have to do with ARMs? It illustrates why ARMs sometimes appeal to the wrong people. During periods of high 30-year fixed interest rates, ARMs permit homebuyers to obtain a larger loan than they otherwise could. A lower qualifying interest rate when combined with higher qualifying ratios (a feature of some ARMs) attracts many marginal borrowers. Because they're struggling from the beginning, unexpected payment increases (called "payment shock") push these types of borrowers into financial distress.

Just as with my XKE, the ARM to these borrowers is emotionally appealing. It enables them to own a home, impress friends and family, and gain immediate gratification. But it may cost more to operate in the short-term than their budget can handle, even though it will likely prove profitable over the long run.

The Myth of Payment Shock

By the time you agree to accept an ARM, the lender will have eliminated any possibility for payment shock. The loan rep will show you a monthly payment schedule outlining the maximum amounts you could ever pay, and the dates when those maximums could go into effect. If your payments at some time did reach those levels, you could not justifiably claim to be shocked any more than I could have justifiably claimed to be shocked when my Jaguar required expensive and continuous repairs.

ARMs versus GPMs

Many borrowers confuse ARMs with graduated payment mortgages (GPMs) because GPM borrowers experience an increase in the payments over time. With a GPM, however, you pay less during the first year so you can qualify for a larger loan; then, during the next four years, your monthly payments increase gradually. Thereafter, they stay the same for the next 25 years. Your lower monthly payments during the early years of home ownership offset the higher payments you'll make during the later years. For example, see Table 4.1.

Table 4.1 **Monthly Payments (8%, 30-Year, $100,000 Loan) Ordinary Fixed-Rate vs. GPM**

Years	*Typical Level Payment*	*Graduated Payment*
1	$769	$580
2	769	623
3	769	670
4	769	721
5	769	775
6–30	769	883

The GPM is offered with a variety of payment schedules and is available on FHA and VA loans, and some conventional mortgages. Like an ARM, the GPM will usually help you buy more home. But unlike an ARM, you won't face any uncertainty about the amount of your future payments. An ARM's monthly payments will adjust up or down according to swings in the maket interest rates (subject to any floors or caps). Your GPM's monthly payments will steadily go up, unaffected by changes in the market interest rate, until they hit their scheduled plateau. Also, during those early years of lower payments, your mortgage balance may actually go up. Before you accept this type of loan, just as with an ARM, closely review your payment schedule and amortization schedule. Don't beware, but be aware.

Borrowers Be Aware

We should change the general advice from "beware of ARMs" (or GPMs) to "be aware of ARMs." As an intelligent borrower, you know that ARM payments can decrease or increase. Smart ARM borrowers stay prepared for the ups and enjoy the downs. They do not say, "Gee, I'm shocked. I never expected rates to go up this much."

No one should ever use an ARM to primarily achieve temporary affordability. Instead, use it when a close look at your needs, benefits, and potential costs places ARMs in the advantage.

The Upside of ARMs in Down Markets

In the late 1980s, the California housing market was steaming. Even though interest rates were fluctuating around 9 to 10 percent, homebuyers kept pushing prices higher and higher. Then the recession of the early 1990s hit California hard. Mid- to upper-price-range homes fell in value by 15 to 30 percent. Unemployment approached double digits. On the bright side, by 1993–94, mortgage interest rates dropped to as low as 6.0 percent. Great time to refinance, right?

Yes, it certainly was, but falling home prices, layoffs, and job uncertainty blocked most recent homebuyers from this opportunity. Many couldn't qualify for a new loan because of job loss or feared cutbacks. Among those who could requalify for a refinance (refi), most couldn't swing the deal. Their houses would no longer appraise out at a high enough amount.

So, who did gain from this mess? Homeowners who in the late 1980s had chosen ARMs. Their interest rates slid down. Some were able to convert their ARMs (see *Mortgage Secret #38*) to a 15-year or 30-year fixed-rate loan at the then historically low rates that prevailed. Although no homebuyers like to consider down markets, they happen, especially in California and other sometimes volatile urban markets such as New York City, Boston, and Washington, D.C. In those situations, ARMs give homeowners an advantage over fixed-rate loans, yet this advantage is rarely pointed out.

Obviously, few real estate agents or loan reps want to frighten homebuyers with talk of downturns, but informed borrowers must think through the full spectrum of outcomes that experience has proven possible.

SECRET # 30

For the short term ARMs usually prove best.

Sometimes you can accomplish a better result with a fixed-rate assumable. Mortgage experts typically give this advice: "If you're going to stay in your home for less than, say, five to seven years, take out an ARM. You're certain (or at least almost certain) to avoid payment shock and save big dollars at the same time." That's good advice for most people, but an important fixed-rate exception exists that could prove more advantageous than an ARM. First, though, let's look at the standard ARM advice.

ARMs for the Short Run

The shorter the length of time you plan to own your home, the more you should consider an ARM. You can nearly always find an adjustable that will cost you less than a 30-year fixed-rate loan if you plan to sell within seven years. Take a look at 5/25 or 7/23 (sometimes described as 30/5 or 30/7) adjustables.

These types of ARMs fix your interest rate and monthly payments for the beginning five or seven years of the loan. They then periodically adjust to keep your rate in line with the market. Even this limited type of adjustable may cut your rate by .5 to 1.5 percent as compared to a fixed-rate mortgage. For instance, at a time when 30-year fixed-rates were at 7.25 percent, I saw several 5/25 ARM plans with interest rates as low as 5.75 percent.

On a $100,000 loan, your payments for a 7.25 percent 30-year fixed-rate loan would have cost $682 a month. If you selected the 5/25, your payments would drop to $583 a month. Although the rate differences between 30-year fixed-rate loans and various types of ARMs change daily, it pays to at least take a look. If you plan to sell or refinance within seven years, the chances are good that an ARM will limit your risk at the same time it reduces your monthly payments. And, if your income is going up, you should be able to handle any increases in your ARM's monthly payments until rates come back down.

An Assumable Low-Rate Fixed-Rate Can Boost Your Resale Value and Lead to a Quicker Sale

Without a doubt, ARMs for the short run typically make sense. But when making this decision, compare the ARM to the short-term advantages you might achieve with an assumable fixed-rate loan. For example, say that at the time you're thinking of buying, interest rates sit near their ebb. Everyone says, "Now's a great time to buy." But you expect your employer will transfer you within three to seven years, or that you will move for some other reason. Should you buy, and if so, should you obtain an ARM or a fixed-rate?[3] As to buying, that answer is easy. Absolutely, yes. Please permit me a digression.

Short-Term Buying Strategy

When I was offering my Stop Renting Now!™ seminars, most attendees I met had thought of themselves throughout life as "temporary" renters—no matter how old they were. And (surprisingly to me) most attendees were in their thirties and forties. They had drifted from temporary personal situation to temporary personal situation. They told themselves, "Well, when I know for sure where I'm going to be and what I'm going to be doing, then buying makes sense."

Unfortunately, while indecisive renters drift, housing prices do know where they're going—and that's up. So rather than dropping further behind if you're facing an uncertain situation, develop a short-term buying strategy;[4] then finance it with either an ARM or a new assumable fixed-rate mortgage if you're in a low-interest-rate environment.

Why an Assumable Fixed-Rate?

A low-interest-rate assumable will play into your short-term strategy. This loan will help your property sell quicker and at a higher price. If you've selected the home wisely, you could probably sell without listing the house with a brokerage firm. Because only FHA and VA now offer new assumable fixed-rates, you may pay more than you would for a conventional (Fannie/Freddie) fixed-rate, but in this short-term situation the FHA/VA premium might prove worthwhile.

Alternatively, don't originate a new fixed-rate and incur all of those up-front costs. Look for a low-rate FHA/VA loan that you can assume. At a time when market rates were at 10 percent, I sold a property with an assumable 8 percent fixed-rate in two days simply by word of mouth. I never hired a sales agent or even ran a newspaper ad. On another occasion when market rates were at 16 percent, I bought a property with

---

3. As *Mortgage Secrets* reveals, your financing choices extend far beyond this simple comparison, but let's keep these examples manageable.

4. Such strategies are discussed in my book, *Stop Renting Now* (available at www.stoprentingnow.com).

an assumable 13.75 percent in a for sale by owner (FSBO) situation during the first week he had placed the property on the market. That "subject to" property that I bought (Chapter 3) with a 10 percent (way below the current market rate) interest rate also was a word-of-mouth transaction.

When you plan to move within three to seven years, ARMs usually do make good sense. But experience also shows that in some situations, low-rate assumable fixed-rates can also prove useful to facilitate a short-term ownership strategy.

SECRET # 31

ARMs for the long run: How to lower costs and alleviate risk.

An ARM will probably save you money if you plan to sell within seven years, but you also might save money over the longer term. Here's why.

Imagine you're faced with a choice between a 30-year fixed-rate loan at 8 percent and a 7/23 that starts at 6.75 percent. You want to borrow $100,000. With the fixed-rate plan, your payments will cost $733 a month. With the 7/23, you'll pay $648. For at least the first seven years, you'll save $85 a month, for a total of $7,140.

Instead of pocketing this monthly savings of $85, though, add it to your monthly mortgage payments. Even though you're only required to pay $648 a month, you pay $733 ($648 + $85 = $733). This tactic causes you to pay down your outstanding mortgage balance much faster. By making these extra payments, your mortgage balance after seven years would have fallen to approximately $83,000. On the other hand, your mortgage balance with the fixed-rate plan at 8 percent would have dropped to just $92,480. Obviously, if you sell at this point, you're way ahead of the game with the ARM.

But what if you don't sell? As long as your new adjustable rate stays below 9.5 percent, your monthly mortgage payments won't amount to any more than $740—about the same as you've been paying. At 10.5 percent, your payments would increase only to $798 a month. Now, what if interest rates are lower when your loan adjusts after seven years? Not only will you have accumulated an additional $9,480 in home equity, but your monthly payments won't increase and may actually go down.

These figures are illustrative only. Because the *relative* costs of ARMs as opposed to fixed-rate loans change frequently, you must work numbers with your mortgage loan advisor that are current at the time you buy your home.[5] Still, this basic fact holds true: For some homebuyers, the right ARM can put them thousands of dollars ahead of where they would have been with a 30-year fixed-rate mortgage.

SECRET # 32

You can (sort of) forecast interest rates.

To get some idea how high your ARM rate might rise (or fall), you need to forecast the movements in the interest rates; however, most mortgage pros say that no one can predict interest rates, so why even try.

In one sense, the mortgage pros are right. Neither you, I, nor anyone else can know for certain where mortgage rates will sit six months or six years from now. But that fact doesn't mean reasoned estimates won't prove better than off-the-wall swags. Mortgage rates don't land where they do for completely arbitrary reasons. Primarily, the level of mortgage interest rates ties directly into the rate of inflation.

The Real (CPI-Adjusted) Rate of Interest

To compute the inflation-adjusted, real interest rates, you subtract the year's increase in the Consumer Price Index (CPI) from the average nominal mortgage rate—that is, the rate lenders charge. When real interest rates are relatively high, you can reasonably expect nominal rates to fall or at worst remain relatively stable.

Nominal Interest Rates

Recent mortgage costs have seemed historically low only because most people don't know that from the 1940s through 1965, U.S. mortgage

5. As noted elsewhere, in 1981, ARM interest rates actually exceeded fixed-rate loans.

rates ranged between 4.0 percent and 6.0 percent. During some periods of U.S. history, mortgage interest rates have dropped as low as 2.5 percent.

The mortgage rates of 8.0 to 14 percent that prevailed throughout most of the 1970s, 1980s, and 1990s do not represent a good norm against which we should judge today's low rates. High nominal interest rates prevailed throughout most of the past 30 years because we also experienced (and then came to expect) historically high rates of inflation.

CPI-Adjusted (Real) Rates

In other words, to truly understand whether current interest rates sit high or low, adjust the nominal (quoted) rates for the annual rate of increase in the CPI.[6] The cost of money is cheap when *real* mortgage rates are low, and expensive when *real* rates are high.

As you can see from Table 4.2, mortgage borrowers today are paying relatively *high* real rates of interest. Viewed correctly, history suggests that, as long as the chairman of the Federal Reserve Board, Alan Greenspan (or his successor) keeps inflation low, nominal *and* real interest rates are likely to continue their downward trend during the next 5 to 10 years.

Table 4.2 **Comparing Nominal and Real Rates of Interest**

Year	*Nominal Rate* (%)	*CPI Increase* (%)	*Real Rate* (%)
1945	4.00	2.3	1.70
1950	4.50	1.3	3.20
1955	5.00	–0.4	5.60
1960	5.00	1.7	3.30
1965	5.89	1.6	4.29
1970	8.56	5.7	2.86
1975	9.14	9.1	.04
1980	13.95	13.5	.45
1990	10.08	5.4	4.68
1995	7.86	2.8	5.06
2002	6.50 (est.)	2.0 (est.)	4.50 (est.)

6. The nominal mortgage interest rate less the annual percentage increase in the CPI equals what economists call the *real* rate of interest.

With the Federal Reserve's dedicated resolve, the mortgage rate levels of the 1940s, 1950s, and early 1960s could return.

The odds remain good that ARM rates will not push past their annual or lifetime caps anytime soon. In terms of expected inflation, ARMs do not appear to present much risk of payment shock.[7] In contrast, look at the period from 1970 to 1980 when inflation leaped up. Real rates fell way below their historical norms. As a perfectly foreseeable response, mortgage rates skyrocketed.

Disinflationary Trends

At least five major reasons support a forecast of low inflation, and correspondingly, moderate mortgage interest rates (say within the range of 5 to 8 percent):

- The Fed's concerted effort to keep inflation in check.
- Increasing amounts of money flowing into the bond market as skittish investors shy away from stock market volatility.
- Worldwide overcapacity in major industries, such as computer, telecommunications, steel, auto, textiles, and farm products.
- The eight-plus million Americans between the ages of 40 and 60 who will be shifting from consumption to saving as they prepare to accumulate enough money for retirement.
- Most labor unions no longer enjoy enough power to push up wage increases faster than gains in productivity (just the opposite of the late 1960s through the early 1980s). In addition, high levels of immigration will keep costly wage increases in check.

Are there also calamitous scenes that could be painted? Certainly. But like Scarlett O'Hara, let's think about those another day. For now, *Mortgage Secrets* sees a positive outlook. History, current evidence, and reasonable forecasts all support that view.

---

7. This discussion does not intend to revoke my earlier caveats to marginal borrowers. No one can guarantee that rates won't jump up two or three points, but no evidence now exists to support that forecast.

SECRET # **33**

Watch out for low teaser rates.

Start looking for ARMs, and you're sure to run across some quite competitive low rates. Do such rates represent a good deal? Maybe, maybe not. That's what you must watch out for.

Some Teasers Merely Bait the Hook to Catch the Gullible and Desperate

Occasionally, lenders advertise very low ARM rates to make their phones ring. I recently called about such an ad for a 2.95 percent ARM. As it turned out, the loan did guarantee that monthly payments for the first year would be based on a 2.95 percent interest rate. On closer inspection, however, the mortgage came attached with the following strings:

- *Negative amortization.* If the underlying index for the loan went up during that first year, the additional amounts owed would be tacked on to the outstanding principal balance.
- *Prepayment penalty.* If the borrower paid off the loan within the first three years, he would pay a 3, 2, or 1 percent penalty for years one, two, or three, respectively.
- *Qualifying rate.* For purposes of calculating the qualifying ratios, the lender would use P&I payments based on a 5.7 percent interest rate.
- *Lifetime cap.* Over the life of the loan, the mortgage rate could increase (theoretically) to as high as 13 percent.
- *Loan size.* Minimum loan amount recommended was $400,000.
- *Loan rep knowledge.* I had to push hard to extract the details of this loan product from the loan rep. Either he did not really understand the loan, or he didn't want the inquirer to understand it. He did, though, try to switch my interest to several other products the company was offering that "might better meet my needs."

Most likely, in this case, the lender did not really want to make this loan except to a few specialized niche borrowers. The lender was using it as a bait-and-switch come-on.

Sometimes, though, lenders do want to hook borrowers with teaser-baited ARMs—especially those borrowers who lack understanding, or who desperately want to finance a home with a seemingly affordable loan. It's those instances about which you must inquire closely to learn all features of the product (as *Mortgage Secrets* shows you throughout the remainder of this chapter). When some lender offers you loan rates or terms that sound too good to be true, look for the strings. You'll probably find some long ones. But not always.

Some Teasers (Low Rates) Do Make Good Loans

Recall the Klars from Chapter 3. Their very low rate ARM did provide a near certain benefit-cost advantage. Why do lenders sometimes overwhelm their competitors with an unbeatable product? Here are several reasons:

- *Rebalance the portfolio.* Lenders may internally decide to stuff their loan portfolios with certain percentages of ARMs as opposed to fixed-rates. If fixed-rates become overweighted, these lenders may push hard to quickly rebalance with exceptional ARM offerings.
- *Achieve growth targets.* Like all businesses today, mortgage lenders set growth targets that may require the sacrifice of profit to sales (volume of originations).
- *Gain market share.* Similarly, if a lender wants to quickly grow its market share (or stop a slide), it may develop several aggressive ARM products.
- *Make deals.* To win friends and influence referrals, lenders may cut especially good deals for customers of favored Realtors or home builders.
- *Change its image.* As an example, the large mortgage lender, Countrywide Home Loans, has been known primarily for its fixed-rate loans. To change this image, it began to aggressively offer ARM products.

Mortgage lenders operate in an extraordinarily competitive marketplace. To attract notice or make a big move quickly, they sometimes do place one or more of their products "on sale." Keep a sharp lookout, question closely, and maybe you can find a true teaser bargain.

SECRET # 34

Your start (teaser) rate isn't your contract rate.

Unknowing ARM borrowers get hit with payment shock when their teaser rate runs out. That's because they fail to distinguish their start (teaser) rate from their initial contract rate. Too often, sharpshooting loan reps permit this borrower confusion to continue lest they lose their mark.

Teasers versus Contract Rates

Although lenders may lure borrowers into ARMs with a teaser rate, for purposes of calculating future rate increases or decreases, the lender will use the initial note rate as spelled out in the mortgage contract. The greater the difference between the teaser rate and the contract rate, the greater the potential shock for the unsuspecting.

Contract Shock

To illustrate, consider this example. The lender in *Mortgage Secret* #33 offered a teaser start rate for 12 months at 2.95 percent. The current index (see *Mortgage Secret* #35) rate for this loan was 1.8 percent. The loan carried a margin of 2.75 percent. Add the index rate (1.8 percent) to the margin (2.75 percent), and you find that the initial contract rate totals 4.55 percent. Therefore, if the index remains unchanged during the first 12 months of the loan, the monthly payment will still jump up by 22 percent.

The payments for a $200,000 loan would figure out as follows:

Teaser rate payment @ 2.95%/30-year term = $822.

Contract rate payment (assuming no change in the index) @ 4.55%/30-year term at end of year 1 equals $1,001.[8]

8. All figures are approximate due to rounding.

Now, instead of remaining constant, assume this index moves up one point to 2.8 percent. Add the margin of 2.75 percent, and the adjusted contract rate becomes 5.55 percent for a second-year payment amount of $1,135. That's $322 a month more than the first-year teaser payments.

No Real Surprise to the Informed

Now you see what critics of ARMs call payment shock. But this supposed shock only resulted because the naïve borrower didn't pay close attention to the details of this loan. In fact, given the extremely low yields on short-term maturities during 2002, one should not be surprised to see this index move up to at least 3 or 4 percent during the next several years.

In fact, with an inflation rate of, say, 2.0 to 2.5 percent, indexes based on short-term yields such as the one-year Treasury were showing negative real rates of return (see *Mortgage Secret #32*). Short-term rates were unusually low in 2002 because of concerted attempts by the Federal Reserve Board to slash interest rates and stimulate the economy. Also, many investors were parking hundreds of billions of cash in money market funds as they took a wait-and-see attitude toward stocks, bonds, and other investments. As a result, during 2002, mortgage borrowers (especially short-term borrowers) flocked to ARMs tied to short-term yields. As long as they recognized and could handle the certainty of rising payments when the initial teaser period ended, these borrowers were making a smart choice.

SECRET # **35**

There's no one best index.

Every adjustable-rate mortgage is linked to an index. Some of these indexes move up and down slowly (typically less than one point per year). Others can move as fast as one point a month. Unfortunately, too many mortgage advisers tell would-be borrowers to select a slow-moving index so that they face little risk of, yes, you guessed it—payment shock.

Gentle readers, please permit me to belabor this point: Beware of financial advisors who obsess over the fact that payments on some types of ARMs can jump up quickly. Consequently, they have erroneously urged borrowers into high-cost loan products such as the 30-year fixed-rate mortgage or the cost of funds index (COFI).[9] Instead, you cost-efficiently avoid the possibility of payment shock by knowing exactly how both your interest rate and monthly payments might change. Then financially prepare for the worst as you enjoy the immediate gains which, when averaged over time, will probably produce big savings.

What Indexes Can You Choose?

As with mortgage products, lenders can confound you with more choices than Baskin-Robbins. Listed below are the four most popular ARM indexes:[10]

1. *Treasury Constant Maturities (TCM).* To fund the debts of the United States government, the Treasury regularly issues interest-bearing notes, bills, and bonds of varying maturities ranging from 30 days to 30 years.[11] Most TCM ARMs are linked to the one-year TCM. Three-year, 5-year, and 20-year TCMs also may be available to you. After their fixed-rate period ends, most hybrid ARMs link to the one-year TCM (not the Treasury Bill, as this index is mistakenly called by many).
2. *London Interbank Offered Rate (Libor).* This index reflects the interest rate often used by London banks when they lend short-term to other European banks. American lenders may use it for mortgages because they frequently sell such loans (mortgage-backed securities) to European investors.

---

9. "The cost of funds indexes are better for consumers than [short-term] indexes because they do not go up so quickly when interest rates rise." (*The Mortgage Kit,* Thomas Steinmetz; Dearborn, 2002, p. 77.)

10. Every adjustable rate mortgage is linked to some type of interest rate index. The index is nothing more than interest rates charged or provided on certain designated types of borrowings, such as Libor, or savings, such as COFI.

11. As of this writing, the Feds have discontinued new issues of 30-year bonds.

3. *National Average Contract Mortgage Interest Rate (NACR).* This index averages the mortgage rates charged by lenders on loans for owner-occupied housing (not including new construction). This index moves much more slowly than either the one-year TCM or the Libor.
4. *Eleventh District Cost of Funds (COFI).* This index averages the interest rates that many Western banks (California, Arizona, Nevada) pay their depositors. Similar to the NACR, this index moves slowly.

Quite wrongly, many loan advisors and book authors recommended the COFI index to ARM borrowers throughout the 1980s and 1990s as interest rates consistently trended downward. These advisors emphasized that slow changes in this index would protect borrowers from bearing the brunt of interest rate spikes.

How to Select an Index

Unfortunately, these advisors were still fearful of 1981-sized interest rates; yet, during the second term of President Reagan, all economic fundamentals were in place to push interest rates lower. As of the mid 1980s, *real* (inflation-adjusted) rates for mortgage interest had climbed to 6 or 7 percent. Recall that when tamed inflation meets high historical real rates (*Mortgage Secret #32*), you can safely forecast falling nominal rates—the contract rates that lenders quote.

What This Means for You

To figure which index can reasonably be expected to net you the lowest cost for the least risk, examine where the index sits relative to its history, and relative to the rate of inflation.

For example, as I write, the Libor and one-year Treasury sit at near 40-year lows. Plus, both of these indexes sit below the rate of inflation. Given these relationships, one can reasonably conclude that the risk of significant increases greatly exceeds the potential for further declines. Without tight caps (see *Mortgage Secret #37*) and a short time frame, say less than three years, *Mortgage Secrets* does not recommend either of these indexes today. Increases look far more probable than decreases.

On the other hand, with three- to five-year ARMs priced at 4.25 to 4.75 percent as opposed to about 6 percent for a 30-year fixed-rate, such loans look very attractive because you're guaranteed the low rate during that entire introductory period. Again, though, this advice presumes a relative short-term holding period, and also presumes that you don't want the assumable fixed-rate mortgage alternative explained in *Mortgage Secret #30.*

As to COFI, it also sits so low today (2.821 percent) that long-term upside moves seem far more likely than further downward drift. In closely comparing rates today, no ARMs look especially attractive for the long run; however, if 15- and 30-year fixed-rate loans unexpectedly bounce back up to 7.0 to 8.5 percent, while inflation stays below at 2.5 percent or less, the relative costs, risks, and benefits could shift back to ARMs.

Compare, Compare, Compare

To sum up, selecting the best index requires you and your loan rep to review your needs and the loan market with these issues in mind:

- Time horizon: Determine your relevant planning horizon (job transfer, trade-up home, refi possibilities, family changes, and so on) that will affect the number of years you might hold your mortgage.
- Review what's available: Look at the available ARM and fixed-rate loans that might fit your needs.
- Historical perspective: Compare the respective ARM index rates to where they stand now relative to their history.
- Index versus CPI: Compare the respective ARM index rates to the current and expected rates of inflation.
- Payment increases: Go through period by period to calculate potential payment increases.
- Qualifying and affordability: Eliminate loans that would not work because you could not qualify or afford them.

No one can simplify the process of choosing an ARM product and its corresponding index[12] partly because no permanent rules or relationships exist.[13] You can, however, examine the evidence. Make your calculations and then choose the loan that appears most likely to optimize your total outcome—including wealth building through mortgage paydown.

SECRET # 36

Don't ignore the margin.

The total interest rate you will pay for your ARM includes the index rate plus the margin. The margin pays lender's overhead, operating expenses, and profit, as well as the costs lenders incur due to borrower defaults and foreclosures.

Typically, ARMs apply margins that range between 2.25 and 2.75 percent, although I have seen margins as low as 2.125 percent and as high as 3 percent. (Margins on loan products targeted toward borrowers with stained credit can range considerably higher.) Because the National Average Contract Mortgage Interest Rate Index is calculated from mortgage rates (as opposed to other types of baseline rates), ARM loans tied to this index apply no margins.

When comparing the same ARM product and index among various lenders, make sure to ask for the applicable margin. This step magnifies in importance when you're comparing similar products and indexes that differ with respect to their teaser rates. Say you find two lenders offering COFI ARMs. One lender offers a teaser rate of 3.95 percent for six month. The other lender offers a 4.5 percent teaser for three months.

---

12. Many ARM products do not permit a choice of index. They're offered as a package of index and features that you choose or reject in total.

13. In fact, during the early 1980s, short-term interest rates exceeded long-term rates, which is called an inverted yield curve. This situation occurs when inflation presently rages, but investors believe it will diminish over the longer run. Generally, long-term rates exceed short-term rates to protect investors against an unexpected, money-cheapening rise of the CPI. Investors fear that rising consumer prices will erode their buying power (the value of their money) when eventually borrowers pay back the money investors put up today.

Superficially (all other features equal), the lender with the 3.95 percent teaser looks best. But remember, that teaser could be a come-on. The lender uses it to distract you from the fact that that lender will be adding to the COFI a high-end margin of 3 percent. In contrast, if the competing lender offers a 2.5 percent margin, that's the lender who is offering the better deal.

SECRET # 37

All caps aren't created equal.

ARM caps limit how high the lender can raise your monthly mortgage payment. Many ARMs set their caps at 2/6. With these caps in place, the lender could not increase your loan's interest rate more than two percentage points at a time; nor more than six percentage points throughout the life of the loan. However, you must go further in you investigation than just learning the monthly payment/lifetime caps that apply to any given loan. You must ask:

- *How often can the lender adjust the monthly payment?* Loan payments may adjust monthly, quarterly, semi-annually, or annually; or payments may stay fixed for 3, 5, or 10 years and then adjust annually or more frequently.
- *Does the loan involve negative amortization (neg-am)?* Your ARM's at 5 percent; interest rates skyrocket, and your loan's index jumps by 3.5 percent. "Whew!" You think, "Thank goodness for my personal cap. The lender can only raise my loan's interest rate two points to 7 percent." True, but if that loan shackles you with negative amortization, you don't escape the pain of a higher rate—you merely postpone it. For now, the lender adds the interest deficiency (1.5 percent) to your outstanding mortgage balance. Instead of owing less, you owe more.
- *What is the baseline rate?* Your ARM may include two initial rates: the teaser rate (say 3.5 percent), and the contract rate (say 5.0 percent). Which of these rates provides the baseline? If your lifetime

cap is 6 percent, how high could your rate go: 9.5 percent (6.0 + 3.5) or 11 percent (6.0 + 5.0)? A similar question also applies to the loan's periodic adjustments. If your payment caps limit annual increases by two points, what base does the lender start with? Contract rate, or teaser rate?

- *Can borrowers do better than 2/6 caps?* Yes, you can. Although conventional ARMs (Freddie/Fannie) typically carry 2/6 caps, FHA/VA ARMs apply 1/5 caps. You may even find periodic caps as low as .5 percent and lifetime caps of 2 or 3 percent.

Nearly all ARMs include caps of one sort of another, but caps by themselves don't tell the full story. To truly compare ARMs, closely examine just how much protection those caps really give you. There's no Declaration of Independence for ARMs. All caps are not created equal.

SECRET # **38**

That flashy convertible could prove to be a clunker.

Historically, ARMs became popular among marginal borrowers when fixed-rate loans start climbing. "Well," the loan rep tells the disappointed homebuyer, "I can't get you qualified at 9.5 percent for that 30-year fixed-rate loan, but here's what we can do. We can qualify you at 8.0 percent for the ARM. And what's great is that when interest rates come back down, you can convert this ARM into a fixed-rate 30-year loan."

At What Cost and Rate?

Have you at last found that ever-elusive free lunch? Probably not. On occasion, the convertible option pays off; however, as a rule, its glamour outshines its horsepower. Few borrowers ever exercise their option to convert. Here's why:

- *Higher interest rate.* Most borrowers think they can convert at the market rate. Not true. If, for example, at the time of conversion, fixed-rates have dropped to 7 percent, your converted fixed-rate would probably carry an interest rate premium of .25 to 1.0 percent—or a total rate of somewhere between 7.25 and 8.0 percent.

- *Conversion fee.* Lenders will charge a conversion fee that may range from a low of $100 up to as high as 1 percent of the outstanding balance on your loan.
- *Up-front cost.* You also typically pay for this conversion privilege at the time you take out the ARM—chiefly through a higher starting interest rate or higher loan origination fees.

When Can You Exercise the Convertible Option?

Anytime you want to? Not necessarily. Most frequently, the option to convert lasts only between the thirteenth and sixtieth months (fifth year) of a 360-month (30-year) loan. Some conversion options terminate earlier than 60 months. While many ARMs do permit you to convert anytime within that four-year window of opportunity, others limit the conversion to the annual anniversary dates of the loan. If interest rates hit rock bottom in June and your anniversary date's in November, you could be out of luck. To comply with the lender's conversion rules, you will need to provide timely notice as spelled out in the loan agreement.

If a loan rep offers a conversion option completely without charge, take it. But if this feature requires an up-front cost, or if the option stands critical to your decision to accept an ARM, stay focused on the substance. Remember, that flashy convertible that you're depending on could prove to be a clunker.

SECRET # 39

APRs tell you nothing about ARMs—and very little about fixed-rates.

The Federal Reserve Board and the Office of Thrift Supervision have published a booklet called *Consumer Handbook on Adjustable Rate*

Mortgages, available online at www.hsh.com. Unfortunately for its readers, this *Handbook* continues to reinforce numerous widely held misconceptions about mortgages. Consider this verbatim quotation:

> Because all lenders follow the same rules to ensure the accuracy of the annual percentage rate (A.P.R.), it provides consumers with a good basis for comparing the costs of loans.

When you compare the costs of mortgage loans, you will see the term annual percentage rate (APR). To comply with government truth-in-lending laws, mortgage-interest-rate advertising must include this figure. The APR always exceeds the stated interest rate because it supposedly accounts for your total cost of borrowing (interest, fees, points, and certain other expenses). Presumably, by comparing APRs among various loan products and lenders, you will be able to select the lowest-cost loan.

Real life proves more complex. APRs that apply to ARMs make no sense. Under the law, they are calculated as if the ARM interest rate will not change during the full life of the loan (except for the scheduled boost up from the teaser rate to the initial contract rate). Yet, the very idea of an *adjustable*-rate mortgage means that the interest rate will change. So, APRs for adjustable-rate mortgages give us mathematically precise, yet totally irrelevant figures. Accurate APRs for ARMs cannot be calculated in advance.

In its effort to force lenders to tell the truth about the costs of their mortgage loans, the government misleads borrowers. When comparing ARMs, you cannot rely on the stated APRs. You may find a COFI ARM with an APR of 7.86 percent and a one-year Treasury ARM at an APR of 7.21 percent. But because no one knows how these respective ARM indexes will change over time, no one can accurately predict which one represents the lowest-cost loan.

Moreover, contrary to what the Fed's consumer booklet says, all mortgage lenders do not compute APRs to include the same costs. In fact, the law remains quite ambiguous on many types of expenses—and some lenders take advantage of this fact to lowball their APRs. Ignore the ARM's APR. It means nothing to consumers.

Fixed-Rate APRs

Although it might appear that the APR would apply accurately to fixed-rate mortgages, that is true only in the unlikely event you pay off the loan balance precisely according to its schedule over the full life of the loan. If you pay ahead (or behind) of schedule, your actual APR will increase. Similarly, if you sell your house or refinance your mortgage, your actual APR will exceed the APR figure the government requires lenders to calculate.

In mandating APR disclosures, the government was addressing a real need: Help consumers compare the total costs of mortgage loans. In practice, you must look beyond the APR. To obtain the best loan at the lowest cost, you must compare loan products according to your personal financial situation, your tolerance for risk, and the expected period over which you plan to hold your loan (see *Mortgage Secret #24*).

CHAPTER 5

Perfect Your Credit Profile

In the past, mortgage applications were either approved or rejected. Today, lenders are adopting risk-based pricing. If your credit profile looks platinum class, you could whiz through the loan process in less than an hour. The lender may even offer to loan you 125 percent of your home's value. As a preferred borrower you'll choose from among the lowest-cost, lowest-interest-rate mortgages. The lender may waive mortgage insurance and also loan you whatever amount you need for a down payment.

What about those borrowers whose credit profiles range anywhere from "bottom of the barrel" to "looks pretty good?" Lenders have fashioned loan products, interest rates, costs, down payments, and documentation to fit them, too. But the more risk the lender sees, the more onerous the terms, fees, costs, and paperwork. On a $100,000 loan, borrowers tagged most risky could pay interest costs of $5,000 to $10,000 more *per year,* plus an additional $4,000 to $6,000 to cover origination points, fees, and expenses.

To obtain your best loan with the lowest interest rates and costs, start now to perfect your credit profile. In today's world of mortgage lending, your credit profile will strongly influence every decision the lender makes about you and your loan:

- Acceptable size of down payment
- Qualifying ratios

- Type and cost of appraisal
- Mortgage insurance premiums
- Quantity of verifications and documentation
- Interest rate
- Loan product
- Escrow requirements

For many borrowers, perfecting a credit profile may require only a few months and minor tweaks. For others, the process may take two years or more, plus a revolutionary change in their spending, borrowing, saving, and financial discipline.

Over time, people who do effect these changes will reap rewards totaling hundreds of thousands of dollars. Experience proves that the faster you perfect your financial profile, the faster you will grow your net worth—not just through mortgage savings, but also through your new attitude toward saving and investing money, rather than spending it.

SECRET # 40

Emphasize all five Cs of credit approval.

Want to convince a lender to shower a huge pile of cash on you—a total stranger? Then think about your loan profile the same way a lender does:

- Consistency
- Character
- Capacity
- Collateral
- Credit

By far, the most important of these five Cs is credit, and that's the primary topic that *Mortgage Secrets* will address in this chapter. Nevertheless, credit doesn't stand alone. Even when you lack a platinum power credit score, you can still dress yourself up for success.

Consistency: Fast Track or Flake

Have you job hopped or job flopped? Have you lived in more places than you can remember? Did you jump through six majors before you finished community college? Do you suffer bouts of binge spending and borrowing? Does your background look more like a tossed salad that's been thrown against a wall than the impeccable dinner presentation of an expensive French restaurant? If so, you've got some explaining to do.

Loan reps and underwriters want to make sense of your life as it's displayed on your mortgage application. They want to evaluate where you've been and where you're headed. To satisfy their penchant for consistency, figure a theme or angle that ties your loose ends together. Give the lender confidence that six months after you've closed your home loan, you won't abandon your house to join a Hare Krishna colony, or move to Soho and fulfill your dream of becoming a romance novelist. The lender wants to envision your steady path toward job promotions and career advancement. In borderline cases, a good story can make the difference.

Character Counts

Remember J.P. Morgan's first rule of lending: "I wouldn't loan money to a man I did not trust on all the bonds of Christendom." Don't you feel the same way? Well, so does your lender. You've got to prove to the lender that you're trustworthy, and you'll honor your obligations and commitments. Your credit score provides one indicator, but you can bolster this score (if necessary) with other types of written information, such as:

- *Employer reference.* If your lender requires a completed verification of employment (VOE) form, ask your supervisor to enclose a letter that commends your dependability, integrity, and responsibility at work.
- *Credit blemishes.* Explain how misplaced bills, your vacation, a move of residence, or other non-character-indicting reasons account for these lapses that you deeply regret. Even better, discuss the new bill-paying systems that you have now put in place to prevent future lapses.
- *Credit wreck.* Explain serious problems as once-in-a-lifetime, beyond-your-control events that you coped with as honorably as

possible. If actually due to irresponsibility, emphasize that you've learned your lesson the hard way and now are a different person. Supply objective evidence to support your "new you" claims.

- *Personal references.* In the old days of mortgage lending, younger borrowers were awarded loans merely on the basis of family character and reputation.[1] "Why, I've know Luke Jr.'s family for 30 years," says the loan rep. "They're great people. Loan approved." In our big-city, automated world, personal references to lenders seldom count for much. Nevertheless, if you've established good rapport with someone who could prove influential, it wouldn't hurt to enlist their help.

Unless you provide alternative documentation, the lender will infer your dependability from the shading provided by your record of credit and consistency. When such evidence paints too dark a picture, you should add some brighter colors to the mix.

Capacity: How Much Mortgage Debt Can You Safely Carry?

As you previously learned (*Mortgage Secret #7*), lenders use qualifying ratios to help them determine how much money to loan you. Recall that you can improve these ratios in a variety of ways:

- *Income.* Increase the amount of your qualifying income.
- *Debt.* Decrease the amount of your *dis*qualifying monthly payments.
- *Interest rate.* Use a loan program or product that offers a lower qualifying interest rate.
- *Compensating factors.* List and explain all of the reasons that the lender's methods of calculation actually understate your real borrowing capacity.
- *Decrease PITI (MI) (HOA).* Because principal, interest, homeowners insurance, mortgage insurance, and monthly homeowners association dues all conspire to increase your qualifying ratios, take

1. Many loan applications used to include spaces for personal references similar to those found on some job applications.

aim at each of these items. Shop for homes that require lower insurance, lower property taxes, lower mortgage insurance premiums, or lower homeowners association fees. You can also reduce your qualifying principal repayment through longer terms (say, 30 or 40 years as opposed to 15 or 20), GPMs (*Mortgage Secret* #29), and balloon loans (*Mortgage Secret* #69).

Keep in mind the most important theme of *Mortgage Secrets:* Qualifying and affordability depend on you! You need not become a Sister Carrie blown about by winds of fate. And if, after working your ratios down as far as you can, you still don't qualify with one lender, switch to another lender or loan program that accepts higher ratios.

Collateral: We Don't Want the Property, but We Do Want You to Want It

Except for some ruthless, predatory loan sharks (*Mortgage Secret* #82), lenders don't want your property. Most mortgage loans focus on *credit.* In a worst case, lenders will foreclose as a means of last resort, but they rarely expect to get their money back from doing so. Why then do lenders require an appraisal?

One reason for an appraisal is to protect against fraud. The lender checks to see if the property seems to be worth the price you're offering to pay. Without this check, scam artists can bilk mortgage lenders out of billions (as with the savings and loans in the mid to late 1980s).[2] The lender also wants to make sure that you're committed to the property. To that end speaks the loan-to-value ratio. From the lender's perspective, the more of your own cash you invest in the property, the less likely you'll mail the keys to the lender when times get tough.

Never Tell the Lender a Foreclosure Will Yield It a Profit

Borrowers with spotty credit err egregiously when they expect their large down payment to substitute for commitment and credit.[3] These

2. This instance of massive widespread fraud included many dishonest loan reps, appraisers, developers, loan underwriters, lawyers, and other insiders.

3. Except when borrowers are dealing with predators, or so-called hard money lenders.

borrowers typically say something like this to the loan rep: "Why should you care about my credit? I'm putting 30 percent down. If you foreclose, you're going to make money." If you adopt this approach, you will alienate the lender, and your loan app will get deep-sixed.

You will never persuade reputable lenders to make a loan by emphasizing how much money they will reap if they foreclose. Lenders don't want to foreclose. They do not want an inventory of real estate owned properties (REOs). And they certainly do not knowingly make loans to would-be borrowers who do not appreciate those facts.

Show Your Commitment

Use a larger down payment to show your *commitment* to the property. Emphasize how much the home means to you. Detail the improvements you plan to make. Relate how much effort you put into finding a property whose features exactly match what you've been trying to find for the past two years.

A higher down payment can to a limited degree offset less-than-perfect credit, but never think of it as a profit incentive for the lender in case you don't pay as agreed.

Investor Loans, Ditto

This same advice applies to real estate investors. Traditionally, lenders require investors to put more money down to diminish the possibility that the investor will abandon the property when rent collections fail to cover property expenses. Experience proves that the vast majority of homeowners will struggle far more to keep their properties during economic downturns or personal setbacks than will investors. I have never heard of an investor who obtained a mortgage by trying to persuade the lender how much money it could make through foreclosure of the property. Investors, show your commitment, too.

Credit Counts Most

With very strong credit, lenders will relax all of the aforementioned requirements. Strong-credit borrowers need to worry far less about high qualifying ratios, low down payments, self-employment (difficult to determine income), piles of verifications, inconsistent life patterns, or character flaws. Strong-credit borrowers win the lowest interest rates, the best terms, and the fastest approvals. These borrowers need never suffer the claw marks of predator lenders.

So now we'll turn to the information you need to move toward this platinum power credit status.

SECRET # 41

Credit scores can shape your destiny.

During the past four or five years, most mortgage lenders have tried to assess the creditworthiness of their potential borrowers through the use of credit scoring. Fannie Mae, Freddie Mac, FHA, VA, and numerous large portfolio lenders such as Washington Mutual all follow some form of this so-called "black box" credit evaluation.

For borrowers whose scores pop out at, say, 780 or higher, great! Just make sure you've not messed up any of the other four Cs of credit approval, and you're home free at the lowest interest rates and costs available (provided that you understand the mortgage process and don't let some sharpshooting loan rep get you in his sights). If your score totals between 660 and 720, however, you may not get the best terms available with the least amount of hassle. And if your score falls below, say, 620, some lenders will push you into the subprime (much more expensive) mortgage market unless your other four Cs look pretty good. Below 600, watch out for predators or try for protection with FHA or VA.

What Is Credit Scoring?

Through credit scoring, lenders try to minimize individual human judgment in the mortgage lending decision. Credit scoring data from auto loans, department store accounts, and credit cards prove that computer statistical programs can distinguish platinum, gold, copper, lead, and plastic far better than back-office loan clerks or front-office loan reps.

To create these credit scoring programs, math whizzes study the credit profiles, borrowing habits, and payback records for hundreds of thousands of people. They then search for statistically significant correlations that tend to rate borrowers along a continuum from walk on water (say, 800 or higher) to let's pray they drown (say, 500 or lower). Supposedly, credit scores may range from 350 to 900, but more than 75 percent of Americans fall within the range of 600 to 800.

Credit Scoring Is Spreading

If you've received a preapproved credit card in the mail, or secured instant credit at Sears, Home Depot, or Best Buy, you've been run through a credit scoring program. That's why the store could make the credit decision so quickly with only minimal information from you (social security number, name, address). Now, even insurance companies (especially auto) are turning to credit scores to decide whether to insure you and, if so, at what price. Employers, too, have started running credit scores on job applicants and, in some cases, current employees.

We are approaching the time when people will no longer say, "You are what you eat." Instead, they'll remark, "You are your credit score." Therefore, you must do all you can to bolster your score. And if your score now shines out in platinum territory, learn to do what's necessary to keep it there. In the United States of tomorrow, Mensa will become old hat. Far more prestigious and practical to be invited into the FICO 800 club. (Fair, Isaac and Company—FICO—is the leading supplier of credit scoring computer programs.)

SECRET # 42

Your credit score doesn't necessarily represent your credit strength.

Contrary to what increasing numbers of loan reps (and others) believe, your credit score doesn't necessarily represent your credit strength. You may never have paid a bill late in your life and still earn a credit score of less than 660.

Credit Scoring Doesn't Rate You Personally

The credit scorers select certain characteristics that you share with others who have (or have not) paid their bills as scheduled; then, based on these selected characteristics, the scorer's mathematical formula assigns you a number. Supposedly, this assessment accurately gauges the risks you present to the lender—but it doesn't. Why? Because you are a unique individual. Although you share some similarities with this computer sample of borrowers, you also differ in many ways of which the credit scoring programs have no knowledge. These unaccounted-for differences may give you far more (or far less) borrowing credibility than your credit score indicates.

You can easily see the parallel here with SAT scores and other college admission tests. If you fail to register a top score, you can kiss Stanford good-bye—unless, that is, you write a superlative admissions essay and bolster your application with distinguishing achievements.

I'm Not a Number

Remember Bob Seger's classic hit, "I'm Not a Number." When you apply for mortgage credit, make that song your anthem. Certainly, do all that you can to boost your credit score, but never deal with a lender who confuses the total *you* with your credit score.[4] By the same token, never assume that your astute loan rep and underwriter will intuitively recognize your worthwhile qualities. Just as the aspiring Stanford applicant must document why she deserves admission, you, too, must persuasively document why the lender can trust you to pay back that $250,000 you're asking to borrow.

SECRET # 43

You can discover your credit scores.

In the late 1990s, when mortgage lenders first began widespread use of credit scores, the credit score providers told lenders to keep the scores

4. Unless, perhaps, your credit score makes you look better than you deserve.

secret from the borrowers. The score providers would otherwise cut off the lender. This secrecy created a howl of protest from consumers, but the law was on the side of the credit repositories. The Fair Credit Reporting Act clearly exempted mandatory release of credit scores.

Nevertheless, eloan.com braved the storm and began releasing scores to its customers. True to their word, the credit score providers threatened to throw eloan.com out of the fraternity. Not only did eloan.com refuse to buckle under, the California legislature entered the fray and mandated release of credit scores to Californians. Shortly thereafter, Fair, Isaac (FICO) set up its Web site www.myfico.com. Now, for $12.95, anyone can learn their FICO score as created from credit data held by Equifax, one of the three major credit repositories.

Not All You Need

Unfortunately, you can't depend on the myfico.com number alone. When a lender or its automated underwriting system runs your credit, it uses a tri-merged credit report from all three credit repositories (Equifax, Experian, and Trans Union). The lender will actually receive three credit scores for each person who applies or coapplies for a mortgage (six scores will be generated for a couple, nine scores for three partners, and so forth).

Often, the three scores provided for each individual won't vary much from each other. But sometimes they do. That's because Equifax, Experian, and Trans Union don't share credit data with each other. Different data yield different scores. Big differences in credit data may yield big differences in credit scores.

What Should You Do?

At present, you can't get your credit scores from Experian or Trans Union; however, this secrecy will change shortly due to mounting consumer and political pressure on the credit scoring providers. You can, though, go to www.truecredit.com or other similar sites where less than $50 will get you a well laid-out, relatively easy-to-understand tri-merged credit report. You can then discover whether the Trans Union or Experian files include any data not found in the Equifax report that you'll get at myfico.com.

Saving Money?

If you don't want to spend the money to obtain credit information, you've got several other alternatives:

- *Eloan.com.* This pioneering mortgage Web site will provide you a free, no-obligation credit score that simulates, but doesn't replicate, the Equifax-FICO score (trade-named Beacon).
- *Consumerinfo.com.* This Web site operated by Experian will give you a free credit report, but it also will automatically enroll you in a $79.95 credit-monitoring service. Cancel this service within 30 days and you owe nothing.
- *Free reports.* Various states require credit bureaus to provide reports for free, or at nominal cost. Also, under federal law, you may receive free reports from each of the repositories if you're unemployed and looking for work; you're on welfare; or you've been turned down for credit during the past 30 days.
- *General commentary.* For the latest (usually critical) commentary about credit scoring and credit reporting, go to www.creditscoring.com and www.creditaccuracy.com. Also, the Federal Trade Commission maintains consumer information on all types of credit issues at www.ftc.gov.

SECRET # 44

You can improve your credit scores.

When credit scoring first caught the public's attention, credit score providers not only refused to tell borrowers how they rated in the system, they also refused to tell how the system itself operates. Today, that refusal still stands. Until Congress or state legislators force the issue, credit scoring remains a black box operation.

Credit scorers place your credit data into their programs, out pops a number, but they won't tell you how or why they calculated that figure. You're left in the dark.

Turning Up the Lights

Fortunately, even though the credit scorers have not shined much light into their black boxes, mortgage loan reps and underwriters who see everyday results are beginning to develop some keen insights. In addition, while still cloaking their systems in secrecy, credit scorers have reluctantly released some clues over which borrowers can puzzle.

Indeed, at myfico.com, after you've paid your $12.95, the Web site info will give you some pointers on how to improve your Beacon-FICO score. To learn how much your score actually does improve (if any) over the next 12 months, you will need to pay another $38.85. For that price, you get four more Beacon-FICO reports. Turns out that turning up the lights a little will prove to be a real moneymaker for Equifax and Fair, Isaac. Millions of Americans must now click on to myfico.com and *pay* to glimpse their credit destiny.

I say "glimpse" because the info provided still doesn't go nearly far enough. It's more like, "try this and (pay us) see what happens." You really can't tell ahead of time the specific score boost that their suggested changes might bring about. Nevertheless, piecing together clues from myfico.com and several helpful loan reps, here are the best tips currently available:

- *Number of open credit accounts.* You can have too few or too many. The optimum number probably ranges between four and six. One highly paid, credit-perfect (no lates) executive I know scored 640. After closing 6 of her 12 credit card accounts, her score went to 780, but it took six months before her score climbed up to that level.
- *Balances.* Open accounts with balances reduce your score more than open accounts *per se.*
- *Balances/limits.* Numerous accounts with balances close to the limit will bring down your score.
- *Credit inquiries.* Whenever someone checks your credit file, it counts against your score; however, multiple checks within, say, two weeks may not hurt as much as if it appears that you're merely shopping different lenders for one loan. Your personal inquiries don't affect your score.

- *Payment record.* Obviously, late payments hurt your score, but supposedly FICO doesn't distinguish between late mortgage payments and late payments on your Visa or student loan. (Mortgage lenders, though, most certainly do care. Always pay your mortgage or rent first.)
- *Recency counts.* Late payments two years ago don't hurt as much as two months ago.
- *Black marks.* Multiple lates on multiple accounts, collections, unpaid judgments, and tax liens devastate your score.
- *Kiss of death.* Go straight to credit scoring purgatory if you're within two years of a past bankruptcy discharge or a foreclosure sale. Chapter 13 bankruptcy plans and credit counseling debt management plans also count heavily and negatively.

Myfico.com also shows that some categories weigh more heavily than others:

- Age of credit (15%)
- Mix of credit (10%)
- Amount of balances (30%)
- Payment history (35%)
- Recent credit inquiries (10%)

These clues shed some light on the credit scoring process, but far too little. Perhaps most importantly, they display why perfect credit in the sense of no late payments does not necessarily generate a high FICO score. To improve your score, you must not only pay your bills on time, but you must also manage your credit according to the likes and dislikes of the FICO (or other) credit scoring program.

SECRET # 45

Garbage in, garbage out (GIGO).

Researchers everywhere know of GIGO (garbage in, garbage out). Clearly, this axiom applies to credit scoring. These programs retrieve raw data from the files of Equifax, Trans Union, or Experian. If your credit file data include errors, as do at least 30 percent of all files, your credit scores will also err.

Examine Your Credit Reports Now

Seventy-five percent (or more) of mortgage loan applications require tri-merged credit reports and, correspondingly, three credit scores per borrower. Because each credit repository holds more than 200 million files and registers billions of computer-generated entries every year, you are unlikely to find three flawless, perfectly matched reports. Yet, inconsistencies and mistakes can slow down or derail your mortgage approval.

What to Look For

You're looking for errors, but what kinds of errors? More than you might think, as seen in the following list:

- *Inconsistency.* Evaluate whether the reports differ significantly from each other. Does each report accurately show your credit accounts along with an appropriate "open" or "closed."
- *Late payments.* Make sure that all late payments shown were in fact late. Also, check the category of lates—30, 60, 90 days or over. Sometimes creditors overstate the number of days payment(s) have been late. Watch for rolling lates; you miss a payment, then get back on schedule. Every subsequent payment may show up as late.
- *Balances.* Verify that the outstanding balances and credit limits don't overstate your credit position. Remember, when balances push against limits, your credit score goes down.
- *Disputed claims.* Have you justifiably refused to pay any creditor's bills? Health clubs (and other service contract providers) often continue to bill (and report unpaid) fees for membership that customers canceled long ago.
- *Credit experience counts.* Do the reports accurately indicate the length of time each account has been open?

- *Omissions.* Have you established excellent credit with a credit card, landlord, or retail merchant that does not show up in your credit files? Increasingly, creditors withhold excellent payment records and balance information. Why? If your credit score goes up, that lender's competitors will start mailing you with offers to switch to their better terms or higher limits.
- *Tax liens.* This type of claim nearly always must be paid before your loan closes.
- *Judgments.* Ditto for judgments unless statute of limitations has passed.
- *Collections/write-offs.* Ditto for collections and write-offs (perhaps subject to statute of limitations).
- *Time limits.* Does any derogatory information show up in the files in violation of these legal time limits: Credit inquiries (two years); foreclosure (seven years); lates, collections, write-offs (seven years); judgments and tax liens (usually until statute of limitations runs out). To calculate time limits, work back from the date of last activity on the debt. Also, creditors often sell their bad debts to credit vultures. These outfits may improperly report debts beyond their lawful date of removal. Beware: You can trigger a new time limit by partial payment or settlement. Bankruptcy starts the clock on the date of discharge, not filing.
- *Other information.* Verify all other information, such as names, addresses, employment, date of birth, and so on.
- *Consistency with application.* Remember, your loan underwriter will likely verify the data in your credit files with the liabilities and other information you list on your mortgage application. Do they match up?

What to Do Next

Should you discover errors, omissions, or inconsistencies that bear negatively on your credit score, act immediately to start the correction process. If you wait until a loan rep initiates inquiry about these items, you could lose your loan and the home you have agreed to buy. Some problems can disappear in a matter of days, but others may take months to clear up.

Contact the Credit Source and the Repository Simultaneously

Most credit advisors tell you to notify the credit repository, point out the change you deserve, and formally (in writing) seek compliance with your request. Good advice except for one critical fact: Credit repositories primarily report only that information given to them by your creditors. Unless the repository has botched the data it's been given (a quite possible problem), the repository must contact the (mis)reporting creditor. If the creditor does not respond within 30 days, the repository must remove the disputed item.

However, if the creditor says, "Sorry, no mistake on our part," the record remains as is. The problem's back in your lap—but now 30 days may have passed by. To head off this potential delay, contact the original source of the (mis)information simultaneously. Ask them to give new, corrected info to the repository. Upon request, some friendly creditors will even reverse derogatory entries for customers they do not want to lose.

On the other hand, if you're dealing with a hostile or indifferent creditor, you could face a prolonged battle. In that case, the loan underwriter will either waive the black mark upon suitable explanation from you; offer you a higher-cost, less-desirable loan; or flat out decline approval until you obtain the creditor's correction or release.

To close their mortgage in a timely fashion, many borrowers have had to pay disputed claims. Acting early prevents forced settlements on eat-crow terms. Carefully review your credit report now. Avoid having to put forth last-minute pleas under deadline conditions.

Credit Scores Adjust Slowly

Your credit score may take 30 to 60 days to incorporate new or changed credit file data. In the meantime, if your loan program requires a 660 score and your uncorrected score stands at 648, you could be out of luck. Your computer clerk underwriter may refuse to manually override the computer.

The mortgage industry is working to cut down this score adjustment period for corrections to less than a week. One such system (www.scorefacts.com) will notify loan applicants by e-mail that their credit scores fall below loan program minimums. Borrowers will next log on to a secure Web site, examine their credit files that gave rise to the deficient score, and then initiate the correction process.

Scorefacts promises a new score within 72 hours after it receive documentation from a creditor that confirms and corrects the mistake you have alleged. But here's the catch: This technique won't work for disputes. It won't work when the creditor fails to respond in a timely manner, and it doesn't work to achieve the score boosts you could attain through more attuned credit management.

Credit Scores Adjust Like Molasses to Changes in Credit Management

After correcting your credit reports, you next should improve your credit score by changing your credit profile. Unfortunately, such changes can take at least six months, and sometimes as long as a year or two. Pay your bills more conscientiously; close excessive accounts; reduce the amount of your outstanding balances—but total payoffs of all accounts may hurt because you want to maintain active credit experience—and resolve disputes, liens, judgments, and write-offs. No one can quickly overcome the stains that soil a credit report when they lawfully belong there. Just clean them up the best you can. At the same time, manage your credit as if the FICO folks were looking over your shoulder—because they are.

SECRET # 46

Credit repair firms can't fix your credit or boost your credit scores.

"Erase bad credit" the credit repair ads say. The Federal Trade Commission (FTC) says something quite different. "Don't be misled by credit repair ads. . . . Promises to repair or clean up a bad credit file can almost never be kept." How do these firms get away with making false promises? They just operate until the government shuts them down; then they open shop again under a new name.

Even worse, many of the tactics these firms do try can land their clients in jail. For example, one trick they pull is to get you a new credit file under a different (false) social security number or business tax number. If caught (and you will likely get caught in our ever-more-automated, no-privacy world), the Feds can prosecute you for identity fraud or obtaining credit through fraudulent representations. Anytime you fib, deceive, mislead, omit, overstate, or understate to obtain credit from a federal- or state-regulated financial institution, you commit criminal fraud.

You can repair your credit by following the steps outlined in *Mortgage Secrets* or other books by reputable authors and publishers. Also, Countrywide Funding, the huge mortgage banking firm, has published an excellent (and free) credit repair manual. Keep in mind "credit repairs" in the sense used here doesn't mean jettisoning lawful negative entries from your credit file. It means correcting wrongful entries, adding legitimate entries, and careful credit management that complies with the rules manufactured by Fair, Isaac and other credit scoring systems.[5]

SECRET # 47

Credit counselors can scam you, too.

As credit repair firms finally begin to get the tar and feathers they deserve, many similar operations now do business as credit counselors, debt consolidators, and "get out of debt for dimes on the dollar" firms. Similar to their credit repair brethren, these firms typically overpromise, overcharge, and underdeliver.

Rather than detail all of their seedy practices, let me pass along the recommendations of Clark Howard, the most informed consumer intelligence expert in the country. For credit counseling and debt repayment

5. Although FICO currently dominates the field of mortgage lending, numerous other scoring systems will soon challenge Fair, Isaac. Such systems will be forthcoming from Fannie Mae, Freddie Mac, and FHA, to name just a few.

plans, Clark recommends the not-for-profit Myvesta (locate at www.myvesta.com) or Consumer Credit Counseling Service (CCCS).[6] CCCS charges its clients a nominal fee of less than $25.

If you ignore this advice and select some other counseling or debt management advisor, get all promises *in writing.* Do not accept glowing hype. Read your written contract very carefully in the comfort of your home. Federal law (the Credit Repair Organization Act) gives you three days to rescind. Do not pay any money up front.

SECRET # 48

Credit counselors and debt management firms do not improve your credit record or boost your credit scores.

Why go to a credit counseling–debt management service? Three reasons: To get help with budgeting; to seek legal advice about bankruptcy and creditor collection practices; and to prevent or stop creditor collection efforts. If you've got good credit, budgeting assistance can help you retain it. If you've bruised or busted your credit, however, debt management or consolidation plans will not redeem you any time soon. To most creditors, you either pay your bills on time or you don't.

They may agree to accept less money than you owe on revised terms as the best outcome for a bad situation, but your credit file will still get hit with a write-off. If in collection, that, too, will remain. As a rule, neither Fannie Mae's nor Freddie Mac's conventional underwriting standards will approve mortgage applicants who are participating in debt workout plans (including Chapter 13 bankruptcy). In fact, conventional loans generally require two years of nearly clean payments *after* completing debt rehab.

FHA and VA lenders, though, do take a case-by-case approach. If you've got a good story to explain your past credit problems, neither

6. Formerly known as Debt Counselors of America (DCA). Myvesta's Web site offers a cornucopia of credit advice and information.

FHA nor VA will reject you arbitrarily. After at least one year of paying as agreed, liberal government program lenders may accept your application. Essentially, these lenders (and most others) want to hear how your credit problems arose from a run of misfortune, not perpetual irresponsibility.

SECRET # **49**

Bankruptcy (Chapter 7) doesn't ruin your credit.

Many hapless borrowers are talked into ill-fated debt management repayment plans including Chapter 13 bankruptcy. They are told that bankruptcy (Chapter 7 liquidation) will ruin their credit. It stays in the credit file for 10 years. In response, these troubled debtors quake with the fear of stigma and the thought of becoming a credit leper.

While it is true that both Chapter 13 (debt repayment) and Chapter 7 (liquidation) will show up in your credit report for 10 years, it does not follow that Chapter 7 bankruptcy ruins your credit for 10 years, or even 2 years.

What's the Best Outcome?

If your bills get out of control, you should consider a debt repayment plan only when you own substantial assets that you would lose in a Chapter 7 filing. Experience shows that more than 50 percent of the people who enter debt management plans fail to successfully complete them. Consequently, they've continued to harm their credit and merely postponed the day of reckoning.

On the other hand, if you want to rebuild your credit as quickly and securely as possible, Chapter 7 often makes more sense. After you obtain a Chapter 7 discharge, you're debt free, except possibly for past-due taxes and certain types of judgments. Now, instead of plugging $300 to $3,000 a month into paying off debt, you can put that money into savings. Within a year or two, you'll be much further ahead financially than if you were still stuck in a payoff plan. As to credit profile, cash in the bank and no (or very limited) debt give you a better credit profile. Fannie and Freddie will each consider Chapter 7 bankrupts two years after discharge. FHA/VA will consider such persons after one year. In other words, when you're really drowning in debt, Chapter 7 can put you on the path to mortgage approval and financial stability faster and more effectively than a debt repayment plan.

Won't We Lose Everything?

Every state exempts many of your valuable assets from loss in a Chapter 7 bankruptcy. You may emerge from Chapter 7 with your home equity, retirement plans, automobile, life insurance cash values, and the tools of your trade. But even if you did lose everything, wouldn't your new debt-free, anxiety-free net worth actually rank higher in importance than your previous liability-laden financial statement?

Not an Endorsement of Bankruptcy

You may read the previous paragraphs as a billboard for bankruptcy lawyers. That is not the intent. The intent is to warn you against the ill-fated debt repayment programs that keep so many good people mired in debt and financial struggle to no avail.

Remember, most reputable not-for-profit credit counseling agencies are funded by banks. Although these organizations employ dedicated people who would like to help you, their jobs depend on encouraging borrowers to elect partial debt repayment rather than Chapter 7. As to the disreputable for-profit and not-for-profit debt management companies, they make their money from credit repair fees and by taking a slice of your monthly debt management payments. The debt counseling industry does not gain when creditors file Chapter 7.

If you are (or become) overwhelmed by debt, weigh your options according to the alternative that will move you to where you want to be most quickly and surely.

Beware of Changes to the Bankruptcy Law

For the past five years, banks and credit card companies have liberally greased the palms of congresspeople in hopes of buying a new bankruptcy law that will force nearly all bankrupt debtors into debt repayment plans. Even though every disinterested bankruptcy expert and consumer advocate in the country has condemned this proposed legislation, the banks seem close to shamelessly winning the political battle. The banker's vision: "Get people into debt and keep them there for the rest of their lives." For the right price, Congress seems willing to make the bankers' wishes come true.

SECRET # 50

Your ex-spouse can ruin your credit (and other tales of double counting).

Are you divorced, married, or planning a wedding? Might you buy a property with a partner or significant other? Then you're going to face the multiple scores and multiple-person problems of credit scoring and mortgage approval.

The Ex-Spouse Dilemma

If a sharp lawyer handled your divorce, you cut up all joint credit cards and closed all joint accounts. If you and your ex owned a home with a joint mortgage, one spouse bought the other spouse out and refinanced solely in his or her own name. Without these precautions, you're still on the hook for these debts, and they will count against your qualifying ratios when you apply for a mortgage. If you haven't yet eliminated this potential debt overload, work out something now.

Even worse than debt overload (for purposes of qualifying), your ex-spouse's poor repayment habits on joint debts will show up to bruise your credit. Similar problems can also confront married couples who are separated (either legally or by informal agreement). When ending your personal lives together, also abolish all joint credit accounts. In some instances, a lender will permit you to explain away poor credit where full responsibility actually falls on your ex, but the lender will not overlook joint credit obligations that remain open. If the law imposes eventual liability on you for the debt, as far as the lender's concerned, it's your debt, or it's your credit line for as long as it remains open or unpaid.

One Borrower, Multiple Credit Scores

Earlier, *Mortgage Secrets* discussed the fact that any given borrower will earn a credit score from each credit repository. Should the credit data in these files materially differ, the corresponding credit scores also will differ. This fact brings up the question: Which score will the lender choose to use if one or two of your scores fall below program minimums? To a certain extent, it will depend on the persuasive story you tell. In other instances the lender may average the scores or select the middle score. This lender tendency to average or discount your highest score again underlines the importance of getting all low-scoring files updated and corrected prior to the time you apply for your mortgage.

Multiple Borrowers, Multiple Scores

Even when you and your spouse (co-borrower) show more than adequate income to buy and finance the property you want, both borrowers will need credit scores or explanations that surpass lender standards. Without meeting this requirement, the low-score borrower must withdraw as a co-borrower. The lender will then limit the loan amount to the qualifying capacity of the high-score borrower.

You can work around this, though. Buy a two- or four-unit property, or a home with an accessory apartment, and use lease income from the rental units to bolster the high credit scorer's qualifying income. Also, you could bring in another strong credit person (parent, sibling, friend) to serve as cosigner or co-borrower; however, the amount and repayment performance for that mortgage will impact that person's future credit record and borrowing power. (Typically, *Mortgage Secrets* strongly advises against cosigning or co-borrowing in these types of situations.)

Credit scoring and automated underwriting greatly ease the pain of securing a mortgage for the top 20 to 30 percent of U.S. homebuyers; however, for the majority of people (say with FICO scores below 720), credit scoring imposes something more than merely paying bills on time. It means keying into FICO or other credit scoring systems because you and your co-borrower will only achieve the lowest interest rates, best terms, and least hassle when you perfect your play according to the rules laid down by these new sultans of mortgage credit.

CHAPTER 6

The Lowdown On Low Downs

If you think that you haven't saved enough money for a down payment, you can put away your worry beads. In this chapter, *Mortgage Secrets* explores many ways to get over, under, or around the problem of too little cash, but it also reveals how little- or nothing-down mortgages can seriously increase the costs of your financing. Fortunately, *Mortgage Secrets* also suggests techniques that can alleviate or even eliminate these costs.

SECRET # 51

You can buy with little or nothing down.

No matter where you live, there's a low- or no-down-payment home finance plan waiting for you. The *Baltimore Sun* recently featured a major article titled, "Turning $5,000 into a House." The article featured at least 25 ways to buy a home with little or nothing down. And the *Los Angeles Times* and *San Francisco Examiner* run similar feature articles on a recurring basis.

"Five percent, 3 percent, and even nothing-down loans," says the *Los Angeles Times,* "are becoming the alternative for many buyers as private industry and government team up to help more people into home ownership." The *Baltimore Sun* article began with the same message:

"Banks, nonprofit housing groups, and local, state, and federal governments are so eager to help income-earning people become homeowners right now that they've developed scores of buying programs that give almost anyone an opportunity to own a house."

The *Baltimore Sun* and the *Los Angeles Times* are right on. Right now, providing that you shape up your fiscal fitness, you can become a homeowner without a large down payment. What's more amazing, the down payment, small as it may be, need not come from your own pocket. Some home finance plans allow you to raise all or part of your down payment through loan, gift, grant, rent credits, or do-it-yourself (sweat) equity.

SECRET # 52

No matter how much you earn, FHA may hold the key to your home financing.

By far, the most well-known low-down-payment home finance plan is offered by the United State Department of Housing and Urban Development/Federal Housing Administration (HUD/FHA). Yet, in contrast to popular belief, FHA does not limit its loans to people of low or moderate incomes. For example, in perpetuating this myth, one of Florida's largest newspapers continues to describe FHA as a program for low-income homebuyers. Not true. No matter how much you earn, FHA may provide the key to your home financing.

What Is FHA?

When Realtors and mortgage lenders talk about an FHA loan, they typically have the FHA 203(b) mortgage in mind. With close to 1,000,000 new FHA 203(b) loans made last year alone, this program is the largest low-down-payment loan available throughout the United States.

You can get into this type of FHA mortgage for just 4 or 5 percent out-of-pocket cash—sometimes a little more, sometimes a little less. On an $85,000 home, you would pay around $3,250; to finance a $125,000 home, you'd pay approximately $6,000; and a home priced at $175,000 would require cash of around $8,250.

How Much Will FHA Finance?

If you would like to buy a low- to mid-priced home, carefully consider the FHA 203(b) program. In this context, the meaning of "mid-priced" depends on where you live because FHA sets tailored loan limits for each locale around the country. In high-priced cities such as Los Angeles, San Diego, Washington, D.C., and Boston, the FHA maximum loan currently tops out (for single-family houses, condos, and town homes) at $280,749. In the lowest-priced areas of the country, the maximum FHA home loan comes in at $154,896. Because FHA limits vary, consult with a Realtor or mortgage loan advisor in the area where you would like to own. You can then compare these limits to home prices to see if the FHA 203(b) can work for you. (Note: Much higher FHA limits apply in Hawaii.)

Reconsider Rental Properties

As another choice, again consider buying a duplex, triplex, or fourplex. As long as you live in one of the units, you still can take advantage of a relatively low down payment. Again, here are examples of maximum FHA loan figures for these properties:

	Lower Cost Areas	**Higher Cost Areas**
Duplex	$198,288	$359,397
Triplex	$239,664	$434,391
Fourplex	$297,840	$539,835

Naturally, if you do buy a two- to four-unit property, you won't have to qualify for the loan using just your monthly earnings. The rents that you collect from the property will also count. Because the first home I bought was a fourplex with an additional detached carriage house, I enthusiastically endorse this multiple-unit approach to home ownership.

Other FHA Advantages

Besides a low down payment, FHA borrowers enjoy many other advantages, such as:

- You can roll many of your closing expenses and mortgage insurance premiums into your loan. This cuts the out-of-pocket cash you'll need at closing.
- You may choose from either fixed-rate or adjustable-rate FHA plans. (As an aside, note that FHA ARMs give you lower annual and lifetime caps—1/5—than most other ARM programs.)
- FHA authorizes banks and other lenders to use higher qualifying ratios and easier underwriting guidelines. After you've shaped up your finances, FHA will do all it can to approve your loan. FHA wants you to become a homeowner.
- If interest rates drop, and as long as you have a clean mortgage payment record for the previous 12 months, you can "streamline" refinance your FHA loan at lower interest rates without a new property appraisal—and without having to requalify.
- If you can persuade your parents or other close relatives to offer the down payment to you as a gift, you won't need to come up with any closing-table cash from your own pocket.
- Unlike most nongovernment loans, FHA mortgages are assumable. Someone who later agrees to buy your home need not apply for a new mortgage. When mortgage interest rates are high, an assumable low-rate FHA mortgage will give your home a great selling advantage.

FHA Drawbacks

FHA mortgages display two drawbacks. For one, you'll have to pay FHA mortgage insurance premiums (MIP) to protect the lender should you fail to make your mortgage payments. This mortgage insurance initially will cost around 1.5 percent of the amount you borrow, such as $1,500 on a $100,000 mortgage. Remember though, if you don't have the cash, you can add this premium onto your mortgage loan balance. As another cost, your loan interest rate will be boosted by one-half percent to cover additional mortgage insurance premiums that you'll make along with your monthly mortgage payments.

The Verdict on FHA 203(b)

What's the verdict? Yes, FHA 203(b) loans can generate costly settlement expenses and mortgage insurance premiums. Granted, too, FHA paperwork can sometimes make you tear your hair out as you hassle with bureaucratic detail. But if you rely on a specially skilled FHA lender (called a DE, for direct endorsement underwriter), your hassles can probably be alleviated. Regarding higher loan costs, don't forget you'll also gain numerous offsetting benefits such as a mortgage your future buyers may assume, a streamlined refinance when interest rates fall, low down payments with sometimes no cash from your own pocket, and liberal underwriting.

In weighing these costs and benefits, anyone who wants to become a homeowner should definitely consider this home finance plan. Mel Martinez, the secretary of the United States Department of Housing and Urban Development (the parent of FHA), is pushing for favorable changes in the 203(b) program. Lower costs, higher limits, and faster closings are three important goals. Both Secretary Martinez and President Bush are trying to give the FHA a starring role in the national strategy to make home ownership a reality for every American who is willing to make the personal and financial commitment to do so.

SECRET # 53

Discover FHA's best-kept secret: The 203(k) program.

Like many renters, Quentlin Henderson of Orlando, Florida, hoped to own his own home someday. Yet, with little savings, Quentlin thought he wouldn't realize his hopes for at least three to four years. He never dreamed that within six months he would actually own a completely renovated, three-bedroom, two-bath home of 2,288 square feet—more than two-and-a-half times as large as his 900-square-foot apartment.

How did Quentlin manage this feat? He discovered the little known, but increasingly available, FHA 203(k) mortgage loan program. FHA 203(k) allows buyers to acquire and improve a run-down property with a low- or no-down-payment loan. "The house needed a new roof, new paint, new carpeting; and a bad pet odor needed to be removed," says Quentlin. "There was no way I could have paid for the house plus the repairs at the same time. And there was no way I could have otherwise afforded a house this size."

Locate an FHA 203(k) Specialist

To use a 203(k) plan, your first step is to locate a mortgage loan advisor who understands the current FHA 203(k) purchase and improvement process. In the past, FHA often stuck borrowers in red tape for months without end. Now, however, with recent FHA streamlining and special computer software, Robert Arrowwood of California Financial Corporation reports that up-to-date, direct endorsement (DE) firms like his can "close 203(k) loans in four to six weeks instead of four to six months."

Search for Good Value

After you've located 203(k) advisors who know what they're doing, your next step is to search for a property that offers good value for the money. In Quentlin Henderson's case, his Realtor found him a bargain-priced, six-year-old house that was in a sorry state because its former owners had abandoned it as a result of foreclosure. "The good news for people who buy such houses," says Bob Osterman of HUD/FHA's Orlando, Florida, office, "is that purchase prices are generally low so that after repairs are made, the home's new value often produces instant equity."

Not surprising, the term "instant equity" was also used by John Evianiak, a 203(k) homebuyer in Baltimore. "Not only can you buy a house and fix it the way you like," John says, "but you can buy a home for much below its market value, put some money into it, and create instant equity. There were a lot of other houses we checked out, but we were going by the profit margin."

Greg Gerin, a 203(k) loan specialist with Prosperity Mortgage, says his typical loan is with buyers who spend $50,000 to $100,000 for a home, add $20,000 to $25,000 in improvements, and then end up with a home appraised at $100,000 to $150,000. But Greg adds that one recent customer borrowed $147,000 to pay $98,000 for a home and cover $50,000 in renovations. Upon completion that home appraised at $188,000.

Inspect, Design, Appraise

After you locate a home that you figure can be bought and rehabbed profitably, you next must come to terms with the owners on price and other conditions of sale. With agreement in hand, the home is then inspected, a formal plan of repair and renovation is designed, and the home is appraised according to its value *after* your improvements have been completed. The amount of your loan is based upon your purchase price plus your rehab expenses up to 110 percent of the home's renovated value.

Eligible Properties and Improvements

As long as you plan to pay more than $5,000 in rehab expenses, you can use a 203(k) mortgage to acquire and improve nearly any one- to four-family property. In fact, using 203(k) money, you can convert a single-family home into a two-, three-, or four-unit property; or you can convert a multifamily property into, say, a duplex or single-family home. As long as you are creating value, you can adapt the property as you like. Under some conditions, however, you can borrow more than your home will be worth after you complete your improvements. That's not a sensible strategy when you want to build appreciation fast and create home equity wealth.

In terms of specific repairs and renovations, the 203(k) mortgage permits an endless list of possibilities. As long as you stay away from luxuries such as saunas and hot tubs—although you can spend to repair these items if they're already installed—you can do about anything you want. Here are some examples:

- Install skylights, fireplaces, energy-efficient items such as thermopane windows and heavier insulation, or new appliances such as a stove, refrigerator, washer, dryer, trash compactor, and dishwasher.

- Finish off an attic or basement.
- Eliminate pollution or safety hazards such as lead paint, asbestos, and underground storage tanks.
- Add living units such as an accessory apartment or mother-in-law suite.
- Recondition or replace plumbing, roof, or HVAC systems.
- Improve aesthetic appeal with paint, carpet, tile, and exterior siding.
- Install or replace a well or septic system.
- Landscape and fence the yard.

"One of the great features of this program is that it doesn't restrict the niceties," says Michael Noel of Pinnacle Financial. "If you want to install upgraded kitchen cabinets, you can do that. If you want to add crown moldings, you can do that. You can't borrow the money to install a swimming pool, but you can use the money—up to $1,500—to fix up a swimming pool."

Buy with Little or Nothing Down

Down payment requirements for 203(k) loans generally match the same rules that apply to FHA 203(b) mortgages; however, the 203(k) plan also gives first-time buyers a pure no-down-payment possibility. Here's how this works:

Say you locate a house that has great potential. The house can be bought for $85,000; after rehab, its market value appraisal will increase to $125,000. Next, you or your Realtor could locate an investor or contractor who will buy the house and take responsibility for the improvements. If this investor or contractor will pledge to sell the rehabbed home to a qualified first-time buyer, FHA will loan a total of $119,250 against this property. Upon completion of repairs, you then buy the property from the investor and assume the $119,250 FHA 203(k) mortgage. FHA calls this first-time buyer plan Escrow Commitment Procedure.

You achieve a no-down-payment purchase. The investor or contractor gains because he or she has only spent $85,000 for the house plus, say, $17,500 for the value-creating improvements—a total investment of $102,500. That leaves a profit for the investor of $16,750. Of course, the exact numbers will vary according to each specific property, but the basic procedure remains the same.

Many investors, in fact, are now entering the FHA 203(k) program and locating properties on their own for repair and resale to first-time buyers. "Investors love the program," says Jackie Carlisle of Malone Mortgage in Oakland, California. "Most of them can do their own work and get paid for it. It's the best game in town for rehab money."

Of course, if you do buy from an investor, he or she's the person who will profit from the rehab work, not you. Make this choice for only two reasons: if you can't come up with the small cash-to-close that FHA requires, or if you want a freshly renovated property, but can't take the time or risk to perform (or arrange) the work yourself.

SECRET # 54

Too many vets pass up VA loans.

If you're a veteran with eligible active military service, or if you have served at least six years in the reserves, why are you still renting? The VA mortgage is truly one of the best benefits offered to those who have worn our country's uniform. Last year alone, a record 600,000 veterans took advantage of this loan program. Here are several of the great benefits you'll get with a VA mortgage.

- *No down payment.* With a VA loan, you can finance up to $203,000 without putting any money down. If you want to buy a higher-priced home, you need only come up with 25 percent of the amount over $240,000. For instance, if the home you want to buy is priced at $300,000, you'll need a down payment of $15,000 (.25 X $60,000)—or just 5.0 percent of the purchase price.
- *Liberal qualifying.* Similar to FHA, VA loans offer liberal qualifying guidelines. Many (but not all) VA lenders will forgive properly explained credit blemishes. The VA loan also permits higher qualifying ratios. I've seen veterans with good compensating factors close loans with a .48 total debt ratio.

- *Closing costs paid.* New home builders and cooperative sellers will often pay all of the veteran's settlement expenses. In fact, builders frequently advertise that veterans can buy homes in their developments for just $1 total move-in costs.
- *Assumable.* Similar to FHA, a nonveteran buyer may assume your VA mortgage when you sell your home. Also like FHA, if interest rates fall, you can streamline a no-appraisal, no-qualifying refinance.
- *No mortgage insurance.* Unlike FHA, you won't have to buy mortgage insurance when you use a VA loan. You will, however, have to pay a one-time "funding fee" ranging between 1.5 to 2.75 percent of the amount you borrow. If you don't want to pay this fee in cash at closing, you can tell the lender to add it to your mortgage loan balance.

As with many types of mortgages, VA loans require mountains of paperwork as well as compliance with various guidelines that look into job history; property condition; home value report, called a Certified Residential Value (CRV); and seller prepaids. That's why you should work with a Realtor and mortgage loan advisor who are skilled and experienced in the day-to-day job of finding homes and getting VA loans approved. "The devil is in the details," says loan consultant Abe Padoka. "Make sure you work with professionals who know the ins and outs of the VA home buying and loan approval process."

SECRET # 55

The USDA offers a prime choice for low- to moderate-income homebuyers.

"I'd like to write to the president about expanding this program," says Tom Dixon of Catawba County, North Carolina. In referring to the United States Department of Agriculture's Rural Development Administration mortgage, Tom enthuses that, "It's a great program . . . this loan can get people into their own houses. This loan makes a tremendous difference to their lives. Under this program, anyone who has a steady job and good credit can afford a house. That's the wonderful thing about this loan."

Although most people have heard of FHA home financing, relatively few know of its cousin, formerly known as the Farmers Home Administration (FmHA). But if you can live in a small city or rural area outside a Metropolitan Statistical Area (MSA), the Rural Development Administration could provide your easiest route into home ownership. In contrast to FHA, RDA offers several low- or no-down loan programs. In addition, if you earn less than 80 percent of a rural county's median income, RDA will subsidize your monthly mortgage payments.

Funding amounts and specific eligibility requirements for RDA mortgages change frequently. To learn what's current available in your area, call a local Realtor or mortgage lender who is familiar with RDA loans. Look in the yellow page mortgage ads for FmHA or Rural Development Administration loans. For great financing on low- to moderate-priced homes, it's tough to beat FmHA (RDA).

SECRET # 56

Community lending goes mainstream.

When nationally syndicated (*Nation's Housing*) columnist, Kenneth Harney wrote, "Mortgage lenders devise more ways to say yes," he was primarily referring to various types of community loan products. "If you don't own a home because you believe that your income, cash savings, or job history rule you out, think again," Harney advises. "Banks, thrifts (same as savings and loans), and other mortgage lenders are actually rewriting their rulebooks to get you into home ownership."

Basic Community Homebuyers' Programs

The most widely available community lending initiative is sponsored by the Federal National Mortgage Association (Fannie Mae), and is offered by hundreds of mortgage lenders throughout the country. Several features of this program are as follows:

- For loans up to $300,700, you may put down 5 percent of your purchase price; but, only 3 of this 5 percent needs to come from your own savings or other available assets. If you can raise the other 2 percent as a gift from your parents, or maybe a grant or loan from a government housing agency or not-for-profit housing group, that's okay with Fannie Mae.
- Some, but not all, lenders will judge your credit on a case-by-case basis. You'll need good-to-excellent credit at the time you're planning to buy, but past blemishes and setbacks may be forgiven if you've since proven you can manage your finances responsibly.
- This program is designed for households who earn less than 120 percent of an area's median annual income. In larger cities, this figure typically falls somewhere between $50,000 and $80,000. If you earn "too much," you still might use this or a similar program by buying a home in an area that's targeted for revitalization or gentrification.
- Depending on the strength of your credit score and compensating factors, your total debt ratio can go up to .40—or maybe higher. In addition, this type of loan doesn't require cash reserves after settlement; however, that's still a good idea, if you can figure out how to do it. Also, any cash reserves you can put aside will count as a compensating factor.
- Under the community lending program sponsored by Fannie, you'll need to buy private mortgage insurance. Depending on the loan amount, your premium for mortgage insurance could add $500 to $1,000 (or more) to your closing costs, and perhaps $50 to $150 (or more) to your monthly mortgage payments. If you're really cash short, however, your lender may permit you to pay these and other closing costs with a gift, grant, or borrowed funds.
- To participate in this program, you must complete four to six hours of homebuyer education. You can meet this requirement by attending qualified homebuying seminars that are regularly sponsored by participating mortgage lenders and Realtors. As an alternative, you can schedule a one-on-one homebuyer counseling session offered by mortgage lenders or not-for-profit counseling centers.

To own your own home through the community homebuyer's plan sponsored by Fannie Mae, call a Realtor to learn which lenders in your area participate in this program. Alternatively, watch your newspaper for announcements of lender and Realtor homebuying seminars (usually offered weekly or monthly) and homebuyer fairs (usually offered in the spring of each year). Fannie's Web site also includes much valuable information on community homebuyer programs.

Other Community Lending Programs

In addition to the previous suggestions, you might call banks, savings institutions, and various mortgage companies in your area. Ask to speak to a loan officer or assistant vice president who has knowledge of that lender's community lending or Community Reinvestment Act (CRA) loan programs. Some lenders also refer to these or similar easier qualifying loans as "first-time buyer" programs.

Because community lending has grown quite quickly, your efforts to locate the right program may take your fingers for a walk through the Yellow Pages—but your reward will make the trip worthwhile. "We are making money, we have no delinquencies or REOs, and we are in the risk management business," says Tobias Washington, a senior executive with Washington Federal Savings and Loan. "We thought we needed to step out of the box a little more. People are basically honest and they need homes." So step out of the box, they did. Washington Federal introduced a 1 percent down payment program for first-time buyers for homes priced up to $200,000.

Although your area lenders may not offer a 1 percent down payment community lending or first-time buyer program, you're almost certain to turn up relaxed qualifying, 3 to 5 percent down home finance plans. Leave no stone unturned. Ask Realtors, loan officers, and friends who have recently bought homes. Closely read the mortgage loan ads in your local newspapers. Ask your Realtor to look through the monthly or quarterly magazines published in your state's association of Realtors. Often, these publications include articles and ads that describe easier qualifying, first-time buyer home finance plans.

SECRET # **57**

Not-for-profit housing groups help people in need buy and finance homes.

If you earn less than the average income for your area, there's another type of community effort to help you over the down payment hurdle. In nearly every city in the country, not-for-profit housing groups are helping low- to moderate-income families become homeowners.

One of the best not-for-profit groups is Habitat for Humanity. Its most famous volunteer worker has been former president Jimmy Carter. As a Christian service organization, Habitat's "thousands of volunteers around the world have eagerly opened their hearts [and checkbooks] and picked up their hammers to build houses in partnerships with God's people in need."

Similar to most not-for-profit housing groups, Habitat accepts applications from hopeful homebuyers. It then chooses those families whose character and sense of responsibility well suit them for home ownership. If selected, you'll buy a Habitat home with a $500 to $1,000 cash down payment, and 300 to 500 hours of work helping the volunteers build your home.

Other Not-for-Profit Efforts

Habitat is just one of hundreds of local and national not-for-profit groups who help low- to moderate-income families buy and finance homes. In addition, many local Catholic, Christian, and Jewish groups work to help low- to moderate-income families become homeowners. Nationwide, the five largest black religious denominations, representing 43,000 churches, have joined with a variety of corporations to form the Revelation Corporation of America. Revelation plans to finance thousands of homes in minority neighborhoods. Ask your minister for more information.

Susan Cook and Family

"Originally I went out to rent a house but they wanted $600 or $700 a month for something much smaller than this," says Susan Cook, a

36-year-old divorced mother of four, as she surveys the home she recently bought with the financial help of the not-for-profit Portland Housing Center in Portland, Oregon. "I just fell in love with it," Susan continues. "It was big enough, and I had some friends who had bought a house in the area so I was real comfortable with this neighborhood. I wanted to have something of my own so I wouldn't be under the thumb of some landlord. I couldn't see paying someone else rent. . . . Now, I can do things to my house and always know it's going to be mine," Susan adds.

Although Susan was earning just $1,200 a month and had little or no savings, Realtors Peggy and Alan Glickenhouse and Peg Malley at the Portland Housing Center worked up a home-buying plan that could get Susan and her family into the home they wanted. In fact, the Glickenhouses offered to sell Susan a home they owned at a price of $49,000. After Susan got her credit cleaned up, the Portland Housing Center's down-payment assistance program contributed $3,000 toward her home buying cause. Susan borrowed another $1,000 from her parents.

Susan got her 30-year mortgage through an FHA 203(b) loan. Her payments (PITI) came in just at $370 a month—much less than she would have paid to rent. And of course, unlike rent, that $370 monthly payment is fixed for 30 years. Susan will never struggle to meet another rent increase.

In praise of successes of not-for-profit assistance programs, Portland Realtor Board vice president John Gronewold says, "It's not just a business thing. The more people who own their own homes and improve their neighborhoods and communities, the better it is for all of us."

Anything in Your Area?

What are the not-for-profits doing in your area? In every city in the country, groups similar to the Portland Housing Center, Habitat for Humanity, Neighbor Works, and others are working with mortgage lenders, Realtors, community organizations, church groups, and neighborhood associations to convert renters into homeowners. Could you benefit from their help? Ask around. If you're willing and able to meet your housing and other credit obligations, a not-for-profit group might offer the financial and homebuyer counseling assistance that will move you up to home ownership.

SECRET # **58**

Local governments assist with down payments.

In Oakland, California, several years back, Lynne Jerome and husband Brian Conan had for years wanted to become homeowners. But they could never put together enough for a down payment.[1] "We tried," says Lynne, "but it was always out of our reach." With Lynne studying for a graduate degree and Brian's work as a truck driver, their family income was just at $33,000 a year—which doesn't go far in the expensive California housing market.

"We always paid a lot of money for rent each month," says Lynne, "probably comparable to a mortgage payment, but instead of a mortgage we took out student loans to cover school expenses. We hated throwing money down the drain for rent and couldn't see any long-term benefits of paying rent. We always took as much care of the property we rented as we would have our own home. Every time we would go outside and work in the yard or paint a room, it made us cringe because we could have been doing these things to our own place instead."

Fortuitously, Lynne and Brian no longer rent. Thanks to Fannie Mae's HomeOakland Initiative, this couple and their one-year-old daughter have now become homeowners. To buy their $163,500 Craftsmen bungalow, they received a 2 percent down payment grant from the city of Oakland and a $35,000 mortgage assistance grant. "Without the HomeOakland Initiative," says Lynne, "we would probably be working close to retirement before we could have afforded to buy."

In explaining Fannie's efforts, Larry Dale explains that, "Working together, cities and Fannie Mae can harness the expertise of nonprofits, Realtors, government agencies, mortgage lenders, and private developers. This combination of resources and combination of efforts is expected to have a far more positive impact on the community than previous, relatively uncoordinated efforts have had." In following through with its Central Cities Initiative and Opening Doors Outreach Campaign,

1. Could negative self-talk have blocked their efforts? Quite likely (see *Mortgage Secret #4*).

Fannie has put together partnership agreements with mayors and local lenders in the country's 25 largest cities. To learn more about Fannie's outreach, look for a *House* Your City program where you live.

Down-Payment Assistance Doesn't Just Apply in Major Cities

Mortgage Secrets has emphasized Fannie's initiative only because it's the largest and most widely publicized effort that encourages local governments to offer financial assistance to first-time homebuyers. Yet, many large and small cities and counties haven't waited for Fannie to lead the way. They've been operating down payment or other financial assistance programs.

In Cobb County, Georgia, for example, Donna White and her two children recently bought in the Parkside at Village on the Park new home development. To help swing the deal, Donna enlisted sales agent Jeannie Tucker to come up with some creative finance options. "We'll work with a homebuyer any way we can," says Jeannie who prides herself on keeping up with all the special mortgage programs in the Atlanta area. "Many people have good credit and can manage house payments, but they just don't have that down payment."

To help Donna raise down-payment money, Jeannie put her in touch with Max Stone, a loan officer at Traditional Mortgage Corporation. With Max handling the paperwork, Donna was approved for down-payment assistance offered by Cobb Housing Inc.'s First HOME program. "Most of my business right now is first-time buyers," reports Max. "These creative financing options involve lots of extra paperwork and take more time. But because of these programs, some borrowers get in a home who wouldn't have otherwise."

SECRET # 59

Even Fannie and Freddie accept little- or nothing-down loans.

In the mid 1990s, both Freddie Mac (see www.homesteps.com) and Fannie Mae (www.fanniemae.com) committed to broadening the variety of little- or nothing-down loan programs. Since then, in addition to their standard 5 percent down product, they have pioneered community homebuyer programs, 3 percent down loans, and now even 103 percent loan-to-value (LTV) loans—meaning qualified borrowers can go through closing with almost no cash out of their own pocket. For a full view of their current programs, visit these companies' Web sites.

Tougher Credit Standards and Lower Cost PMI

These Fannie and Freddie low-down-payment loans do apply tougher credit standards than either FHA or VA, but their loan limits reach substantially higher. Also, borrowers whose credit scores top 680 (possibly 620) will probably pay less for private mortgage insurance with Fannie and Freddie loan programs than they would with FHA.

On the other hand, borrowers with FICO scores of less than 620 may find that FHA's mortgage insurance premiums (MIP) now fall below the premiums of the private insurers who guarantee Fannie and Freddie's low-down-payment mortgages (LTVs greater than 80 percent). That's because some PMIs recently kicked up their costs to give marginal borrowers a real wallop—an increase of nearly $200 per month on a $200,000 mortgage.

SECRET # 60

Cut the cost of PMI by learning where rates break.

Private mortgage insurance adds another layer of costs to your monthly payment on homes financed with little or nothing down. Mortgage insurers, however, do not charge all borrowers the same amount of premium. Instead, they use risk-adjusted pricing. In a manner similar to the way lenders risk-adjust interest rates, mortgage insurers vary their premiums according to risk factors such as:

- Loan-to-value ratio (LTV)
- Borrowers' credit scores
- Amount of the mortgage

- Total debt ratios
- Borrowers' financial shape such as net worth, cash reserves, job stability, and so on

For example, if your total debt ratio goes above, say, .38, the mortgage insurer adds to your monthly premium. Likewise, rates may break, respectively, at 5 percent down or less (95 percent LTV); 10 percent down or less (90 percent LTV); 15 percent down or less (85 percent LTV), or less than 20 percent down (greater than 80 percent LTV).

Should it turn out that your total debt ratio went to .40, and you were putting $10,000 down on a home priced at $101,500 (90.15 percent LTV), you could save considerably by tweaking your numbers. Place just a little more down, figure a way to reduce your monthly payments, and you will slip into a lower rate category. Of course, the same principle holds true for your credit score. A borrower with a credit score of 617 may pay a higher mortgage premium than if his score were 630. Learn where the PMI rates break, and with a little financial juggling, you might save $30 to $50 a month—or more.

SECRET # 61

Before you obtain a PMI little- or nothing-down loan, understand the high cost you'll be paying.

Many homebuyers (especially first-timers) get so enthused about buying with less than 20 percent down that they fail to appreciate the high cost of low-down-payment PMI mortgages. To keep the numbers simple, imagine you buy a $100,000 home and borrow $95,000. In that case, most lenders will require you to purchase PMI. In contrast, if instead of putting $5,000 down, you put $20,000 down, you pay no PMI.

The True Cost of Low Down Payments

To obtain that low-down-payment loan, you'll pay the lender yearly interest on that extra $15,000, plus you'll pay the annual premium for the

		Yearly Costs
Mortgage interest (6.5% @ $15,000)		$ 975
PMI premium		1,500
Total cost		2,475
Cost as a percentage of amount borrowed	=	$\frac{\$2,475}{\$15,000}$
	=	16.5%

Figure 6.1 The Cost of Mortgage Insurance Expressed as a Percentage

PMI. Recall (*Mortgage Secret #60*), mortgage insurers risk-adjust their premiums according to the borrower's credit profile. In addition, overall rating and premium schedules change as insurer loss experience hits peaks and valleys. Consequently, you can't apply the following numbers shown in Figure 6.1 to your situation at the time you get your mortgage. You can, though, use exactly the same technique to calculate the true cost of your low down payment:

For that extra $15,000, your interest and mortgage insurance costs total $2,475, or 16.5 percent. In today's market, that's a high cost of funds. But I've seen low-down loans where the effective cost goes above 20 percent. Before you jump for a low-down-payment loan with PMI, calculate your true cost of that marginal amount of money you're borrowing in excess of an 80 percent LTV; then compare that cost (the effective rate) to the cost of raising money through a second mortgage or family loan.

SECRET # 62

Reduce the high cost of low down payments with a second mortgage.

These types of financing arrangements are often referred to as 80–10–10, 80–15–5, or even 75–15–10. The largest figure represents the LTV of the first mortgage; the second figure reflects the LTV of the second mortgage; and the third figure is the percentage of cash you put down. As a rule, the sellers make the best source for this second mortgage. Given the high cost of PMI, you often can pay the sellers an interest rate of 8 to 12 percent and still come out ahead. As long as you keep the first mortgage LTV at or below 80 percent, the lender typically does not require mortgage insurance.

Second Mortgage Specialists

If at all possible, get the sellers to carry back financing. But what if the sellers cannot (or will not) assist with seller financing? You can then turn to a lender who offers second mortgages. Here's what Eagle Mortgage says in a promotional brochure that this company mails to Realtors:

> If you knew how to lower the monthly payments on a home purchase for your "A" credit homebuyers, while helping them build equity in their new home faster—would you be interested enough to listen . . . . what if you could also help your marginal "B" and "C" credit customers close the gap between their 60% to 70% loans and the funds they have available for their down payment? Our purchase-money seconds are an alternative financing method that can provide your homebuyers with up to a 90% total loan-to-value (LTV) financing . . . . With No PMI!

Eagle Mortgage, like hundreds of other lenders located throughout the country, can help reduce the down payment gap and drop your first mortgage balance low enough so you can avoid buying private mortgage insurance. Sometimes second mortgage lenders will charge you larger loan fees and a higher interest rate than most sellers, but if seller-assisted financing isn't available, locate a reputable mortgage lender who knows how to structure an 80–10–10 or similar loan package (tiered financing).

SECRET # 63

Use pledged collateral to eliminate PMI.

If you don't have enough money for a big down payment, and you can't (or don't want to) buy mortgage insurance or obtain a second mortgage, you've got another possibility. It's called pledged collateral. "We don't care where the collateral comes from," says Elmer Frank of First American Savings, "As long as we feel secure, we'll consider the loan. We've taken stocks, bonds, mortgages, retirement accounts, and once a Mercedes 300 SL Gullwing. We did though refuse to accept a racehorse."

Pledged Retirement Accounts

In terms of popularity, Elmer Frank adds, "Retirement accounts have become one of the most frequent sources of pledged collateral for our first-time homebuyers. We don't even require that the account belong to the buyers. We'll accept funds from any close family member. On no-down-payment mortgages, we usually like to see 30 percent, but for good customers, we've gone as low as 20 percent."

"In other words," Elmer continues, "we'll give homebuyers a no-down-payment, 100 percent loan, if, say, those buyers (or close relatives) move enough of their 401(k) funds to our bank to offset 20 or 30 percent of the home's purchase price. Last week, we closed a loan for a young couple in their thirties who bought a $165,000 home. Between them, they earn $70,000 a year, but they had little savings because they've been rapidly paying off their student loans. We financed their full purchase price without PMI, and the wife's mother deposited $45,000 of her 401(k) monies with us.

"The couple will pay First American $1,507 a month for principal, interest, homeowners insurance, and property taxes, but we didn't require them to buy mortgage insurance. We'll pay the mother a market rate of interest on her 401(k) funds. As long as the couple keeps their loan current, we won't touch the pledged collateral. After the couple's mortgage balance falls below an 80 percent LTV and as long as they've kept a clean payment record, we'll release our lien against the 401(k) certificates of deposit."

Other Types of Pledged Collateral

Retirement funds aren't the only source of pledged collateral you can use to offset your lack of a down payment. As Elmer Frank points out, his bank (like many mortgage lenders) will accept nearly any type of asset such as savings accounts, stocks, bonds, perhaps even a valuable antique automobile. If your parents have built up a large equity in their home, many lenders will accept that equity as pledged collateral.

If your parents or other close relatives would refinance their home or other real estate, you might be able to use a blanket mortgage to buy a home with no down payment. Imagine your parents owe $130,000 on their home now valued at $210,000. You want to buy a home priced around $85,000. Many mortgage lenders would loan you and your parents $215,000 so your parents could pay off their old mortgage balance of $130,000, and you could buy the home you want at a price of $85,000 ($130,000 + $85,000 = $215,000).

The lender would then record a blanket mortgage for $215,000 to cover both homes that together have a value of $295,000 ($210,000 + $485,000). You and your parents would share responsibility for making the monthly payments. You would have bought your home with no cash down and without having to pay mortgage insurance premiums.

SECRET # 64

Search for sellers with low-equity assumables.

You've already seen (*Mortgage Secrets #20*) that in periods of relatively higher interest rates, you can slash your interest costs by assuming a mortgage that carries a below-market interest rate. In addition, assumables can help you buy with little or nothing down. Just locate a seller who has bought (or refinanced) recently with a low-down, high-LTV assumable mortgage. Within the past three or four years, FHA and VA have originated millions of low- and nothing-down home finance plans.

Because the original loan balances often add in closing costs and fees, most of these buyers (now sellers) have built up little equity in their homes. In many instances, you can assume for less than 10 percent cash out of pocket. In those cases where sellers do own substantial equity, you might ask for a seller second or arrange a second mortgage through a mortgage lender.

SECRET # **65**

You can avoid PMI with a higher interest rate mortgage.

Fannie and Freddie require PMI on all home loans they buy with LTVs greater than 80 percent (less than 20 percent down); however, lenders who do not sell into the secondary mortgage market can make low-down-payment loans without PMI. These portfolio lenders frequently use that advantage to create a competitive edge over Fannie/Freddie affiliated lenders. Here's the catch: The "no PMI" lenders typically price their loans about .5 percent higher than the Fannie/Freddie interest rate.

Does this pricing make for a good deal? Maybe. It depends on the amount you would otherwise be required to pay for mortgage insurance. But two other factors also play a role. First, from a tax angle, the higher-interest, no-PMI loan proves advantageous. Whereas you can't legally deduct PMI premiums—although some borrowers do it and hope they don't get caught—you can deduct all amounts you pay for interest.[2]

Second, and this point tips toward PMI, under certain conditions (*Mortgage Secret #103*), you can cancel your PMI; therefore, you probably won't pay the PMI premium for the full term of your loan. In contrast, you will pay the higher interest rate until the date you pay off the loan (home sale, refinance, or full payoff through amortization).

Similar to so many other issues and decisions that pertain to mortgages, someone must run the numbers for each specific PMI as opposed to higher interest alternative. For those who are willing to make this effort, or those willing to ask a trusted loan rep, the reward could net cost savings for most people of several thousand dollars (or more).

2. Subject to the high income, $1,000,000 loan tax rules.

CHAPTER 7

Win Big Savings with Seller Financing, Foreclosures, and REOs

Robert Bruss, the nationally syndicated columnist, real estate attorney, and investor, was recently asked, "Where's the best place to get a mortgage? At a bank, savings and loan, or credit union?" Bob Bruss answered, "None of these is the best. The best source of financing for your home is the seller." If you can persuade the sellers to help with your financing, you can often get easier qualifying and lower costs. Likewise, here's what Realtor Robert Deimel says about seller financing in a recent issue of *Real Estate Today:*

"In today's complex marketplace, sellers and buyers don't always see the opportunity. That's why innovative sales people often are necessary to bring owner will carry (OWC) into the mix of financing possibilities. The key to making more transactions happen is to understand how to encourage sellers to offer the carrot of seller financing."

What are these benefits of seller-assisted financing? With OWC, buyers line up to gain these benefits:

- *Easier qualifying.* Although many lending institutions have eased up on their qualifying criteria, they're still tougher than most sellers.
- *Flexibility.* Price, interest rate, monthly payments, and other terms are set by mutual agreement. You and the sellers can put together a financing package in any way that works for both of you.

- *Lower closing costs.* Sellers seldom require points, origination fees, and loan application costs. Unlike lending institutions, sellers don't have to cover office overhead.
- *Less paperwork.* Although sellers may ask for a credit report, they won't require a stack of forms, documents, and verifications.
- *Quicker sale.* Seller financing can help sellers get their home sold more quickly. Plus, for properties that require extensive repairs or renovations, seller financing can make the difference between a sale and no sale.

The types of seller-assisted financing that you might use to buy a home are as varied as you or your Realtor's imagination. But be aware—not all owners who will accept OWC financing advertise that fact. Indeed, Robert Bruss says, "I've bought many houses with seller financing, but I can't recall a single one that was advertised 'seller financing.' Until they saw my offer, none of the sellers had informed their agent that they would help finance the sale."

Regardless of whether sellers have advertised OWC, keep the possibility in mind. You won't know for sure until you've put forth an offer. The following are several examples of seller-assisted financing taken from the pages of newspapers:

Lease With Option to Buy $450/mo. 1 year rent toward down payment on purchase price of $56,000.

315 DOVER—OWC. Completely Remodeled Brick bungalow, foyer, 2+ BR, large kitchen and living room, oak cabinets, dishwasher, range, recessed lighting, gas frplc, owner finance. big yard w/privacy fence. CALL 460–0020 Broker

$6950 DOWN on this 3 Bdrm ranch with ceiling fans, fncd yrd. Just redone in pale grays with new carpet, paint, etc. Paid off in full in 25 yrs! $695.09 per mo. OWNER CONTRACT! $84,950. 9.75% APR. NO BALLOON! 768–5350. R.E. Lic./owner.

NO QUALIFY
5+ Bdrm, 4 Ba. $295K. Owner Financing, only 48K dn. 4118 Catalina Pl. Call 291–1810/224–6806.

$5000 DOWN, $1695 mo. Poway, 2yr new, 4br. 3ba, pool, 3car gar, $249,500. 1 or 2 year lse. 486–3262

1 Level Beauty $173,500 Contract Terms/Lease Option Wonderful 1 level 2 bdrm plus den/3rd BR, 2BA, A/C, island kitchen, masonry frplc, security, 2 car garage, fncd. More! Westside Realty Co. 579–5001

OWNER MAY CARRY 2ND!! Near schools, best area, 3 BR. Make Offer! Only $140,000
Century 21 440–2020

LEASE/PURCHASE. You can own your home & move now through a flexible lease/purchase w/little down. Lovely 3 BR, 2 BA Cape Cod w/bsmt on a beautiful, prvt, wooded ac lot. Convenient location. Hurry! Low $90s. Buddy Boone 972–8782. Remax 979–1700

OWNER FINANCE
2+ acre estate. Large brick home with full bsmt, pool, workshop, and more—$164,900. Low down payment. V. Purser 491–6142 METRO BROKERS 843–2500

Loan reps will never tell you about the possibilities of seller financing because they don't originate these types of financing agreements, nor can loan reps tell you about foreclosures or REOs (foreclosed real estate owned by lenders, mortgage insurers, or government agencies). Yet, these properties often combine bargain prices and bargain financing. How about this Realtor ad for HUD homes:

CALL THE HUD SPECIALIST
COMMITTED TO SERVE

I have the **knowledge and experience** to provide the best service!
Why Rent When You Can Own!

Specializing in first-time homebuyers
Quick Closing within 14 days
No Closing Costs
Low Interest Rates

- **All you need to purchase your Dream Home**
- Steady Employment
- Previous Slow Credit & Bankruptcies OK
- $500 to $1000 Down
- **Let HUD pay you to own a home**
- $300 to 3% Down Payment
- $1,000 Renter's Bonus
- Purchase Below Market Value

Can you find a super deal similar to those described in this ad? Maybe.

Granted, super deals don't come along every day. In strong housing markets, foreclosures dwindle and terms of financing tighten. During the blazing real estate markets of the late 1990s and early 2000s, homebuyers and investors often had to search diligently for great deals with foreclosures and REOs. But times are changing. The *Wall Street Journal* just reported that homeowner delinquencies and foreclosures were beginning to jump significantly. Softening economic conditions always conspire with easier qualifying, low-down-payment finance plans to push weak swimmers into deep water.

If the past helps us forecast the future, the coming years are again likely to produce a strong need for rescuers. When you're interested in building home equity wealth fast, or perhaps merely increasing your affordability, ask foreclosure specialists whether borrower defaults, foreclosures, and REOs are piling up in your area.

Although you can save big with seller financing, foreclosures, and REOs in all times and places, soft markets produce buyer's delight.[1] As high tide approaches, most buyers fear to even put their toes in the water; but if you're willing to take the plunge when others shiver in a blanket of worry, you will earn large rewards.[2] Now let's look at these lesser-known property finance possibilities in more detail.

SECRET # 66

Sellers can nearly always beat the banks at their own game, but you must do more than ask.

Mortgage lenders operate by bureaucratic rules. Sellers, on the other hand, are free to listen to any deal that provides worthwhile benefits.

1. I don't relish the personal hardships created by tough times, but when sellers, borrowers, and lenders need relief, someone else stands to profit. This someone could be you.

2. During the high tide of foreclosures and tough times in California (1993–1996), my books of that day went firmly against the accepted opinion that "homes were no longer a good investment." I strongly urged homebuyers and investors to take advantage of the amazing buying and financing opportunities then available. Those who followed my advice were rewarded with extraordinarily outsized profits.

Lenders require qualifications, paperwork, documents, and verifications piled higher and deeper, while sellers can agree to as few documents and qualifying standards as reasonable in a specific situation. Lenders pay huge costs for fancy buildings, office overhead, loan rep commissions, and executive perks. Sellers incur none of these expenses. In addition to interest, lenders charge thousands in origination fees, closing costs, and mortgage insurance. Sellers expect payment only for interest and maybe a few out-of-pocket costs.

Lenders pay their depositors at least 2 to 5 percentage points less than they charge for mortgage interest.[3] Sellers can match or beat the lender's mortgage rate and still earn a higher net return than placing their funds in bank CDs or savings accounts.

Search for Mutual Advantage

All of the differences mentioned in *Mortgage Secrets #66* give sellers generous opportunity to offer buyers a more appealing home finance plan than institutional lenders. But often, sellers who are well-situated to provide or assist with financing don't realize the possibilities and benefits that lie in front of them. Like Bob Bruss, I've entered more than a dozen seller-financed (or assisted) transactions where the sellers weren't previously considering this avenue.

How to Get the Sellers Interested

When you simply out-of-the-blue orally ask most sellers to carry back financing, you will probably receive a quick "No." As a minimum, put your proposal in writing as part of your overall offer to buy the property. Don't expect oral concessions on this issue right away. (Prior to writing an offer, however, I do frequently pose feeler questions such as, "Have you given any thought to offering financing with the property?")[4] Most importantly, prior to writing an offer, learn the seller's needs and selling motives such as:

---

3. For borrowers with low to moderate credit scores, this differential can reach 6 to 10 percent, or more.

4. For more on negotiation, see pp. 150–175 of my book, *The 106 Common Mistakes Homebuyers Make*, 3rd ed. (Wiley, 2002); and pp. 150-175 and my book, *Investing in Real Estate*, 4th ed. (Wiley, 2003).

- Do they want or need a quick sale?
- Do they have a pressing need for cash?
- Would an 8 percent (more or less) return seem attractive to them?
- If an investor-owned property, what kind of capital gains tax liability will the sellers incur from an all-cash sale? Would an IRS-approved installment sale save the sellers considerable taxes?
- What do the sellers plan to do with the proceeds of sale?
- How do other pressures such as time, money, family, or work bear on the sale?

These questions merely suggest lines of inquiry. Overall, your goal is to tactfully discover as much about the sellers as you can and then draft your written offer to play into their most pressing needs. Explain point by point how your offer alleviates their principal concerns without giving rise to new ones. Are you a credible buyer? Does the proposal create too much risk? A skilled Realtor should help you achieve this end. Remember, a confused mind always says no. Eliminate seller doubts with clear and compelling reasons.

What Type of Seller Financing?

Use any type of seller financing that meets the needs of buyers and sellers without imposing undue risks or benefits on one party or the other. It's this ability to draft a financing agreement from a half dozen or more seller-finance techniques that gives OWC its advantage over bank financing.

To that end, the sellers could offer financial assistance through a standard first mortgage or trust deed similar to those available at thousands of lending institutions. In addition, a seller-finance purchase might include any or some combination of the following: assumption (*Mortgage Secret #20*), "subject to" (*Mortgage Secret #21*), refinance blend, second mortgage, balloon mortgage, contract-for-deed (installment sale), lease option, lease purchase, or wraparound.

SECRET # **67**

Ask the seller and lender to cooperate with a refi blend.

Some years back, Patrick O'Brien had his home up for sale. His listing price was $110,000. He owed around $72,300 on his old mortgage, which carried an interest rate of 7 percent. Mortgage interest rates at that time were 12.5 percent. Because of these high market rates, many buyers who would have liked to buy Patrick's home couldn't qualify for new financing. To solve this problem, Patrick talked to the branch manager of his mortgage lender. He persuaded her to refinance his home with an assumable fixed-rate mortgage of $88,000 at an interest rate of 10 percent. In effect, this 10 percent rate blended Patrick's old interest rate of 7 percent with the then-current market rate of 12.5 percent.

The mortgage lender profited because it got the old money-losing 7 percent mortgage off its books. Patrick gained because he could now offer his home to prospective buyers with attractive (relatively speaking) financing. At 12.5 percent, an $88,000 mortgage requires a payment of $939 per month. At a rate of 10 percent, an $88,000 mortgage requires a payment of $772 per month. Three weeks after his blended refinance, Patrick sold his home for $112,000. With their income of $35,000 a year, the buyers easily qualified to assume Patrick's mortgage. At the then-current rate of 12.5 percent, the buyers would have needed an income of $40,000 (or more).

In some future climate of high interest rates, find a seller like Patrick O'Brien who has a low-interest mortgage that's nonassumable; approach the lender and try to negotiate a refinance blend. It's another way to beat the affordability problem in times when mortgage interest rates have risen. Or reverse perspectives—if in some future period of high interest rates when you're the seller who holds a below-market mortgage, you could approach your lender as did Patrick O'Brien. This technique works best with portfolio lenders. Originating lenders are not permitted to change the terms of mortgages that have been sold into the secondary market and then repackaged into an investment pool of mortgage-backed securities.

SECRET # **68**

Bridge the assumable gap with a seller second.

Using the preceding example, let's say that Patrick O'Brien's pre-blend $72,300 mortgage could be assumed. Qualified buyers could take advantage of that low 7 percent interest rate, but with a price of around $110,000 the buyers would have needed close to $40,000 cash to pay Patrick enough to cover his high amount of equity. Most first-time buyers would find it tough to raise $40,000.

As another possibility, though, Patrick (or a mortgage lender) could have financed some or all of that $40,000 as a second mortgage. For instance, if the buyers had $20,000 in cash, they could offer Patrick a price of $110,000 to be paid as follows: $72,300 mortgage assumption; $20,000 in cash; and a seller second mortgage of $17,700.

Now the question becomes, "What will be the interest rate and repayment schedule for this $17,700 second mortgage?" The answer: Whatever terms can be negotiated to make both parties comfortable with the transaction. No hard and fast rules apply. I have seen second mortgages with interest rates as low as 6 percent and others as high as 16 percent. Sometimes a second mortgage is paid back in monthly payments over a period of three years or less. Sometimes it is structured over a term of 15 to 20 years. In the final analysis, the terms of a second mortgage typically evolve according to what you can afford, what the sellers can be persuaded to accept, and what terms are necessary to make the sale work.

For now, just remember that a second mortgage can move you closer to affordability. Use it when you need to cover the gap between the available first-mortgage financing (assumed or newly originated) and your home's purchase price. Recall, too, it will often pay to use a second mortgage along with new financing to keep the loan-to-value ratio of your first mortgage at or below 80 percent. With a less-than-75 to 80-percent loan-to-value ratio, the lender probably won't require mortgage insurance.

SECRET # **69**

Avoid the bang of a bursting balloon.

Sellers who agree to carry back a second mortgage frequently insist on a payoff term of seven years or less. These sellers want their money, and the sooner the better. From your viewpoint, a short-term second mortgage usually won't make much sense. The short term sends the monthly payments too high, but here's a solution to this problem. It's called a balloon mortgage.

When you use a balloon mortgage, you typically pay small monthly payments. You then pay the full outstanding balance owed after perhaps five or seven years. Say the sellers have agreed to carry back a five-year second mortgage for $25,000 at 10 percent interest. You want your monthly payments to be as low as you can get them. The sellers want to receive as much money as they can as fast as they can. Here are five possible payback schedules.

- *Fully amortizing.* Under this schedule you would amortize (pay off completely) the $25,000 second mortgage with 60 equal installments (principal and interest) of $531 per month. The sellers might like this schedule, but you might have a tough time paying $531 a month on top of the payments for your first mortgage. Some kind of balloon might be the solution.
- *Partially amortizing (15-year term/5-year balloon).* Under this schedule, you make monthly payments of $268 per month. After five years, you pay the outstanding balance of $20,280.
- *Partially amortizing (30-year term/5-year balloon).* Under this schedule, you make 60 monthly payments of $219; then you make a final balloon payment of $24,100.
- *Interest only.* Under this schedule, you do not make any payments on principal. You pay interest only of $208 for 60 months; then you pay the entire $25,000.
- *No monthly payments.* This type of balloon requires no monthly payments. Instead, interest builds and is added to the original bal-

ance of $25,000. At the end of five years, the total accumulated interest and principal due would equal $41,133. Although this type of no-monthly-payments-plan for the second mortgage can increase affordability, few sellers are willing to accept it.

The great advantage of negotiating second mortgages with balloon payments is flexibility. You can tailor a payment schedule to reasonably fit the needs of both you and the sellers. Just one important caveat: BE CAREFUL! Most buyers do satisfactorily pay their balloon balances through either a refinance or the sale of their property as part of a move-up strategy. And balloons do help bring home ownership within reach. If not structured with a pessimistic view of the future, however, balloons can create more problems than they solve. Allow yourself plenty of time (at least five years) and plenty of breathing room. Don't base repayment of the balloon on wild rates of home appreciation or speculative salary increases. Overinflated expectations can cause a balloon to burst with a bang.

To reinforce this point, consider these other informal terms for balloon loans—a dynamite stick with a short fuse; a suicide loan with the bullet coming at the end.

SECRET # 70

Buy on the installment plan.

Among the most famous lines in American film history is Oil Can Harry's repeated warnings to Pauline, "If you don't give me the deed to your ranch, I'm going to tie you to the railroad tracks." Oil Can Harry knew if Pauline signed over the deed to her ranch, that deed would transfer the property's title to Harry. Although Oil Can Harry's no-money-down approach to property ownership was somewhat unorthodox (not to mention illegal), typically whenever someone buys real estate, they receive a deed at the time of purchase. With the deed comes ownership.

In some sales, however, buyers don't receive a deed at the time of purchase. Instead, they buy a home (or other property) on the installment plan. In this type of purchase, buyers usually pay the sellers a small down payment and then promise to continue paying monthly installments. In return, the sellers give the buyers possession of the property, and promise to deliver a deed to the buyers after they have completed their scheduled payments. This type of home purchase agreement is known by various names such as *contract-for-deed, installment sale,* or *land contract.* For buyers who don't meet the qualifying criteria of a lending institution, a land contract can be an excellent way to buy property. I know from experience.

Why Sellers Are Willing

When I turned age 21, I wanted to acquire real estate as quickly as possible. At the time I was an undergraduate college student. I had little cash, no full-time job, and no significant credit record. My immediate chances for getting a bank to write a mortgage for me were zero. But this fact didn't deter me. I searched for properties that could be purchased on an installment contract. By the time I completed my Ph.D., I had bought around 30 houses and small apartment units. The cash flow from these properties paid many of my college living expenses—and yes, for my Jaguar XKE.

Now you might wonder why some property owners are willing to sell on an installment contract. Shouldn't they just deal with buyers who have the cash and credit necessary to get a loan from a bank? In my experience, I found sellers willing to sell on a contract for some combination of seven different reasons:

- *No bank financing available.* A home may not qualify for bank financing. The property might stand in poor condition, be located in a less-desirable neighborhood, or be functionally out-of-date (rooming house, apartment units with shared bathrooms, irregular floor plan, and so on). Also, many lending institutions won't write mortgages on condominiums or townhouses where more than 30 or 40 percent of the units in the complex are occupied by renters instead of owners.
- *Quick sale.* One of the best ways for an owner to sell a property quickly is to offer easy terms of financing. The contract-for-deed is the easiest and quickest type of home finance plan available.

- *Higher price.* Property owners who offer easy financing can often sell at a higher price than they otherwise could expect to receive. Many buyers will trade off price for terms.
- *High interest on savings.* Sellers who plan to deposit the cash they receive from a sale in certificates of deposit or money market accounts can get a higher return on their money by financing a buyer's purchase of their property. A 7- to 10-percent return from a real estate installment sale certainly beats a 5 percent return from a certificate of deposit.
- *Low closing costs.* With a contract-for-deed, sellers and buyers pay far less in closing costs. You avoid nearly all the expenses that a mortgage lender would charge.
- *Tax savings.* When the seller is an investor, an installment sale of a property produces a smaller income tax bite than does a cash sale.
- *Repossession.* Should the buyers default on making their monthly payments, the installment contract typically gives sellers a relatively quick and inexpensive right to repossess the property.

Follow These Guidelines

When you and the property you buy meet the standards of a lending institution, favor that alternative unless the seller's terms are just too good to pass up. On the other hand, if bank financing is not available, by all means consider using a contract-for-deed. Buying from a seller on the installment plan beats renting. Cash-short buyers can also win with this strategy: Buy a rundown property on contract and then create value through improvements. Next, refinance based on the now-higher value of the property. If you do consider the possibility of using a contract-for-deed purchase, follow these guidelines:

- *Buy the home, not the financing.* Don't let easy credit draw you into the purchase of an overpriced property. When circumstances warrant, you might in good judgment pay a price slightly higher than market value. But you would not want to pay $5,000 for a 1995 Ford Mustang from Easy Ed's "buy here, pay here" used car lot just because Easy Ed will sell it to you with nothing down and low monthly payments. This same principle applies to home buying. Beware of the guru's tactic to gain seller financing, "You name the price; I'll name the terms." Verify value through an appraisal or other professional opinion.

- *Beware of hidden defects.* A property that seems priced right might suffer hidden defects. Take care to obtain experienced and knowledgeable estimates for any repairs or renovations that you plan. Never ballpark or casually figure the costs necessary to bring a property up to the condition you want it. Get professional property inspections and cost estimates before you buy.
- *Contract terms are governed by law.* A contract-for-deed places you and the seller in a relationship that is governed not only by the contract language, but also by state laws and court decisions. Under an installment sale, your rights and responsibilities differ from those you acquire when you finance a home with a mortgage or trust deed.

Before you sign an installment sale agreement, consult a real estate attorney who is experienced in reviewing these contracts. Lacking knowledge of this specialty, too many lawyers warn against buying a home on the installment plan. (Using similar logic, such lawyers would advise against marriage because divorce can be so painful.) This type of lawyer looks at risks without considering benefits and opportunities. Get a lawyer who understands both; then negotiate a contract that can work for you and the sellers. Over the years, millions of Americans (especially low- to moderate-income Americans) have successfully bought homes and small rental properties on the installment plan.

SECRET # 71

Try it before you buy it.

The "try it before you buy it" technique is called the lease option. It combines a lease agreement for a home, townhouse, or apartment with an option (a contractual right) to buy that home at a later date. In the early 1980s, Robert Bruss, the nationally syndicated real estate columnist and investor, called lease options "the most overlooked and underused" home finance possibility. At that time, most homebuyers, home sellers, and real estate agents remained clueless about this technique.

Times have changed, and awareness has mushroomed. Whenever I travel throughout the United States, I always check through the local real estate classifieds. In most cities, there are now real estate agents who regularly handle lease options and other low-down-payment home finance plans. I have also seen lease options promoted by home builders and developers of new condominiums and townhouses. In San Francisco, one recent ad from Bay Crest Condominiums boldly announced, "If You Can Afford to Rent, You Can Now Afford to Own: Exciting New Lease/Purchase Option." No question, lease options can bring home ownership closer to reality for many renters in several different ways, such as:

- *Easier qualifying.* Qualifying for a lease option may be no more difficult than qualifying for a lease—sometimes easier. Generally, your credit and employment record need meet only minimum standards. Most property owners (sellers or lessors) will not place your financial life under a magnifying glass as would a mortgage lender.
- *Low initial investment.* Your initial investment to get into a lease-option agreement can be as little as one month's rent and a security deposit of a similar amount. At the outside, move-in cash rarely exceeds $5,000 to $10,000, although I did see a home lease-optioned at a price of $1.5 million that asked for $50,000 up front.
- *Forced savings.* The lease-option contract typically forces you to save for the down payment required when you exercise your option to buy. Lease options often charge above-market rental rates and then credit perhaps 50 percent of your rent toward the down payment. The exact amount is negotiable. After you have committed yourself to buying, you should find it easier to cut other spending and place more money toward your "house account."

- *100 percent financing possible.* You also can reduce the amount of cash investment you will need to close your purchase in another way: Lease-option a property that can be profitably improved through repairs, renovation, or cosmetics. By increasing the home's value, you may be able to borrow nearly all the money you need to exercise your option to buy. For example, assume your lease-option purchase price is $75,000. Say by the end of one year, your rent credits equal $2,500. You now owe the sellers $72,500. Through repairs, fix-up work, and redecorating, you have increased the home's value by $10,000. Your home should now be worth around $85,000. If you have paid your bills on time during the previous year, you can finance your purchase with the full $72,500 you need to pay off the sellers. As another possibility, you could sell the home, pay the sellers $72,500, and use the remaining cash from the sale to buy another home.
- *Reestablish credit.* A lease option also can help renters buy who need time to build or reestablish a solid credit record. Judy and Paul Davis wanted to buy a home before prices in their area once again rose above their reach, but the Davises needed time to clear up credit problems created by too much borrowing and Judy's layoff. The lease option could be the possibility that helps the Davises achieve their goal of home ownership.

SECRET # 72

Buy and lease simultaneously.

In south suburban Chicago, the not-for-profit New Cities Development Corporation has sold 200 of its rehabbed homes using a lease-purchase agreement. "The buyer profile for this method of financing," says Jim DeBoth of Mortgage Market Information Services, "covers a wide range of people—from the moderate-income buyer to anyone who earns a good income, but who has little or no savings." Cooperating with New Cities Development in these house sales was Suburban Federal Savings.

"We've had a 100 percent success rate," reports Peter Ruhl, an executive of this thrift.

How Does the Lease-Purchase Work?

In this particular situation, New Cities found buyers for their homes who wanted to own, yet lacked money for a down payment. These buyers were counseled about home ownership. They then were qualified for a mortgage by Suburban Federal. Next, the buyers signed a lease-purchase agreement for their homes, moved in, and began making rental payments large enough to cover their future PITI plus $100 to $200 a month extra. After these extra payments (called rent credits) had built up enough to fund a 5 percent down payment, Suburban Federal would close the homebuyers' loans and New Cities Development would convey title. These families moved smoothly from leasing to owning.

Lease-Purchase Agreements versus Lease-Purchase Options

Although some people use these two terms interchangeably, technically there's a big distinction. With a lease-purchase agreement, you're actually agreeing to buy a property. Your lease period just gives you time to build up cash or rent credits for a down payment, or perhaps time to shape up your financial fitness. With a lease-purchase *option*, more frequently called a lease option, you can walk away from the home at the end of your lease period. You would forfeit any option money or rent credits you have paid, but the sellers couldn't require you to buy the home if you chose not to.

Several Key Issues

To buy a home through a lease-purchase or lease-option agreement, here are several key issues to talk over with your Realtor, an attorney, and the sellers.

- *Purchase price.* Ask your Realtor to verify that the price you're offering is in line with other comparable homes that have recently sold in the neighborhood. When you apply for a mortgage at some future date, your home must appraise high enough so your loan

LTV ratio will be approved. Some lease-to-own sellers grossly overprice their properties.

- *Move-in cash.* Whether you lease-purchase or lease-option a property, you'll have to negotiate the amount of your move-in money. This cash will be credited toward your purchase price if and when you eventually buy. Typically, if you choose not to buy, the sellers will keep all or part of this money.
- *Lease period.* How much time will you need before you're able to buy? Sellers often want to close relatively quickly—sometimes within 6 to 12 months. However, make sure you give yourself enough breathing room. If you can't come up with your mortgage financing at the end of your lease period, you may lose your move-in cash. On the other hand, if you can close sooner than the date in your agreement, most sellers would gladly accommodate you.
- *Rent credits.* As noted above, many lease-purchase/lease-option sellers now apply rent credits toward your purchase price. These monthly credits also can count as part or all of your down payment; but remember that lenders won't count the full amount without question. They count only lease amounts paid in excess of market rent levels. You pay $1,000 a month, market's at $800, the lender will allow $200 per month. If you're planning to use rent credits as part of your cash to close, make sure your lease agreement fits within your lender's guidelines.
- *Right to assign.* Include a "right to assign" clause in your agreement. If you don't complete your purchase, you can sell (assign for a payment) your right to buy the property to someone else at your option (or purchase) contract price. That way you won't forfeit all of your rent credits and move-in cash. In fact, if the property has appreciated, you can assign your right of purchase and make a nice profit.
- *Inspections and title check.* When you buy your home, get the property inspected by a specialist who knows houses. Unless you're buying at a steep discount, don't run the risk of unexpected major repairs. Likewise, you'll want a title insurance company to check the seller's rights of ownership. Too many lease option/lease purchase buyers skip these precautions and put themselves at risk,

or they wait until they eventually apply for a mortgage. Discuss this issue with an attorney. Be especially careful about waiting for the title check if you're giving the seller a fairly large amount of move-in cash.

Lease-purchase and lease-option agreements are two more good techniques you can use to acquire a home. Remember, though, both of these techniques raise questions that differ from straight purchase offers. So as mortgage counselor Jim DeBoth advises, "Seek out some counseling if there's anything you don't understand. Done right, a lease-purchase or lease-option agreement may be your low cash route to home purchase."

SECRET # **73**

Beat high interest rates with wraparound financing.

Wraparound financing yields big savings for buyers at the same time that it puts profits into the pocket of the seller. Only the lender gets shortchanged. Here's how a wraparound works to overcome higher market interest rates:

Financial Facts

Asking price	$200,000
Mortgage balance	100,000
Mortgage interest rate	6%
Term remaining (years)	20
Monthly payment	716
Market interest rate	9%

You offer to buy the property for $200,000 if the seller agrees to finance $180,000 at 7.5 percent fully amortized over 20 years. Your payment (P&I) equals $1,450 per month.[5] The underlying mortgage debt re-

5. You also pay for the property insurance, property taxes, maintenance, and upkeep.

mains in place, and its monthly payments will be paid by the seller. To complete the purchase, you sign a land contract, alternatively known as a contract-for-deed or installment note.

Each month the seller collects $1,450 from you and then pays the bank his monthly mortgage payment of $716 for a net gain of $734 ($1,450 less $716). Because the seller has actually financed only $80,000 ($180,000 less 100,000 still owed to the bank), he achieves an attractive rate of return on his loan of 11.1 percent.

$$\text{Seller ROI} = \frac{\$8{,}808}{\$80{,}000} = 11.1\%$$

Yet, you, too, gain. Had you financed $180,000 with a bank at the market rate of 9 percent amortized over 20 years, your payment would total $1,619 per month instead of the $1,450 that you'll pay to the seller. The actual spread between the current market interest rate, the seller's old bank rate, and the interest rate you pay the sellers will depend on the motives and negotiating power of the respective parties. But this example shows how a wraparound can benefit the buyers and the sellers—true win-win financing.[6]

SECRET # 74

Don't dillydally with due diligence.

Mortgage Secrets encourages you to rely on sellers to provide all or part of your home financing. With few exceptions, you will find sellers easier and more pleasant to work with than lenders. Plus, you can probably swing better terms, lower costs, and quicker closings. But the record for these great advantages plays a much different tune on its flip side. Be-

6. If the lender can enforce a "due on sale" clause, this technique does bring about that risk. In that situation, a wraparound works better as a short-term financing strategy. If the lender calls, there may be no long term.

cause many sellers do make OWC transactions quick and easy, too many buyers sign before they fully investigate.

Only later do they learn that the sellers, the property, or both have failed to meet the buyers' expectations. Troubles brew. Costs mount. The buyers' once-joyful spirit morphs into mournful regret, or worse, anger, accusations, and litigation. So, yes, eagerly search out seller financing, but don't dillydally with due diligence. Just as you should with any home purchase, temper your enthusiastic eagerness with cool calculation. Answer these questions:[7]

- *Can you trust the sellers?* Nearly all real estate experts urge sellers to assess the character and credit strength of their borrowers, but so must buyers assess the integrity of their sellers. Some con artist sellers know they can line up buyers around the block with promises of easy terms and no credit check. Be wary of sellers who come on too glib, or sellers who raise your suspicious instincts. Cheats and scammers can populate either side of a real estate transaction.
- *Can you afford the price and terms?* Lenders will test your capacity to pay against their approval formulas and qualifying ratios, but sellers may let you slide by. So, it's up to you to realistically (nay, pessimistically) appraise your finances. Some sellers lure hopeful but unprepared buyers into transactions they aren't likely to complete successfully. Why? To keep their buyers' front-end money, kick them out of the house, and repeat the process with the next wide-eyed innocents that the sellers can recruit.
- *How much will you spend to maintain and operate the property?* Experts warn you to, "Get the house professionally inspected." Good advice, but it doesn't go far enough. Get the facts on the cost to maintain the home, yard, and operating systems (HVAC, plumbing, water, waste disposal, electrical, and so on). Put actual numbers down on paper. Forget ballparking. It's not reliable. Determine precisely: Are you acquiring a money trap or a wise investment?

---

7. My book, *The 106 Common Mistakes Homebuyers Make (and How to Avoid Them)*, 3rd ed. (Wiley, 2002), addresses each of these topics more extensively.

- *At what price would the home sell without OWC terms?* You can sometimes sensibly trade off a higher price for great terms or easy credit, but know exactly what trade-off you're making. It's tough to sell or refinance a property when your debt pitches you upside down.
- *How are you protecting your financial interest in the property?* If you're giving the sellers more than a few thousand dollars up front, run, don't walk, to a trustworthy and competent real estate attorney. At very least make sure a competent and trustworthy title company okays the legal paperwork. (I confess that I have violated this rule on a number of occasions and suffered no harm, but *Mortgage Secrets* cannot recommend this approach to those without experience—unless maybe, you've got an angel on your shoulder.)
- *How much will you pay for homeowners insurance?* During the 1990s, property insurers lost far more money on claims than in any previous decade. Fortunately, they made those losses back and more through their investments. The 2000s have not proved so kind. High losses are still mounting (9/11, mold, storms), but investment gains have stalled (to put it mildly). That means (if you haven't already noticed) insurance premiums are going up and insurers are cutting back on coverages—especially in high-loss, high-loss-exposure locales. Before you commit to buy, verify the availability of all needed coverages at a price you are willing and able to pay.
- *How much will you pay for property taxes and assessments?* Look to the future, not the past. The amount the sellers paid last year could fall far short of the amounts that the tax authorities and assessment districts will bill you next year. (If you itemize, however, you will be able to deduct these taxes. That's at least some consolation.
- *Is the home governed by a homeowners association (HOA)?* Homeowners associations add another layer of costs (and benefits) to a property. How much will the HOA require you to pay each month? Is the HOA fiscally strong with cash reserves, or is it looking at deficits that you and other owners will have to pay? How will the HOA's covenants, conditions, and restrictions (CCRs) and "house

rules" crimp your actions? Pets, parking, kids, basketball courts, tree houses, exterior color schemes, home offices, fencing, landscaping, yard care? You name it. The HOA probably regulates it. Just ignore the HOA? Bad idea. HOAs hold the legal power to assess, fine, and even foreclose when amounts levied remain unpaid.

Most homebuyers and homeowners define affordability primarily in terms of principal and interest—the basic monthly mortgage payment. But your actual monthly costs of homeownership can exceed your base P&I by 50 percent (or more). Most certainly, when you knowledgeably create a plan for financing, you can afford to buy a home. But please, before signing on that dotted line, make sure you can afford the home you buy.

SECRET # 75

Negotiate a preforeclosure workout.[8]

Each year in every community, hundreds (sometimes thousands) of property owners hit the financial skids. Divorce, job loss, accident, illness, business failure, and other setbacks render people unable to make their mortgage payments. Rather than effectively deal with their mortgage problem as soon as trouble hits, most owners hang on too long hoping for a miracle to bail them out. Because miracles are rare, most of these people end up staring foreclosure in the face.

At that point, you may be able to help these potential sellers salvage their credit record and part of their home equity, and at the same time secure a bargain for yourself. Faced with pressures of time and money, these property owners may be willing to accept a quick, credit-rescuing sale at a price below market value. Just as importantly, their lender may let you assume the sellers' mortgage on favorable terms. Because foreclosure typically spells loss for a lender, that lender will

8. *Mortgage Secret #s 75–81* address the topics of foreclosures and REOs. My book, *Investing in Real Estate,* 4th ed. (Wiley, 2003), details these topics more thoroughly.

carefully review offers that credibly promise to improve its current doomed position.

Approach Owners with Empathy

There's no magic system for successfully buying a property from owners facing foreclosure. These owners must contend with financial troubles, personal anguish, and indecisiveness due to mental stress and anxiety. In addition, they probably have already been attacked by innumerable foreclosure sharks, speculators, bank lawyers, and recent attendees of get-rich-quick foreclosure seminars. These owners are living with the shame of a very public failure. For all these reasons, and more, they are not easy people with whom to deal.

Yet, when you develop a sensitive, empathetic, problem-solving approach with someone suffering foreclosure, you may be able to come up with a win-win agreement—but play it right. You won't be the only buyer who pays them a visit. A "Here's my offer—take it or leave it" approach will provoke the owners. It will not favorably set you apart from the dozen foreclosure sharks who try that ploy. Develop your negotiations and offer to preserve what little may be left of the owner's dignity and self-esteem. Share personal information about setbacks you have lived through. Emphasize win-win outcomes. Dire straits or not, no one wants their home (property) stolen from them.

Finding Owners in Distress

Each time a lender sues for foreclosure, the county clerk where the property is located files that suit in the public records. Local newspapers or specialty newsletters often publish the borrowers' names and addresses. Numerous foreclosure Web sites also have been created. Beware, though, most of these sites are rip-offs that require a large fee before viewing. Check out the integrity of the sites and their data before you pay.

You can also go to the county courthouse. Some counties make it easy to find pending foreclosures; others make you search. Either way, the information is always available to the public. You can locate distressed owners with the following techniques, too:

- *Advertise.* You've probably seen some of the sharks who run these types of ads. Make yours different and empathetic.
- *Network.* Pay attention to which employers are laying off. What are realty agents and loan reps saying? Who do you know who knows the people experiencing financial difficulty?
- *Contact debt counseling agencies.* Let them know that you're looking to help someone. You could even hang out around an agency and watch who's coming in and out; then talk with them, and learn their names and addresses.

County records, apart from getting inside info from mortgage servicers, represent the surest way to find owners with loan difficulties. If you can discover who these people are before the lender files foreclosure, you're more likely to wade into shark-free water.

Working with Lenders

Mortgage defaults, payments in arrears, and foreclosures don't look good to a lender's regulators, mortgage insurers, investors, profit picture, or its general reputation in the community. That's why most lenders with trouble borrowers want to resolve their mortgage delinquencies sooner rather than later. To succeed in negotiations with a lender, emphasize your credibility and capacity to provide it permanent relief. In return, the lender may grant:

- *Additional financing.* In high owner equity deals, the lender could advance you funds to buy out the owner.
- *Below-market interest rate.* Below-market rates permit you to assume the owner's low rate, or knock the existing interest rate down a point or two as an incentive.
- *Reduced closing and origination costs.* These minimize transaction fees by waiving or reducing typical loan costs.
- *Short-sale.* If the owners are upside down (owe more than their property is worth), the lender may slice off a part of the loan balance to bring it in line with the property's market value.

- *Rolled-in past-due payments.* To further reduce your out-of-pocket costs, the lender could add all amounts owed in arrears to the mortgage balance, rather than require a cash payment. For purposes of negotiating appeal, however, workout buyers usually should offer to bring the loan current with ready cash.

As in all negotiations, the end result will evolve from the needs, wants, motives, and negotiating skills of the parties. But in all cases, lenders want to turn around a loan that's going downhill. If you're the person who can hit the brakes and maneuver the loan onto a safe route, the lender will reward you for your efforts.

SECRET # **76**

Buy (carefully) at the foreclosure sale.

When a lender fails to successfully work out a loan in default, the property ends up on the foreclosure auction block. Typically, only experienced foreclosure specialists who can accurately calculate the risks can win at this game. Yet, it's true—everybody's got to start somewhere. If after you get to know a property by talking with its owners in your failed preforeclosure workout discussions, you might consider bidding at the public auction.

Bidders who thoroughly prepare their homework sometimes can walk away with great bargains, but not great financing. Most foreclosure sales require cash. You'll need wealth, a ready line of credit, or a money partner. Seldom, though, do homebuyers or investors buy properties at auction. Typically, the foreclosing lender buys. The property then ends up as an REO in the (unwanted) real estate owned portfolio of HUD, VA, Fannie Mae, Freddie Mac, or the lender itself. In these cases, the owners of the REOs face no choice. The properties have to go. This fact gives you another chance to cut a good deal on price, terms, or sometimes both.

SECRET # **77**

Locate a foreclosure pro.

Many mortgage lenders *avoid* (although they do make exceptions) selling directly to REO buyers for two reasons: They don't like the unfavorable publicity, and they want to promote good relations with Realtors. Because mortgage lenders expect Realtors to bring them new loan business, these same lenders can't then turn around and become FSBO (for sale by owner) dealers. "You scratch my back, and I'll scratch yours" sets the rules in business.

As one part of your efforts to find REOs, cultivate relationships with Realtors who specialize in this market. In most cities, you can easily find REO specialists by looking through newspaper classified real estate ads (such as that shown on p. 155).

After you have identified several advertised foreclosure specialists, give each one a call. Learn their backgrounds. Do they only dabble in the field of REOs and foreclosures, or do they make this field their full-time business? When I recently telephoned REO specialist John Huguenard in Orlando, Florida, he talked with me for an hour and a half about property availability, financing, purchase procedures, hot areas of town, rehab potential, estimating repair costs, portfolio lenders, strategies for buying and managing properties, selecting tenants, and a dozen other related topics.

At one point during our conversation, he asked, "I'll bet you haven't talked to any other agents who know as much as I do about REOs and foreclosures, have you? I've been doing this 23 years. Last year, I sold 90 houses and rehabbed 16 others for my own account." Pretty impressive!

Knowledge Counts

John's the kind of real estate professional you want to find. Although many realty agents claim expertise in REOs and foreclosures—"Sure, I can do that for you"—only a few make it their primary activity, day in and day out, year after year. When you work with an agent who's really in the know, you won't have to do your own legwork and door knocking. Your agent will screen properties as soon as—if not before—they come onto the market. You will then be notified immediately.

Plus, specialty agents with in-depth knowledge also will stay on top of the finance plans that portfolio, government, and conventional lenders are offering to homebuyers and investors. For example, John Huguenard knew of portfolio lenders doing 100 percent LTV homebuyer and investor loans for acquisition and rehab.

HUD, VA, Fannie, and Freddie Won't Sell Direct to Buyers

No matter what approach to acquiring REOs and foreclosures you choose to follow, you will benefit by talking with realty pros who make the business a career. If you buy an REO from HUD, VA, Fannie Mae, or Freddie Mac, you *must* process your offer through a licensed real estate agent. Only in certain exceptional circumstances would any of these organizations deal directly with a potential buyer. Moreover, each of these organizations follows its own specific procedures and practices.

SECRET # **78**

HUD may hold the keys to your home or investment property.

Each year the FHA insures hundreds of thousands of new mortgage loans. (The total number of these outstanding FHA mortgages runs into the millions.) FHA loans are originated by banks, savings institutions, mortgage bankers, mortgage brokers, credit unions, and other types of mortgage lenders.

When FHA borrowers fail to repay their lenders as scheduled (absent a successful workout), the owner of the mortgage will force the property into a foreclosure sale. Rather than keep the property in its own REO portfolio, the lender turns in a claim to HUD (FHA's parent). HUD then pays the lender the amount due under its mortgage insurance coverage and acquires the foreclosed property. HUD then puts the property, along with all the others it has acquired in similar fashion, up for bid to the general public.

In some cities such as Atlanta, Georgia, HUD may sell as many as 1,000 properties a year. In the San Francisco Bay Area, HUD's annual sales may total fewer than 150 homes. Depending on the strength of the housing market and the local economy, the number and selection of HUD properties vary widely. Still, every area can be counted on to have at least some HUD homes. To locate HUD properties in your state and county, go to www.hud.gov and then click on HUD homes.

Like all sources of bargain properties, HUD homes do offer profit opportunities; however, no one can bid blindly and expect to snag a great buy. Investors and homebuyers must first do their homework through neighborhood and property value analysis. Only then can you confidently buy properties for substantially less than their market value (after fix-up work).

Although HUD is best known for single-family houses, it also sells these types of REO properties:

- Vacant lot
- Duplex
- Triplex
- Fourplex
- PUD, a Planned Unit Development
- Condominium

To buy a HUD property, you must submit a bid package to HUD according to a detailed set of procedures. Violate a rule, and your bid package is tossed out. That's why you need a foreclosure pro. After HUD opens the bid package, it accepts the bid that nets HUD the most money—except that homebuyers receive priority over investors—even when the investor submits a bid that's more beneficial to HUD.

Financing Programs and Incentives

Ordinarily, homebuyers can finance HUD homes with FHA-insured financing and pay 3 to 5 percent cash out of pocket. Although these cash payments are typical, HUD sometimes runs low- or no-down-payment "specials." Several years ago, all HUD-owned, FHA-insurable properties throughout the state of Georgia were being financed under either FHA 203(b) or FHA 203(k) with just $300 down. Check with HUD-approved real estate sales agents in your area to see what deals HUD may be brewing.

Other Incentives

In addition to low- or no-down-payment specials, local HUD offices may run other types of incentive programs for buyers of HUD properties. To encourage quick closings during a market surplus in Indianapolis, HUD offered a $2,000 early closing bonus (less than thirty days) to investors and homebuyers. In Chicago, HUD offered a rebate up to $1,000 to renters who buy a HUD home for owner occupancy. In Boston, HUD offered a 5 percent purchase price credit on certain designated properties, a $250 bonus to buyers who had arranged a lender's *preapproval,* and a $675 early closing bonus (less than forty-five days). In Baltimore, the early closing bonus was $900, but settlement had to take place within 15 days of contract acceptance. On occasion, to reduce its inventory of unsold homes, HUD offers "clearance sales" at deep discounts. Some years back in Houston, HUD ran a huge "Turkey Day" sale on Thanksgiving.

Local Options

As you can see, HUD can authorize its regional and local offices to modify or loosen HUD's overall financial requirements. If HUD homes are not selling fast enough in Chicago, you can bet that HUD will increase buyer incentives for its Chicago area properties. When sales are booming in a given city and HUD has relatively few properties available, HUD not only refuses to offer incentives, but it may refuse to accept bids at less than a property's list price. You can score the best deal on HUD properties in down markets, but regardless of the market, it's worth your time to investigate the HUD opportunities that may be available in your area.

SECRET # **79**

VA offers deals to both veterans and nonveterans.

The U.S. Department of Veterans Affairs (VA) guarantees the payment of home loans for eligible veterans. This guarantee permits veterans to finance their homes with 100 percent (zero down payment) loans. As with FHA-insured mortgages, however, lenders foreclose when VA borrowers fail to make their payments, and fail to enter a workout and VA financial counseling program. In exchange for a loan payoff from VA, lenders return the foreclosed homes to VA, which then tries to sell them as quickly as possible.

VA's Similarities to HUD

To sell its foreclosed properties, VA follows many rules similar to those of HUD. For example, here are twelve major ways the programs resemble each other:

- VA sells through a sealed bid process. As either a potential homeowner or investor, you may submit multiple bids during the same bid period.
- You cannot *directly* negotiate with or submit a bid to VA. You must submit your bid through a VA-approved real estate agent (your foreclosure pro).
- VA sells its homes on an as-is basis. Even though it may partially disclose a home's defects, it offers no warranties. Caveat emptor.
- VA does guarantee title and permits buyers to obtain a title policy.
- VA accepts bids that yield it the highest net proceeds (not the highest price). If your bid obligates VA with fewer closing expenses or a lower realty sales commission, you can win the bid over others who offer higher prices, but also higher costs (a lower net) to VA.
- Just as HUD/FHA charges FHA buyers an insurance fee, VA charges buyers who choose its financing a 2.25 percent guarantee fee.

- VA accepts bids only on VA forms. Errors in completing the forms may invalidate the bid.
- VA publicizes its homes through combinations of newspaper ads, broker lists, and Internet postings (http://homeloans.va.gov/homes).
- Local VA offices report to regional directors who may issue policies and procedures that differ from other regions throughout the country.
- VA may choose to keep your earnest money deposit if you fail to close a winning bid for any reason other than inability to obtain financing.
- As with HUD home contracts, VA purchase offers do not include a contingency for postpurchase property inspections. You may, however, inspect a property before you bid.
- When necessary, VA evicts holdover tenants or homeowners prior to placing a VA home on the market. At closing, you will receive a vacant property.

Big Advantages for Investors

Although in many ways VA follows rules similar to HUD, it differs in two important ways that work to the advantage of investors:

- VA does not give homebuyers preferential treatment. VA looks for the highest net offered by any credible buyer—homeowner or investor.
- VA offers financing to investors on quite favorable terms. At present in my area, for example, investors can close financing on a VA home with total cash out of pocket of less than 6 percent of a property's purchase price. In addition, VA typically applies relaxed qualifying standards. VA buyers (who need not be veterans) must show *acceptable,* not perfect, credit records. For specifics in your area, talk with your foreclosure pro.

With such favorable terms of financing, VA homes in good (and even not so good) repair frequently sell at top of the market prices; however, many homebuyers and investors still find the program attractive for these three reasons:

1. *High leverage* permits you to accelerate your wealth-building returns.
2. Even at top of the market prices, many VA homes pull in rents high enough to provide a *positive cash flow* from day one of ownership.
3. The VA allows future buyers to assume your VA financing. For buyers who want to "fix and flip," an *assumable loan* makes a great benefit. Plus, in periods of high interest rates, a lower assumable VA rate gives your sales efforts a big advantage.

Overall, VA homes provide an excellent source of properties and financing for homebuyers and investors alike. Make sure you investigate this opportunity in your area.

SECRET # **80**

Let Fannie or Freddie treat you to below-market financing.

Fannie Mae and Freddie Mac, the two largest players in the nation's secondary mortgage market, don't ordinarily make loans directly to homebuyers; but they do buy more than 50 percent of the home mortgages that are made by banks, credit unions, and other mortgage lenders. Sometimes when a loan Fannie or Freddie owns goes bad, Fannie or Freddie may force the originating lender to buy back the mortgage. The lender then ends up with a foreclosed house in its REO portfolio. Lenders, though, who have followed all of Fannie's or Freddie's underwriting guidelines when originally making these mortgages can require Fannie or Freddie to take ownership of the foreclosed houses.

Agent Listings

Fannie and Freddie do not often use the sealed bid sales procedure that's common to HUD and VA. Instead, both companies choose a realty firm and give that firm an exclusive listing. Typically, the realty firm then places the REO property into MLS. The realty agent who takes on responsibility for a foreclosed property first inspects it and then recommends the best way to fix it up to maximize its sales price.

Seldom a Bargain

Because Fannie and Freddie frequently spend thousands of dollars to put a property in top condition and then price that property aggressively, you won't find many bargain-priced buys among their REOs. In fact, only in out-of-the-ordinary circumstances will Fannie and Freddie consider lowball or wheeling-and-dealing types of offers. They even try to price their as-is—no repairs—properties as high as the market will bear.

First-Time Homebuyers—Special Financing

Fannie and Freddie primarily direct their marketing efforts toward highly credit-qualified homebuyers—especially first-time homebuyers. Rather than use the bargain price appeal, these companies attract buyers with well-presented homes and special financing.

Freddie even permits homebuyers to "customize your Homesteps [the name Freddie gives to its foreclosures] home." Under this option Freddie invites buyers (for a price, of course) to upgrade their home's carpeting, padding, vinyl, appliances, and window blinds. Freddie also sells most of its homes for 5 percent down, no private mortgage insurance (which typically saves buyers $75 or $150 per month), lower closing costs, and a slightly below market interest rate.

All Properties Sold "As Is"

Even though Fannie and Freddie fix up most of their properties, neither offers any type of warranty that guarantees the condition of a property. Unlike HUD or VA, however, as a Fannie/Freddie buyer, you may submit a contract that includes an inspection contingency. If the home qualifies, you also can purchase your own home warranty plan just as you (or the sellers) can with most other home sales.

Investors Accepted

Both Fannie and Freddie will accept offers from investors with no priority listing period that applies only to owner-occupants. Both companies also offer special financing for credit-qualified investors that requires a 15 percent down payment, in contrast to the conventional down payment of 20 to 30 percent for investor-owned properties. Closing costs may come in a little lower, too. Investor interest rates usually sit on the low side of market. You can locate Freddie and Fannie properties, respectively, at www.homesteps.com and www. fanniemae .com/homes.

SECRET # **81**

Buy and finance directly with a lender.

When a mortgage lender "wins" the bid at a foreclosure auction, the foreclosed property ends up as an REO. If the lender can't cash out by turning the property over to HUD, VA, Fannie Mae, or Freddie Mac, it will hold onto it and then sell to a homebuyer or investor.

The Benefits of Buying Direct from a Mortgage Lender

In nearly every instance, you can say one thing for certain about an REO: The lender wants to sell the property as quickly as possible. Mortgage lenders like to make loans and collect payments. They do not like to own and manage vacant houses. As a result, they often will grant buyers of their REOs favorable terms such as low or no closing costs, below-market interest rates, and low down payments.

If the property needs fix-up work that the lender would prefer not to perform, it may accept offers at deep discounts from market value. Just as important, prior to closing the sale of their REOs, lenders normally clean up title problems, evict unauthorized occupants, and bring all past-due property tax payments and assessments up to date. Some lenders, too, permit buyers to write contingency offers subject to appraisal and professional inspection.

Safer Than Buying at the Foreclosure Sale

Buying an REO directly from a lender typically presents no more risk than buying directly from any other property owner.[9] Normally, you can buy an REO much more safely than you could have bought the same property at its foreclosure sale. Depending on the lender's motivation, its internal policies and procedures, and the property LTV at the time of the foreclosure sale, you might even be able to buy at a lower than market value price.

Why a Lower Price?

Let's say the market value of a property at the time of its foreclosure sale was $165,000. The lender's liens against the property totaled $160,000. To win the property away from the lender at the foreclosure sale, you would have had to bid more than $160,000—a price that's too high to yield a good buy.

After the lender owns the property, however, and tallies its expected holding costs, Realtor's commission, and the risks of seeing the (probably) vacant property vandalized, it may decide to cut its losses. It may accept an offer from you within the range of $140,000 to $150,000—especially if you offer cash that you can borrow from some other mortgage lender.

Finding Lender REOs

In desperate times REO lenders often turn to mass marketing and highly advertised public auctions to unload their REOs. In stable to strong markets, they generally (but not always) play it low key. If it can be avoided, no lender wants to publicize the fact that it's throwing down-on-their-luck families out of their homes. Absent tough times and mass advertising, you can find REOs in three different ways: follow up after a foreclosure sale; cold call lender REO personnel; locate Realtors who typically get REO listings.

---

9. Several exceptions might include: states where the foreclosed owners may have a right of redemption; if the foreclosed owners still retain some legal right to challenge the validity of the foreclosure sale; or if a bankruptcy trustee or the Internal Revenue Service (tax lien) is entitled to bring the property within their powers. Rarely would any of these potential claims be worth losing sleep over; however, prior to closing an REO purchase, you might want to run these issues by legal counsel.

Follow Up after Foreclosure

You can easily learn of lender REOs by attending foreclosure auctions. When a lender casts a top bid for a property in which you're interested, buttonhole the bidder and start talking business. Or, try to schedule an appointment to see the officer who takes charge of the management and disposition of REOs. When you show the lender how your bargain offer will actually save or make money for the bank, you'll be on your way to closing a deal.

Beware of the stall. Nearly every financial institution is run by standard operating procedures, management committees, and other precautionary rules that frequently work against sensible decisions. If you run into a bureaucratic stonewall, you must persevere. The reward of following through doesn't just lie in getting a good deal on a property now. More important, you will build personal relationships that will open the bank's doors for you in future transactions.

Cold Call REO Personnel

All mortgage lenders experience at least a few borrower defaults. No one has yet designed a foolproof system for predicting which loan applicants will fail to pay. It follows, then, that at one time or another, all mortgage lenders must end up with REOs—even if eventually they pass them along to HUD, VA, or some other guarantor.

Sometimes, too, lenders pick up REOs without going through foreclosure. During the last major real estate downturn, many lenders would open their morning mail to find the keys to a house, a deed, and a note from the distressed owners, "We're out of here. It's your problem now."

To find REOs that lenders have acquired through foreclosure or deed-in-lieu transfers, you can cold call mortgage lenders. You might ask for a list of their REOs. This technique, though, seldom turns up much. For various reasons, lenders may keep a tight hold on this information.[10] Nevertheless, it doesn't cost to ask.

Until you establish relationships with REO personnel, you may find the following approach works better: Rather than ask for a complete list

10. Also, most lenders don't want to waste time with all of those investor "wannabes" who have just read a "nothing down" book or "graduated" from a foreclosure guru's seminar.

of REOs, narrow your focus. Tell lenders what you're specifically looking for in terms of location, size, price range, floor plan, condition, or other features. In that way, a lender can answer your request without disclosing the full number of REOs within its inventory.

* * * * *

From this chapter you can see that you can acquire and finance properties without ever applying and qualifying for a loan in the traditional way. I have financed many of my properties using the techniques presented here. With perseverance and some luck, I'm sure that you, too, can succeed as a homebuyer or investor with one or more of these approaches.

CHAPTER 8

Beware: Fine Print "Gotchas" at Work

The following is a question and answer posted on a large mortgage lender's Web site:

Q. "Do I need to know anything about the home loan process before I apply?"

A. "No. Not only is our process very simple, but our Web site is full of useful information to help guide you through it. And you can always call our toll-free number to seek further assistance along the way."

Headline of front page article in the *Wall Street Journal* (September 6, 2002): "Citigroup May Pay $200 Million in Fines for Predatory Mortgage Practices." The *Journal* further reports, "Federal Trade Commission (FTC) allegations have been hanging over the company and have provided ammunition for critics of Citigroup's consumer-finance practices. . . . Indeed it isn't likely that this record settlement would placate consumer advocates, who continue to claim that Citigroup's practices haven't improved to adequately protect borrowers."

SECRET # 82

It's a jungle out there.

As the mortgage Web site question and answer shows, some mortgage lenders falsely lead borrowers to believe that obtaining a mortgage is similar to buying a ticket on a Greyhound bus. Remember the ad slogan, "The next time you travel, ride the bus and leave the driving to us." Well, if you think you can leave the driving to your lender, one thing is true: You may very well get taken for a ride—but not on a scenic highway. You may instead end up in a jungle of predatory loan reps and predatory loan products.

In fact, not only have FTC investigations, HUD, and congressional hearings (January 2002) exposed the wild side of mortgage lending, but also the attorneys general of no fewer than 13 states have opened their own inquiries. On behalf of one of its mortgage subsidiaries, Citigroup has already paid North Carolina $20 million to settle charges against it there.

What Is Predatory Lending?

In writing about predatory lending, newspapers focus on the subprime mortgage market (say, unsophisticated borrowers with credit scores below 620). In this ruthless world, loan reps and con artists prey especially on widows, the elderly, the intellectually challenged, and other innocents at home. These hapless souls often get stuck with mortgage points and interest rates that more than double the going rate for smart, credit-strong borrowers. Often these prey lose nearly everything in trying to keep up with their impossibly high mortgage payments—and eventually they still lose their homes.

In a broader sense, though, predatory lenders can skin borrowers at higher levels of wealth, income, and credit scoring. When less than vigilant, these borrowers can encounter sharp practices that may include any of the following:

- Garbage fees, excessive charges
- Bad faith estimates of closing costs
- Undisclosed prepayment penalties
- Misleading assumption clauses
- High cost "no cost" loans
- Lowball rate quotes
- Unfair yield-spread premiums

- Insecure rate locks
- Lowball/highball appraisals
- Deceptive advertising

You might ask, "How can lenders get away with these tricks of the trade?" As the Citigroup case cited in the *Wall Street Journal* article shows, not all predatory practices do escape penalty when they leave claw marks in their victims. In most cases, however, such practices don't violate the law in provable ways. When you close your loan, you may sign, see, or initial a dozen or more documents, forms, and disclosures. Yet, how much time will you take to carefully review and question? Not much, right? The papers will come fast and furious. "Sign here, sign here, sign here, sign here. . . . "

Written Trumps Oral

Later, when you discover an onerous prepayment clause, a $200 fee you don't understand; an impotent right of assumption, or a credit life insurance policy you never knew you ordered, your complaint will fall on deaf ears. Why? Somewhere in the file a document will establish your knowledge and consent. You then respond, "But the loan rep told me. . . ." So there it is, a written document with your signature that conflicts with your recollections of oral discussions. Which do you think will prevail in a regulatory hearing or court challenge?

Nine times out of 10, the paper trail will trump mistaken understandings. Generally, the paper trail loses only when the language of the documents shocks the conscience of the court. Given that lenders employ crafty lawyers to draft their documents, you will find that few judges ever respond with shock. Moreover, in some cases, government itself mandates the use of deceptive forms and disclosures. To name three: the supposedly "Good Faith" Estimate of settlement charges; the APR disclosure (see *Mortgage Secret* #39); and the FHA appraisal and property condition disclosure form. Many borrowers believe that this form assures them that FHA is certifying the property's good condition. In fact, the fine print of the form states that FHA certifies nothing about the property's state of repair.

No, Most Lenders and Loan Reps Aren't Crooks

Okay, let's now talk context and perspective. Nothing in *Mortgage Secrets* intends to imply that most loan reps lie awake nights thinking up ways to cheat their customers. But from Babbit to Willie Loman, salespeople (like lawyers) have enjoyed far more ethical slack than other professions. Whether we name it puffing, salesmanship, competitive spirit, or legal argument, sales people (and lawyers) of all varieties are well known for their half-truths, nondisclosures, and clever, one-sided presentations.

Never forget: A loan rep wants you to buy a product that he or she is selling. A loan rep earns a commission, salary, or bonus based on his or her ability to sell against the competition. Loan reps prosper only when they convince you that they offer a better deal than you can obtain elsewhere. Because it's mathematically impossible for a majority of lenders and loan reps to actually offer the best deal—although nearly all promise to do so—it remains your responsibility to weed out the fakes, flakes, and pretenders.

SECRET # 83

Tell your loan rep to take out the garbage.

In a display of law over fair dealing, the 4th Circuit Federal Court has told mortgage lenders that they can continue to bilk their borrowers for garbage fees. The court could find no legal authority to stamp out this practice. What are these so-called garbage or junk fees? For the most part, they refer to settlement charges that sometimes grossly overstate, magnify, or duplicate the actual amount of the expenses incurred by the lender. Here are several common examples:

- $350 for an electronic appraisal that cost $3.
- $65 for an electronic credit check that cost $9.
- $75 for document delivery that cost $16.
- $500 for administrative expenses that already are covered by a 1 percent mortgage origination fee.

Many consumer critics condemned this ruling, but the court merely applied the law as it is literally written rather than imposing its own idea of fair play. If you want your lender to play fair, it is you who must tell the loan rep to take out the garbage. Closely examine every fee and expense listed on the good faith and settlement statements. Ask questions such as, "What amount did the lender actually pay for this service? Is the service actually necessary? Why am I being asked to pay these excessive charges?" Question every item, and negotiate their removal.

Garbage Fees Vary Widely among Lenders

To show how garbage fees vary, one study surveyed 28 mortgage lenders and found these results:

- 4 @ $100 or less
- 10 @ $100 to $1,000
- 9 @ $1,000 to $3,000
- 4 @ $3,000 to $5,000
- 1 @ $7,500

Although you can't judge a lender solely by the amount of its junk fees, you most certainly can appeal for their reduction—especially if you show a strong borrower profile. As Jack Guttentag (the Mortgage Professor), one of the nation's leading mortgage experts, advises, "This is a 'sloppy' market in which borrowers must stay on guard." (See Table 8.1.)

SECRET # 84

Don't place much faith in the Good Faith Estimate.

Within three days after applying for a loan, your lender must provide you with a completed form called a Good Faith Estimate. Presumably, this estimate reliably itemizes and totals the amount of fees and costs you will pay to close your mortgage loan.

Table 8.1 **Fees Vary Widely**

	Highest ($)	*Lowest ($)*	*Average ($)*
Lender/Broker Fees			
Administration fee	725	45	413.46
Application fee	410	100	266.40
Commitment fee	450	100	268.00
Document preparation	350	50	162.22
Funding fee	300	40	125.57
Mortgage broker fee	895	100	344.17
Processing	850	99	302.71
Tax service	110	10	72.09
Underwriting	595	25	279.93
Wire transfer	335	10	55.27
Third-Party Fees			
Appraisal	375	175.00	269.31
Attorney or settlement fees	820	50.00	373.71
Credit report	65	8.50	36.53
Flood certification	65	8.75	22.21
Pest inspection	400	30.00	86.07
Postage/courier	90	20.00	44.73
Survey	525	25.00	226.59
Title insurance	1,157	161.00	460.23

Based on a $125,000 mortgage from a survey of lenders. This list omits many fees that some lenders charge.

Place no faith in these figures. Place faith only in the integrity of your lender. As a rule, those lenders who provide bad faith estimates suffer no government sanctions for doing so. Technically, bad faith estimates violate sections 3 and 4 of the Real Estate Settlement and Procedures Act (RESPA), but only recently has HUD been patrolling for abuses. And even when found, HUD's complaint must allege intent to deceive. No law or regulation prohibits repeatedly honest mistakes.

On Your Own

For the most part, you're on your own. You not only must thoroughly review the Good Faith Estimate to immediately discover garbage fees, charges, and markups, you also must check it closely against the final accounting of settlement charges that are billed at closing. You should find it no surprise that in the flurry of paperwork at closing, some lenders slip in costs and charges that they previously omitted or understated.

Ideally, lenders should quote a guaranteed lump sum for closing costs and origination fees.[1] The borrowers could easily shop among lenders to compare the total package of (fixed) closing costs, interest rates, origination fees, and discount points; however, lenders know that most borrowers inquire about interest rates and discount points, and leave out any serious mention of other costs which—as you have seen—can run into the thousands of dollars. Until consumers wise up, deceptive lenders can still have their way with them.

Closing Costs Aren't Captured by Truth in Lending (APR Disclosures)

Newspaper and magazine articles frequently tell borrowers to compare loans according to their annual percentage rate (APR). Truth in lending mandates this calculation and disclosure, but as revealed previously (*Mortgage Secret* #39), the APR errs because it incorrectly assumes that the borrower will hold the loan to the end of its term and never prepay any amounts—a quite unrealistic assumption.

Moreover, APR errs because it omits many closing costs that do not count as a cost of credit. That APR you see in the mortgage ads does not, for example, include mortgage insurance, most garbage fees, cost of title or title insurance, or appraisal fees. Yet, as Table 8.1 shows, the amounts of these and other noncredit costs vary widely among lenders.

Naturally, this practice (as authorized by law) loads up deceptive loan reps with the ammunition they need to bamboozle you. They merely focus your attention on their low government-sanctioned APR and remain silent about their excessive fees and costs. Remember, the lender need not give you a Good Faith Estimate until three days after you have applied for your loan and perhaps paid a nonrefundable application fee.

---

1. HUD Secretary Martinez is pushing reform in this direction. To do so, though, HUD must revoke its rules under RESPA that mandate the itemized, good-faith approach.

Don't fall for this trick. Get the loan rep to accurately and comprehensively disclose all costs that you will pay. If the loan rep says he doesn't know for sure, ask for a high-low range. Ask precisely what factors create the uncertainty and when you can expect resolution.

Note: *Mortgage Secrets* advises you not to pay a nonrefundable mortgage application fee unless you're 99 percent certain that you know all loan terms and costs (within tolerable limits), you trust the loan rep without question, your loan closing does not depend on any contingencies other than the title search and property appraisal, and the amount of the application fee does not exceed the customary charge in your area.

SECRET # **85**

What's the real cost of a no-cost mortgage?

Mortgage lenders know that garbage fees and excessive closing costs rankle many borrowers. They also know that cash-short borrowers would jump at the chance to avoid this heavy burden of fees on top of reserve funds, escrow deposits, and down payment. Thus was born the so-called no-cost (or no-fee) mortgage. With the no-cost loan, you merely pay a slightly higher interest rate. For many borrowers, this trade-off sounds pretty attractive. But wait. Before you fall for this cheap trick, run the numbers.

Does No-Cost Save You Money?

You should realize right away that no-cost doesn't mean zero closing costs. Instead, it means "pay me later" rather than "pay me now." Given the fact that you're going to pay one way or another, you must determine which turns out better—paying now, or paying later.

How Lenders Price No-Cost Loans

As you know (*Mortgage Secret #24*), lenders typically give borrowers a range of discount point/interest rate trade-offs such as those shown in Table 8.2.

Table 8.2 **30-Year Fixed**

Rate (%)	*Discount Points*
7.0	0
6.75	1
6.50	2
6.25	3

Although you may not see it, the loan rep's 30-year fixed rate sheet may also show a no-cost loan as follows:

Rate (%)	**Discount Points**
8.0	-2.50

If you're quick with numbers, you can instantly spot the way the lenders have stacked the no-cost numbers in their own favor. At interest rates between 6.25 and 7.0 percent, you pay closing costs plus one point for each .25 percent you would like to drop your rate. In contrast, because lenders know that some borrowers can't resist immediate pleasure (no closing costs) in return for long-term pain (an 8 percent interest rate), they can and do price the no-cost loan to reflect a poor economic trade-off for the borrower.

The negative 2.5 points obligates the lender to credit the borrower at closing with up to 2.5 percent of the loan amount.[2] Yet, even though the lender jacks up the borrower's interest rate a full point, the borrower receives less than the amount a fair pro rata trade-off would indicate.

In other words, if to buy down the interest rate .25 percent a borrower must pay a full point, "buying up" the interest rate means the lender should credit the borrower 1.0 point for each .25 percent increase in rate—or, in this example, 4.0 points as opposed to only 2.5 points.

Example: You agree to an 8.0 percent, no closing cost $200,000 loan. The lender has priced the discount points at a negative 2.50 (-2.50). At settlement, the lender waives all fees up to $5,000 (2.5% x 200,000). As it turns out, absent the no-cost feature, your fees for this loan would actually have totaled $4,250.

2. Typically, lenders set the rate/point relationship to exceed all closing costs. The numbers used here are illustrative only.

Do you receive a $750 ($5,000-$4,250) cash-back credit? Not likely. Instead, the loan rep and lender (in some agreed proportion) will split this overage. Your higher-rate, zero-cost loan yields an even poorer trade-off for you.

The Potentially High Cost of No-Cost

In pure dollar and cents, no-cost loans typically are priced to profit the lender greatly—unless you pay it off within, say, two to three years. In the previous example, your payment runs $1,468 per month at 8.0 percent. At an interest rate of 7.0 percent, you would pay $1,331 per month. You pay $137 more each month with the 8.0 percenter. To earn a payback, the lender needs you to keep the loan for at least 31 months ($4,250 ÷ $137 = 31).

In contrast, if you keep this loan for 84 months (7 years), the lender collects, roughly speaking, an extra $7,000.[3] Although the mid- to longer-term economics of a no-cost loan greatly favors lenders, cash-short borrowers and short-term borrowers still find the loan attractive. If you're tempted to go for this trade-off, run the numbers carefully. Figure out just how long you can keep the loan before it turns against you.

In periods when interest rates are trending down, serial refinanceers love this loan—and profit from it—as they ride the trend down with multiple no-cost refinancings. But at some point, the trend reverses. That's when you want to bite the bullet, pay discount points and closing costs, and enjoy the lowest interest rate you can get from now until the foreseeable future. Miss the turning point, and you pay a steep long-term price for your no-cost loan.

SECRET # 86

Does your loan permit unlimited prepayment?

During the 1980s, prepayment restrictions almost died out. But by the late 1990s, they were back in abundance. Why? To keep down t he num-

3. For simplicity, this example ignores principal reduction, which would slightly alter the numbers.

ber of refinancings. As rates trend lower, serial refinancers can cost lenders billions of dollars in lost interest and excessive loan origination costs—especially for zero point and negative point loans, and for ARMs with low teaser rates. The lender then pays the loan rep a large commission it hopes to earn back over the life of the loan. A quick refi means the lender takes an out-of-pocket loss. Your early prepay to refi at a lower rate ruins the lender's day.

Types of Prepay Restrictions

First, the good news. No loan that gains approval by Fannie Mae, Freddie Mac, FHA, or VA will (as of this writing) include any restrictions that limit your opportunity to prepay either in part or in whole. Now the bad news. Generally, these loans do not include those juicy front-end giveaways. And loans that do, increasingly restrict prepay in one of the following ways:

- *Complete prohibition.* No prepay permitted. Period! Although sometimes found in commercial mortgages, these clauses rarely appear in mortgages issued to homeowners.
- *Partial prepay.* These clauses permit you to prepay some stated percentage of the loan each year.
- *Prepay penalty.* You may prepay at any time as long as you pay the lender for the privilege. These types of penalties may run as high as 5 percent of your loan's outstanding balance at the time of payoff, such as $7,500 on a $150,000 balance.
- *Penalty phaseout.* Sometime lenders phase out the penalty over a period of, say, three to five years or longer. On a five-year phaseout, a year-one payoff penalty could cost you 5 percent of the outstanding balance, and a year-five payoff might assess a 1 percent of mortgage balance penalty.
- *Prohibition phaseout.* Likewise, a complete prohibition on prepay might expire at, say, year three or year five.

Read the Fine Print

I once took out a second mortgage at 16 percent. At the time I applied for the loan, I specifically asked the loan rep, "Will I suffer any penalty if

I pay this loan off early?" The loan rep responded, "No, none at all. There's no prepayment penalty." The lender (a major bank) also advertised these loans "no prepayment penalty." However, several years later when rates had noticeably dropped, I called the bank for its payoff amount. Their figure came out about $800 more than my calculations.

"Your numbers are wrong," I told them. "No, they're not," the bank responded. Alas, it turned out the lender was "right." Although the loan did not include any explicit prepayment penalty, it did impose a penalty for prepayment. (Yes, you read that correctly.) The fine print of the contract specified that the lender would calculate early payoffs according to the rule of 78s. This now less-frequently used method of loan amortization overloads interest payments into the first several years of the loan. Thus, lenders who use this technique (legally) cheat their customers. (The rule of 78s does not in any way increase the APR disclosure rate!)

Did I complain about fraudulent misrepresentation? You betcha! Want to guess how well I succeeded in getting my payoff reduced? Zip, zero, nada.

Learn from my mistake. Don't trust a loan rep to honestly address your concerns. Read the fine print of the contract. Every borrower wants to know, "Is it going to cost me extra to pay off this loan early?" Clearly, this bank knew borrowers were concerned about this issue. That's why it advertised, "No prepayment penalty." The bank wanted to deceive its borrowers and found a lawful way to do so.

I can assure you, many lenders use the same tactics today. Rather than fully explain and address your real and commonsense concerns, they answer with half-truths (half-lies?) that can subsequently be resolved in the lender's favor by pulling out the paperwork.

Not Just for Prepayment!

I emphasize again, learn from my mistake: Each time you ask the loan rep a question, refuse to accept a mere oral reply. Tell the loan rep that you prefer to see the written language that will actually rule the issue. Apply this safeguard not just for prepayment penalties, but to every other material issue such as loan caps, adjustment periods, closing costs, rate locks, and the topic *Mortgage Secrets* next addresses—assumption clauses.

SECRET # **87**

An assumable loan may offer much less than you've assumed.

Here's another example from my experiences, only this time the sellers lost and the bank gained. These borrowers had lived in their newly acquired home for nine months; then their employer told them to transfer to Denver.

To qualify for their loan, these sellers had bought down their interest rate for three years to 10 percent—against a market rate of 12.5 percent. Very expensive! "At least," they thought, "we won't have any trouble selling our house. Thankfully, we can offer a buyer our assumable mortgage with that great, below-market 10 percent interest rate." They were right. As soon as I saw the deal they presented, I bought. Unfortunately for the sellers, the bank rejected our purchase contract.

Assumable Loan, Yes. Assumable Rate, No.

Although the lender quickly approved me for the loan assumption, it refused to approve the below-market rate. "Sorry," the bank told the sellers, "we'll only go forward at the 12.5 percent contract rate." Outraged, the sellers responded, "What do you mean? We just paid thousands of dollars for that buydown less than a year ago. You're telling us that we just poured that money down a rat hole."

"Now, now, Mr. Seller, we at the bank are sorry you feel that way, but our hands are tied. The contract clearly states that we will approve assumptions only at the loan contract rate, not the buydown rate. I know headquarters would never let this assumption go through at 10 percent."

"Why did you emphasize to us when we got this loan that it was assumable if it couldn't be assumed at the 10 percent rate," the seller angrily contested.

"We don't recall you asking about that at the time. Did you?"

"No, I didn't ask," the seller shot back, "I just assumed that the rate we bought is the rate the buyers would get."

"Well, as we said, Mr. Seller, we're truly sorry about *your* misunderstanding. But there's nothing we can do."

What Happened?

My purchase contract with the sellers specified that (subject only to loan qualification) I could assume their mortgage at 10 percent. It did not give the sellers an escape hatch. To fulfill their obligation under the contract, they had to again pay the bank thousands of dollars to buy the rate down for me. They were not happy campers. They threatened to sue the bank, but in Dizzy Dean fashion, their lawyer warned that they had only two chances of winning: slim and none. In any event, legal costs would swamp any victory—even in the improbable event that one was achieved.

The Moral: Don't Assume Anything about the Assumption Clause

Your loan rep may point out that the loan you're originating includes a much-desired feature. "It's assumable," she says. You respond, "Sounds good, but tell me more . . .

- At what interest rate?
- What credit and qualifying standards will apply to my buyers?
- What amount of assumption fee must the buyers pay? What other closing costs or settlement fees will be levied?
- Will the buyers retain the contract right to streamline refi if market interest rates drop?
- Will you require an appraisal for the property at the time of the assumption? If so, what's the maximum loan-to-value ratio that will pass muster?
- Is this assumption a one-time shot, or will the new buyers also be able to pass the loan along to their eventual buyers?
- Is the assumption only available to owner-occupants, or can investors also assume the loan?
- (If the loan is an ARM), will the buyers retain the right of conversion? Can the periodic or lifetime caps change for the new buyers?

"And by the way, would you please show me the contract terms, documents, or riders that specifically address each of these questions?"

To know that buyers can assume your loan is really to know nothing at all. The devil may lurk in the details. In those times of higher market interest rates, tighter qualifying standards, or excess housing inventory, assumable mortgages can provide sellers a competitive advantage. They can easily achieve faster sales at higher prices, but only if that assumable conveys benefits that new originations don't offer.

Assume nothing about your assumable. Verify facts.

SECRET # 88

Appraised value doesn't necessarily equal market value.

Prior to funding a loan, nearly every mortgage lender requires some type of property appraisal.[4] To the detriment of their borrowers, lenders often play games with appraisers and appraisals. You must understand that the lender's *appraised value* for a property can come in significantly above or below the property's *market value.* In addition, neither appraised value nor market value says anything about the price you can expect the property to sell for in the future.

Credit, Not Property

For most real estate mortgages, credit stands far more important than property (see *Mortgage Secret #40*). To see the importance of this fact for appraisal, let's eavesdrop on this conversation between a loan rep and an appraiser.

"Hello, Ed., this is Frank over at Fidelity Mortgage. Look, we got a borrower over here with a 790 FICO. He wants a $240,000, 80 percent LTV loan to buy a $300,000 place in Mountview. The price sounds a little steep to me, but we would really like this loan to go through smoothly. See what you can do for us, okay?"

4. Some streamlined refis do omit this step. The topic of appraisals is discussed more extensively in my books, *Investing in Real Estate,* 4th ed. (Wiley, 2003); and *The 106 Mistakes Homebuyers Make (and How to Avoid Them),* 3rd ed. (Wiley, 2002).

"Sure," appraiser Ed responds, "fax the appraisal order to us. I'll get on the job right away. Sales price does seem on the high side, but those homes in Mountview have been appreciating pretty well. I think I've got some good comps. With a little fiddling, I suspect that we can get the number you need. I'll get back to you in a few days. And thanks again for your business. This will make the fiftieth appraisal job our firm has performed for you this year. Let's hope the market continues to roar."

Strong Borrowers Generally Get the Appraised Value Lenders Want

You pay for the appraisal report, but you're not the client. The lender is the client. No appraisal firm that wants to stay in business can regularly provide value estimates that run against its lenders' wishes. That's why the appraisals for strong borrowers nearly always equal or exceed their purchase contract price.

Don't conclude that you're protected by the lender's appraisal. Do your own research. Satisfy yourself by expertly comparing properties, features, and sales prices. Some homebuyers fall in love with a property, agree to pay whatever price the seller is asking, and expect the lender's appraisal to bail them out if they've overpaid. Unless for some reason the lender wants to kill the deal, that won't happen. In the great majority of purchase transactions, credit trumps valuation. Rarely the reverse.

Electronic Appraisals

Increasingly these days, for high credit score borrowers, lenders may not even send an appraiser out to the property. Instead, they obtain the appraisal electronically from a data bank of recent property sales. If your contract price doesn't severely raise eyebrows, the property passes the appraisal test. Although appraisals based on statistical modeling have long been used by property tax assessors, they do not adequately substitute for close, detailed property appraisals performed by a competent and disinterested expert.

From a cost standpoint, though, electronic appraisals win hands down. A typical price for such an appraisal ranges from $3 to $15 versus the $250 to $450 that most appraisal firms charge. If your lender does use a computerized appraisal, however, watch out for overbilling. Some lenders bill you at closing for a standard appraisal fee. HUD says these types of markups (garbage fees) are illegal, but so far the federal courts have ruled otherwise.

SECRET # 89

On occasion, lenders want appraisers to lowball their appraisals.

Although most often you must guard against appraisals that come in too high, sometimes you might encounter a lender's appraisal that comes in too low to justify the amount of your mortgage loan. Consider the experience of homebuyer Phil Tortellori.

"We had spent almost a year looking at houses," says Phil. "We liked a lot of them, but for one reason or other nothing quite excited our fancy. Then one Saturday we drove by a house we knew we had to have. It was priced right—or I should say, *we* thought it was priced right. Unfortunately, less than 10 days before closing, we learned the lender's appraiser had reported a different opinion. Her estimate of the home's value came in $10,000 less than our purchase price.

"To offset this lower appraised value, the lender said we'd have to increase our down payment by $8,000. Or, instead, we could ask the sellers to reduce their price. We had bargained hard as it was, so we didn't think the sellers would agree to come down more. And they wouldn't. As for raising our down payment by $8,000—no way! So, the financing fell through and we had to begin our search all over again."

From time to time, both homebuyers and home sellers have complained of lowball appraisals that killed a sale. In some instances lenders have used low appraisals to turn down loans they didn't want to make. At other times lender appraisers give low appraisals in response to tightened government appraisal regulations. Either way, a lowball appraisal can spoil your homebuying plans.

Prevent Deal-Killer Appraisals

To help prevent this problem, make sure your agent shows you recent sales prices (and terms) of similar homes in the neighborhood. Use these prices to guide your offer. Next, learn the name of the appraiser your lender plans to use. Ask your agent to tell the appraiser the comp sales you relied on to figure your offer. After the appraisal is complete, get a copy from the lender. (You are entitled to a copy of your appraisal under the 1991 Equal Credit Opportunity Act, various state laws, and regulations put in place by the Federal Reserve Board.) Examine the appraisal according to the checks we are discussing in this chapter.

If your lender turns down your loan because of a low appraisal, you can legitimately back out your purchase contract and recover your earnest money deposit. Alternatively, if you think the appraiser has lowballed you, schedule a meeting with the appraiser, or write out your objections to the appraisal and then give them to your lender.

In response, the appraiser can either accept or reject your comments. If he or she rejects them, you can ask the lender to send out another appraiser. If the lender wants your business, it will probably agree to obtain a second opinion. If the lender doesn't oblige, you must increase your down payment, ask the sellers to reduce their price, or apply for a mortgage somewhere else. (To appease your frustrations with the appraiser, write a complaint to the state licensing board; however, that won't help you get the financing you need.)

Lowball appraisals don't seem to be a major problem at this time, but it is a practice for which to stay alert. In sharply rising markets—at least in the past—watch out most for overappraising. With rapid rates of appreciation, lenders, appraisers, and homebuyers get careless. With eyes focused on the future, no one worries much about the price today because it's sure to be even higher tomorrow. (This practice reflects the once-popular view that "inflation cures all mistakes.")

Appraisals Don't Include Personal Property or Seller Concessions

Appraisers limit their value estimates to the house and lot—that is, real estate. If your purchase price includes any personal property (antique Oriental rugs, custom-made draperies, furniture), or if your seller has agreed to pay an abnormally large percentage of your mortgage points and/or closing costs, the lender's appraiser can exclude these amounts from his or her appraised value. With this exclusion, you probably won't be able to borrow the full amount that you would like. So, before you write seller concessions directly into your purchase contract, learn your lender's rules; then ask your real estate agent (or attorney) to figure out the most advantageous way to both get the loan you need and pay the personal property or settlement expenses. Sometimes, you can benefit if you write up a separate agreement to cover these items.

SECRET # 90

Appraisals don't forecast the future.

Maria and Jorge Olson were sitting in the living room of the home they wanted to buy. Five other hopeful buyers sat nearby. The desired home was listed at $290,000. The sales agent for the sellers came into the room. Tension hung in the air. "We're going to start the bidding now," the agent said. Offers started flying. Pandemonium broke lose.

"It was really wild," Maria recalled. "Then, after everyone had had their say and written up their offers, the agent and the owners left the room. When they came back, we just knew we'd won. We were right. The owners accepted our offer of $320,000. We celebrated that evening by going out to dinner at the most expensive restaurant in town. With home values increasing 20 percent a year, we felt that we got a great deal."

Sadly, three years later Maria and Jorge were in divorce court. They needed to sell their home and hired an appraiser. His value estimate came in at $260,000—just about the same as the listing price that several real estate agents had suggested to the Olsons. (Several other agents had estimated much higher.)

Lawsuits against Appraisers Require Proof of Negligence

To say the least, the Olsons were distressed and angry. They wanted someone to blame. They decided to sue their lender, their real estate agent, and the appraisal firm that had appraised the house when the Olsons took out their mortgage. That appraisal showed a value for the home of $325,000. The Olsons knew the market now was soft, but surely prices couldn't have fallen that much. Their lender's appraiser must have overvalued the home, or if prices were really going to fall that much, the Olsons argued, someone should have warned them.

The Olsons lost the court case for two reasons. Expert testimony showed that the original $325,000 value estimate wasn't completely off the wall at that earlier boisterous time. Although one could easily question the appraiser's judgment on several points, the appraisal itself contained no egregious objective errors. Also, the court ruled that neither appraisers nor realty agents could be expected to predict the future. Estimates of market value apply only to the date of the appraisal. Neither the Olsons nor any other homebuyers should count on an appraiser, their mortgage lender, or even their real estate agent to tell them whether home prices are headed up or down.

Appraisers Don't Forecast Values

Throughout the United States, the ruling in this case generally holds. With limited exceptions, homebuyers must make their own forecasts. At best, appraisers describe the current market. Appraisers might believe, "The market is wild with speculation. Buyers are crazy. Within a year prices are going to fall faster than the NASDAQ crash of 2000." But unless specifically directed, appraisers won't put these kinds of comments in their appraisal reports.

Likewise, when performing a market value appraisal, an appraiser wouldn't comment, "This is the best market for homebuyers we've had in years. Home prices are sure to double within the next five years." You could ask an appraiser or real estate agent to give you his or her opinion about where the market is headed over the coming years, but for you to see the future as clearly as possible, examine the market signals discussed earlier.

Many homebuyers think they are getting a great buy if they purchase their home for less than its current market value; however, that's not all to consider. Ask these two questions before you buy: What market signals (or property features) indicate this home will be worth more tomorrow than it is today, and what market signals spell D-A-N-G-E-R? Beware of landing upside down with overappraising and overborrowing.

CHAPTER 9

Achieve Your Lowest Rate

"Hello, Robublind Mortgage Company. What can we do to you today. . . . I mean . . . for you today?"

The caller responds, "What's the best rate you can give me on a 30-year mortgage?"

Readers, please, never shop for a mortgage using the dialing-for-dollars approach. You simply set yourself up for fleecing.

"Okay," you say, "if that approach doesn't work, what does?"

Well, I'm glad you asked because that's the question this chapter answers. To start, let's look at interest rates from the lender's perspective to see how loan reps can make money by overcharging and underquoting.

SECRET # 91

Refuse to yield to the yield-spread premium.

In today's competitive mortgage market, most mortgage originators work on commission. They want to find a loan for you. Otherwise, they don't get paid.

The bad news is that loan originators earn higher commissions when they place you into higher-cost loan products. If your loan rep says, "The best I can do is a rate of 6.25 percent and 2 points," don't take that as a final quote. Just like a car salesperson (or any other type of salesperson), the loan rep may be testing you.

If you accept, great. If you balk, the rep can say, "Oh, wait a minute, I've just thought of something else. Maybe I can get the lender to shave a point off those origination fees. They owe me a favor."

Protect Yourself

To protect yourself from paying too much, ask to see the loan officer's rate sheet. The rate sheet shows the "wholesale" cost of the loans. The bigger the spread between the wholesale rate and the interest rate and fees you pay, the larger the loan officer's commission. In fact, ask the loan officer straight out, "What's the amount of your commission on this loan?" If it's $4,000, you know that more than likely you've been placed into a high-cost loan. If the commission is $1,200, there is far less chance you're being taken for a ride. On most loans, commissions typically should run no more than 1 percent of the amount you borrow.

Of course, neither the wholesale-retail spread nor the amount of the loan rep's commission—taken together or separately—provides the entire picture as to whether you are getting the best possible loan for your needs and financial qualifications, but it is one important piece of the puzzle. Don't passively accept a loan originator's quotes. Investigate and negotiate.

Credit Blemishes

Mortgage lenders classify borrowers into the credit categories of A, B, C, and D. The lower your grade, the more you must pay for a mortgage. But just like in school, the grade you receive depends on who's doing the grading. Even with credit blemishes, one mortgage lender might give you an A-, another might downgrade you to B or even C status—and, correspondingly, persuade you to pay a higher interest rate and fees. (At the same time, of course, the loan rep earns a higher sales commission.)

If you get downgraded because of credit blemishes, don't meekly accept that category. Ask why. Is the loan rep bamboozling you so he or she can make more money, or do you really deserve the downgrade? Also, learn how long it will take—or what you can do—to reach A status. Maybe you should defer buying until you can qualify at lower rates and costs.

Talk with other mortgage companies. If your blemishes consist of nothing more than a few late payments, you can probably find an A grade mortgage. Even when you've suffered more serious setbacks, it's sometimes possible to provide an excuse that will move you into an A category.

Just keep in mind that loan originators can earn higher commissions when they persuade borrowers to accept higher fees and interest rates. If your credit is seriously blemished, you may have to pay more for your loan than A borrowers. Nevertheless, don't meekly accept the downgrade. Learn the specific reasons and then seek second, third, fourth, or even fifth opinions. One mortgage broker told me that as many as 40 percent of B and C borrowers could have been qualified with an A or an A- grade. Also, after you fall into the B grade or lower, your powers of persuasion and negotiation will count heavily. With these higher cost products, when pressed, many loan reps will come down from their sticker prices.

Prepayment Penalty Discount

A loan rep can receive a yield-spread premium (commission bonus) by slipping a prepayment penalty into a run-of-the-mill, 30-year fixed-rate mortgage. Typically, lenders offer these loans to borrowers at a .25 percent discount from the interest rate of a similar loan without the prepay penalty. If you don't know enough to ask about the penalty, however, or don't know enough to insist on the discount, the loan rep earns more money.

Whether you should willingly accept the discounted interest rate in exchange for the penalty depends on the same rate/point questions that always come up: How long do you plan to keep the loan if interest rates don't move down? And, does inflation (or disinflation) seem imminent, leading to higher or lower interest rates?

If the odds point to lower rates, skip the penalty. If higher inflation and higher interest rates look probable, you won't refi any time soon. The trade-off of penalty for rate discount could make economic sense.

SECRET # **92**

Red and yellow, black and white, do lenders treat them all alike?

Critics often complain about two types of mortgage discrimination: stereotypical ("We don't make loans to _____. They're bad risks."), and discrimination through "neutral" rules or practices that adversely impact some identifiable groups of borrowers such as African Americans, Hispanics, immigrants, women, singles, single-parent families, and so on.

As company policy, lenders have nearly eliminated stereotypical turndowns; however, studies do indicate that some borrowers pay more for their mortgages than other borrowers—even when their credit scores and incomes look similar. As it turns out, the borrowers who pay more are the borrowers most likely to fall into some legally protected category. Does this suggest that lenders are engaged in illegal discriminatory pricing? Not necessarily.

Rather, it suggests that some borrowers fail to negotiate their interest rates and loan fees. When the loan rep says, "Gee, this is the best I can do," such borrowers are more likely to accept the loan on the terms offered. They don't realize that they should respond with their own negotiating gambit, "Really, that's the best you can do? Well, Providence Mortgage quoted us a much better deal. Sorry, we're just wasting our time here." Or, "We found rates far less than that on quicken.com. You're not trying to put one over on us, are you?"

No matter who you are, many loan originators will charge you higher interest and fees when you let them. If you fear the lending process, fail to aggressively negotiate, or are uneducated about mortgage loan practices, you are prime game—regardless of your race, sex, ethnicity, nationality, sex, or family status.

To protect yourself, assert yourself (politely, of course). For when some loan reps sense a vulnerable prey, they go for the kill.

SECRET # **93**

Rate quotes: Fact or fiction?

Unlike most products, you won't know the real price of your newly originated mortgage until after you have agreed to buy it. This industry-wide, standard operating procedure enables low-life loan reps to bamboozle you in several ways; but also, it even exposes those borrowers who deal with honest reps to risks they fail to understand. Typically, you *negotiate* interest rates with your loan rep at or around the time you apply for your loan, but the rate you pay can increase substantially from the rate you both have agreed upon. Just as depressing, should rates decline prior to your closing date, you could miss getting that rate break—unless you protect yourself as *Mortgage Secrets* advises you to do.

Low-life and Lowball Quotes

Because lenders compete aggressively with each other, some loan reps try to draw in borrowers by quoting fictional lowball interest rates, points, or closing costs. Or if real, these rates may apply to only a small niche of people. After you're a week or two forward in the mortgage process, the loan rep then discovers a glitch in your credit, employment, tax returns, or qualifying ratios. It doesn't matter how perfect your borrower profile, a loan rep who wants to monkey wrench a deal can always find a way to do so.

Bait and Switch

Upon learning that your loan won't go through as previously agreed, you could threaten to go to another lender. Unfortunately, you're obliged to the sellers for a 30-day close and you're already at day 13. What do you do? If the loan rep has well chosen his mark and talks a good story, you'll agree to switch to a less desirable loan product, or perhaps accept a higher interest rate or costs. Either way, the loan rep makes more money. And if he's really smooth, you will later thank him for the heroic job he performed to save the deal and meet your closing deadline.

Your Defense

Don't shop price alone. Shop for integrity. Verify the experience, reputation, and dependability of the loan rep. Check references, of course, but more importantly, nail down early on the precise loan and terms the loan rep is promising and why he's certain he can deliver on his promises. Listen carefully for hedging. You know the limp, "Well, I'll certainly do the best I can." Watch for mannerisms, eye movement, body language. Does the rep pass the smell test, or do you sniff B.S.?

When thinking over the times I've been duped, one constant remains: The clues were clearly in view if only I had paid more attention. Isn't that fact true for you, too?

SECRET # **94**

What rate will you get at closing?

Other than ARM teasers, mortgage assumptions, and seller financing, few lenders guarantee their rate quotes. Instead, the rate you get is the rate that's set on (or near) the date you close. Alternatively, you can lock a rate by agreeing to pay the lender a fee. After you're on a firm path toward closing, you must decide whether you want to float or lock. If you do want to lock, that opens this set of questions:

- *When to lock?* Generally, you can lock on the date of loan approval—maybe even as early as the date of application—up until a day or two before closing.
- *How long?* Lock periods may run anywhere from 10 to 90 days, or longer if you're buying new construction or building a home.
- *How much?* The longer you lock your rate, the more the lender will charge you. Although some lenders try to grab this fee up front, do not oblige them. Industry standards favor payment at closing.

Whether to Lock

To help answer this question, return to the qualifying process. If rates moved up .5 to .75 percent, would the lender still qualify you for the amount of loan you need? If no, you will probably want to lock. Why risk losing your loan, or having to scurry around at the last minute to reconfigure your qualifying income and qualifying debts? If, however, you've plenty of extra cash to reduce the amount of your loan, if necessary, you can safely accept the risk—as long as any potentially higher monthly payments would not wreck your monthly budget.

Most people who dislike risk prefer to lock, even if upward rate moves wouldn't upset their budget or disqualify them from the mortgage for which they've been approved. If you fall into this category, lock and sleep well. Of course, the downside occurs when rates drop and you kick yourself for being so fearful. Alas, only you know your emotional makeup. Assess yourself; then go with the flow.

When to Lock

Even if you decide to lock, most lenders give you great leeway. Should rates drop the day you receive your loan approval, you might safely wait and see if further drops continue. Ride the trend down and then lock after the next couple of upticks.

Obviously, the rate-lock issue involves short-term interest rate forecasting. Because anyone who perfects this skill can make billions as a bond trader, don't expect flawless timing. Follow the rates, and act when you feel most comfortable in the trade-off between risk and regret.

How Long Should You Lock?

To a certain degree, this question plays into when you lock. Are you counting on a 30-day closing or less? Are you already a week or two forward in the mortgage process? Is your loan approval contingent on any explanations, inspections, appraisal, or documentation? If so, how much time must you or the lender allow to remove these obstacles? Have you verified, corrected, and cleaned up your credit reports prior to applying for the loan (see *Mortgage Secret #44*)? In other words, before you choose a lock period, realistically review what needs to be done and how long it will take.

Too many borrowers lock too soon and for too short a period because they ballpark their scheduling without anticipating where glitches might arise. Also, as explained on p. 220, in a climate of rising interest rates, don't push the timeline too closely. The lender may delay closing solely for the purpose of picking your lock.

How Much?

The longer you lock, the more you pay. On a $200,000 loan, a 30-day lock could cost between $500 and $1,000. A 60-day lock for that amount could run up to $1,500 or more. On the other hand, if you ask for it, your lender may lock for 15 to 30 days with only a nominal charge.

Although 15- to 90-day rate-lock fees shift up and down, they're seldom cheap. Normally, you wouldn't want to add on an extra 30 days "just to be safe." You gain most when you ride trends down; thoroughly prepare for the mortgage process to avoid time-consuming glitches and contingencies, develop a realistic closing schedule, and lock your rate for the minimum number of days that will almost surely get you through closing.

Market Floats Down

Often borrowers lock at a rate, say, at 6.5 percent and then rates go down. When that happens, will you see our rate fall accordingly? No. Not unless your lender has agreed to a rate lock with a float down.

Absent a float down agreement, can you still negotiate for a lower rate? Sometimes, but understand that your lender may have already agreed to sell (deliver) your 6.5 percent mortgage to a buyer in the secondary mortgage market. That buyer expects a 6.5 percent loan. If your lender delivers a 6.0 percent loan instead, it will pay a substantial penalty. If you want a rate lock with a float down, ask for it early on; then prepare to pay for it.

Find a New Lender

If you did not get the lender to agree to a rate lock with float down, you could possibly gain the lower 6.0 percent rate by jumping to a new lender. To do that successfully means that the old lender must agree to immediately transfer your application file to the new lender, and the new lender must agree to accept the file application and close within 15 days. Otherwise, you would need to buy another rate lock. (Unless, of course, falling inflation and weak economic growth signal further drops in interest rates, and you think floating presents an acceptable risk.)

You also would likely forfeit the application fees and costs already paid to the first lender, as well as pay additional application fees and costs to the new lender. All in all, jumping lenders in a purchase transaction will likely prove futile. So, don't leave your float down to last minute negotiations. Ask for it before you need it. With refis, however, you possess more leverage because there's no closing deadline imposed by a sales contract. Also, under federal law, you may rescind your refinance agreement within three business days after closing.

SECRET # 95

Achieve your best rate.

Most often, lenders honor their rate locks. But *Mortgage Secrets* advises you to leave nothing to good faith oral promises. With shady loan reps, or in periods of heavy loan volume, those our-word-is-our-bond rate locks often prove insecure.

Confirm the Lock and Price in Writing

You decide that it's time to lock. You telephone the loan rep; she checks rates and fees. You tell her to lock. She says, "It's done. We've got you 6.5 percent for 30 days. That should give us just about the right amount of time with several days to spare."

You then ask the loan rep to fax or e-mail you the agreed terms of the lock. Alternatively, you fax or e-mail the loan rep your "understanding," and request a response. In fact, this simple written confirmation technique works wonders to prevent later disagreement in any type of important discussion or transaction that occurs via oral communications. (Again, profit from my experience. I once suffered a world of grief when

I acted on a lawyer's erroneous advice given orally. Later, he denied it—as one would expect from lawyers. After that costly mistake, I have scrupulously followed the written confirmation approach.)

Don't Let Your Lock Expire

Borrowers often bust their own locks because they don't timely fulfill the loan rep's requests for documents, explanations, or other paperwork necessary to move the loan process forward. Anticipate, clarify, research, and prepare. Learn what's expected of you, and meet these obligations promptly. On other occasions, lenders don't meet the deadline for one of three reasons:

- *Third-party failure.* Your closing depends on the work of numerous outside parties that the lender doesn't control directly (credit repositories, appraisers, title insurers, surveyors, property inspection services, and so on.). When these people err or delay, the loan process stalls.
- *Lender mistakes or neglect.* Before a third party delivers, the lender must place the order. Sometimes they forget, or the lender may misplace documents, ignore necessary verifications, or employ too few file handlers to expedite its overflowing flood of mortgage applications.
- *Improper intent.* When interest rates jump .50 percent or more above the lock rate, the lender could suffer a serious loss of profit on that loan. Alternatively, if the lender can deliver the loan at a rate substantially above the lock rate, it may gain thousands of dollars in overage or commission bonus. Bottom-line issues can seriously test the lender's ethics. A loan rep only needs to find some quasi legitimate last minute reason to delay. "We're really sorry, but the underwriter now insists that you (or the seller) repair that leaky roof before closing."

By knowing why locks expire, you can head off trouble at the pass. Remain involved in the loan process. Don't badger the loan rep every day, but do ask for a flow sheet of who, what, when, where, and why. Follow the scheduling. Verify that all steps are moving forward on time. Where you see foot-dragging or oversight, push up the pressure—even if it means that you call third-party providers yourself and diplomatically plead for relief.

Next, by the time you lock your rate, the lender should have scheduled the approval process and set a tentative closing date. It's then (if not before) that you want to ask the loan rep whether the lender will honor the locked rate when its own shortcomings create the delay. If so, include that promise when you confirm your lock's terms and fee. If not, you're forewarned. Push the process along or pay the penalty for the lender's ineptness.

Finally, if you sense intent to delay, stand firm. Insist that closing take place as scheduled or you'll use every consumer right and regulatory complaint procedure available. Should that fail, insist that the lender honor the otherwise expired rate lock. Also, search for alternative ways to remedy the cause of the delay. For example, rather than require preclosing repairs, you or the sellers could post a sufficient sum of money into a repair escrow account; or, the lender could merely withhold funds at closing pending repairs. When you think through a problem, you can generally discover multiple ways to solve it and keep closing on schedule.

Refuse to accept intentional (or bureaucratic) foul-ups. Press the lender to create alternatives.

What Does the Lender Mean by "Market Rate?"

Some lenders will lock in your maximum mortgage interest rate, yet will also give you a float down if rates fall between the time you apply and the date your loan closes. "Good news," your loan originator tells you, "rates have fallen and we can now close your loan at 7.75 percent instead of 8.0 percent. You're going to save $26.30 a month."

Yes, that's good news, but it may not reflect the full drop in rates that has occurred. If market rates are really at 7.5 percent, by fooling you into accepting 7.75 percent, your loan originator is going to pocket a nice-sized overage commission. Even with float downs, take care. Make sure you're receiving the full float down to which you are entitled.

SECRET # **96**

Industry pros and government agencies need your help.

To a large degree, the tricks of the mortgage trade continue because they give lenders and loan reps ripe opportunities to profit at the expense of their borrowers. Although various housing, banking, and consumer regulations govern lenders and loan reps, as you've seen, these regulations seldom protect effectively. Even worse, numerous regulations substitute form over substance, bureaucratic rules for common sense, and good intentions for concrete results.

Industry Initiatives to the Rescue?

In a recent issue of *Mortgage Banking*,[1] John Robbins writes, "As mortgage bankers, we know that integrity, trust, and honesty are simply the rules of conduct by which we should all live . . . [government and industry] are currently targeting many unethical practices such as flipping (repeated) refinances that result in fees for lenders without any benefit to borrowers . . . inflating a home's appraised value, packing loans with unnecessary credit insurance, and charging extended prepayment penalties that trap homeowners in high interest rate loans. . . .

"It is commendable that some mortgage banking and brokerage firms are initiating voluntary consumer disclosures on their own. These disclosures detail the loan fees a borrower can expect to pay and how much other settlement costs should total. Some companies also disclose in advance of settlement if closing fees will exceed the initial good faith estimate. Mortgage applicants possess the power to demand similar information from lenders who are not now offering these extra disclosures."

Upfront Mortgage Broker (UMB)

To spearhead this drive for full disclosure of costs, fees, commissions, bonuses, yield-spread premiums, and other types of lender charges and loan rep compensation, Jack Guttentag (mtgprofessor.com) has created the Upfront Mortgage Broker's Commitment (see Figure 9.1). The

1. "Integrity," April 2002, pp. 17–18.

1. The broker will be the customer's representative or agent, and will endeavor to act in the best interests of the customer.
2. The broker will establish a price for services upfront, in writing, based on information provided by the customer.
   - The price may be a fixed dollar amount, a percent of the loan, an hourly charge for the broker's time, or a combination of these.
   - The price or prices will cover all the services provided by the broker. This includes loan processing, for which customers always pay a broker or lender.
   - On third-party services ordered by the broker but paid for by the customer, such as an appraisal, the broker will provide the invoice from the third-party service provider at the customer's request. Alternatively, the broker may have the payment made directly by the customer to the third-party service provider.
3. Any payments the broker receives from third parties involved in the transaction will be credited to the customer, unless such payments are included in the broker's fee.
   - If the broker's fee is 1 point, for example, and the broker collects 1 point from the lender as a "yield spread premium," the broker either charges the customer 1 point and credits the customer with the yield spread premium, or charges the customer nothing and retains the yield spread premium.
4. The broker will use his best efforts to determine the loan type, features, and lender services that best meet the customer's needs, and to find the best wholesale price for that loan.
5. The wholesale prices from which the broker's selection is made will be disclosed at the customer's request.
6. When directed by the customer, the broker will lock the terms (rate, points, and other major features) of the loan, and will provide a copy of the written confirmation of the rate lock as soon as it has been received from the lender.
7. If a customer elects to float the rate/points, the broker will provide the customer the best wholesale float price available to that customer on the day the loan is finally locked.
8. The broker will maintain a Web site on which its commitment to its customers is prominently display
mation the broker wants to convey.

Figure 9.1 Commitment of an Upfront Mortgage Broker
(Courtesy of Jack Guttentag)

UMBs believe that full disclosure will force the tricksters to either reform their ways or get out of the business.

Essentially, UMBs want mortgage lenders to behave more like professionals who work for their clients' best interests while charging a fully known, agreed-upon fee. With true client representation and fixed compensation, the loan reps can design and search for the optimal solution to a borrower's funding needs and wants. When incentives to gouge the borrower are removed, loan reps will walk the straight and narrow. Loan customers will receive better service. Everyone will live happily ever after.

Borrower Savvy Still Needed

Unfortunately, the UMB commitment can't work by itself. Consider this analogy: Lawyers presumably work with even stronger fiduciary duties to their clients, yet everyone who has watched closely knows that lawyers egregiously abuse their clients' interests to line their own pockets with money.[2] Mere fee disclosure in a fiduciary relationship doesn't vanquish chicanery, duplicity, and incompetence. Lawyers triumph over their clients and the general welfare because most people lack sufficient knowledge about the law, rules of procedure, and so-called legal ethics.[3]

Likewise, mortgage borrowers will continue to pay too much for too little unless they gain the knowledge to assert themselves forthrightly and intelligently. Only when consumers en masse learn to ask the pertinent questions—and demand factual, well-reasoned answers—will the tricksters and self-promoters find fewer marks against whom to operate.

Until then, follow the path of John Galt. Become part of the competent minority who refuses to humble yourself with, "Well, we will do whatever you think is best." With *Mortgage Secrets* as your guide, you now can insist on the service and disclosures that will differentiate you from the sheepish borrower who prefers a pleasant, run-of-the-mill loan

---

2. See, for example, the books, *Double Billing, A Nation Under Lawyers, A Feast for Lawyers, Divorced from Justice,* and *Injustice for All,* to name just a few.

3. Can you name one other occupation whose ethics books include an extensive discussion of, "Fostering Falsity," along with instructions on how to do so? See, for example, *Regulation of Lawyers: Problems of Law and Ethics* (Little, Brown & Co., 1989), pp. 488–535.

rep—someone who won't confound their decision making by explaining a variety of choices. Yet, this stronger role requires effort and persistence. Why? Because most loan reps aren't up to the challenge. As salespeople, they expect to "control the customer." When you show that you can't be controlled in the way they would like, they may point you toward their door.

This same situation holds true for real estate agents. During most of the twentieth century, realty agents disparaged knowledgeable buyers. And many still do. Increasingly, though, buyer knowledge (partly due to a plentiful selection of books on homebuying and real estate investing) has forced an upgrade in the real estate sales profession.

Do realty agents know as much as they should? Not by a long shot. But as larger numbers of homebuyers and investors come to expect higher levels of competence and integrity, the industry is slowly edging out the fast-talking tricksters whose only goal is to make a sale. This same trend is beginning to occur in mortgage lending. To start a revolution, we just need to enlist more foot soldiers. Won't you join up?

SECRET # 97

How to (almost) vanquish tricks of the trade.

You may think that you should avoid loan reps who earn commissions, bonuses, and overages. Rather than take a chance on getting snookered, play it safe. Only talk with the salaried loan reps at your local bank or credit union. Not a good solution. Here's why:

- *Less competency.* Most savvy, stand-out-from-the-crowd mortgage professionals prefer commissioned income. Paper-shuffling, by-the-book loan reps prefer salaries in bureaucracies.
- *Higher price.* Because many people believe banks to be a safe harbor in the cutthroat world of commerce, their loan departments charge a premium. They rarely offer the lowest interest rates or fees; however, credit unions often prove the exception, especially for plain-vanilla products. Their lower operating costs

and tax-free status permit them to pass along real savings to their borrowers.

- *Limited choice.* Rather than sell you what you need, salaried reps may push their employer's favored products; or they may push only those products (typically, the 30-year fixed-rate mortgage) that are easiest to explain.
- *Performance standards.* Salaried reps must meet their employer's volume and profit goals. Moreover, whereas you can hire a mortgage broker to work as your "buyer's" agent, the salaried reps can never represent you. They are legally obligated to pursue the interests of their employers.

An Innocent Slaughtered

In recently helping my friend Sue with a refinance, I reviewed all documents that pertained to her current loan that she had obtained 10 years earlier from one of the largest and most reputable banks in the state. This loan carried a 7.75 percent interest rate (in a now 5 to 6 percent market). Sue had taken out her current loan in 1993 as a refinance of her 1990 purchase loan that carried a 9.75 percent interest rate. After working through the numbers, I could not believe how the bank had ripped her off—either through loan rep ignorance, deception, or both. During the past 10 years, that supposedly trustworthy bank's loan rep had cost my friend more than $20,000 (loss of home equity buildup, excessive fees, and interest charges). And this $20,000 was against a loan payoff in 1993 of only $58,000!

Specific Goal

At the time of this refinance, Sue told the loan rep that she chiefly wanted a loan that would get her house paid off as quickly as possible. Sue stated that she was specifically interested in a 15-year fixed-rate loan.

The loan rep told Sue that she would not qualify for a 15-year loan. The rep then proceeded to advise Sue to sign up for a no-cost, 30-year fixed-rate loan. Accordingly, Sue accepted this advice. After all, the loan rep's the expert, isn't she? When Sue closed this loan, she owed $62,100 with a 30-year term. When she had walked into the office, she had owed $58,000 with a remaining term of 27 years. The loan rep had talked her into the worst mortgage possible, given Sue's specifically stated goals. In contrast, that loan (in length, fees, and interest rate) ranked very high in profitability for the bank.

Obvious Misdeeds

Either through ignorance or deceptive intent, Sue's loan rep erred in at least the following ways:[4]

- *Qualifying.* Although Sue's total debt ratios would have exceeded conventional guidelines (15-year term), a little financial planning could have easily restructured those figures to matching the guidelines.
- *Compensating factors.* Most importantly, for the preceding 3 years, Sue had paid every mortgage payment on time—in an amount that exceeded that required by a new 15-year at the then lower interest rates. In addition, Sue had perfect credit and displayed numerous strong compensating factors such as secure job, low housing cost ratio, low personal living expenses, high dependability, and stability.
- *ARM possibilities.* During 1993, many ARM lenders were offering quite attractive interest rates. The loan rep never mentioned any of these options.
- *High interest rate.* During 1993, 15- and 30-year fixed-rate loans in Sue's market were readily available in the 6.0 to 7.5 percent range. At 7.75 percent, Sue's rate was not good.
- *High costs.* Unlike most no-cost loans that trade off costs for higher interest, Sue's loan carried costs in excess of $4,000 (on a $58,000 refi!). Sue's loan product was falsely advertised as no-cost when, in fact, it was merely no cash due at closing. These costs included points of 3 1/8 percent.

---

4. Of course, I'm speaking from Sue's perspective. From the bank's perspective, the loan rep earned five stars.

Neat trick when a lender can do it: High interest rate, high costs, and low amortization (equity buildup). The only thing good about this loan was its lack of a prepayment penalty and few garbage fees. (But with 3 1/8 percentage points, who needs garbage fees?)

Who's Responsible: The Lender or Sue?

If questioned, the bank would admit no wrongdoing. It complied with every required rule, regulation, and disclosure. Sue's file folders for this mortgage brimmed with all necessary documents. Although this loan rep probably was not commissioned, the bank may have paid a bonus for originating no-cost mortgages such as this one.

When I asked Sue how she had selected this lender, she said she had responded to its advertisement. Did she contact any competing lenders? No. Did she call the mortgage company that serviced her current mortgage to learn what they could do for her? No. Why not? Because the bank enjoyed a good reputation and claimed status as the largest mortgage lender in town. If you can't trust a salaried employee of a large bank to give you a good deal, who can you trust?[5]

Who Can You Trust?

The cynic says, "Trust no one." To the contrary, *Mortgage Secrets* advises you to trust yourself. Gain the knowledge and savvy that will enable you to negotiate the optimal loan for your goals. Then trust your loan rep, but only after he or she earns your trust by focusing a preliminary interview on your goals, needs, wants, and capabilities. For how can anyone serve you best who doesn't first learn who you are and what you plan to achieve? Moreover, the true professional will clarify and prioritize. Only when you complete these preliminaries can the loan rep explain and recommend loan programs.

Affordability, budgeting, qualifying ratios, credit and credit scores, types of properties, property locations, interest rate/point trade-offs,

---

5. In recently speaking with a trust [*sic*] officer of a major bank, I said, "You're telling me that you only put your customers into funds and investments that carry heavy front-end loads?" Response: "Of course, the bank has to make a profit. I've got to make a living."

family issues, equity buildup, these factors and many more combine to impact your choice of mortgages. Needlessly, too few borrowers (and loan reps) comprehend how the financing and homebuying decisions you make today will greatly impact your life and your net worth 5, 10, and 20 years into the future.

So, who can you trust? Trust those professionals whose behavior and demonstrated competence leave no doubts about their motives. Trust those who adopt your goals as their own—and then exercise the diligence and expertise to help you achieve them.

CHAPTER 10

Manage Your Home and Home Financing for Maximum Return

From the early 1990s up through 2000, the financial media persistently touted stocks as the number one way to build wealth. Journalists typically quote financial planners who tell homeowners, "Your house is a roof over your head. It is not an investment." Even now with three consecutive bad years for the Dow, the S&P 500, and the NASDAQ, the financial press still tells their readers, "Hang tight and you will be rewarded. Over the long run, stocks can still be expected to outperform all other investments."

While it's true that for the past several years the press has celebrated the fact that hot housing markets have kept the economy from sagging further, it seems that journalists have also felt compelled to somehow work the "housing bubble" angle into their stories. Yes, during 2002, journalists did write repeatedly about the home refinance boom. Only occasionally, though, did they mention how Americans should manage their home purchases, home improvements, and home financing as part of their overall strategy to build net worth. Regardless of all of the hype about 401(k)s, 403(b)s, IRAs, and Keoghs, home equity remains the largest source of wealth for the great majority of Americans. And home financing remains their largest liability.

In fact, Jack Guttentag, finance professor emeritus at Wharton who now writes a nationally syndicated column on mortgages, recently was queried by one of his readers. This reader wondered why the media obsessed over the stock market while giving relatively little attention and advice to the wealth-building issues that relate to homes and home financing.

Jack Guttentag replied,

> "Emphatically, the media give more attention to Wall Street because they believe that consumers actively manage their stock portfolios, and therefore have a continuing interest in what is happening in the market, whereas mortgage borrowers drop their attention once their loan closes. But this view is obsolete. More than half of the mail I receive is from consumers who ask questions about managing their existing mortgages."

Professor Guttentag has just identified what will become a strong trend. Considering the hundreds of thousands of dollars (or more) that individuals and families devote to homebuying and home financing, Americans do need to learn how to manage these sums more carefully. Smart housing and home finance decisions today and continuing throughout your life will pay returns far larger than anything the great majority of Americans could ever expect to see from stocks, bonds, or other investments.[1]

SECRET # 98

Treat your home and your home financing as an investment.

If you read the personal finance articles in magazines and newspapers, more than likely you've seen many articles that tell you to exclude your home equity from your projected net worth at retirement. Financial planners or the journalists who quote them say that homes make for relatively poor investments; and because you will still need a place to live after you retire, money tied up in a house certainly won't do you much good.

1. For proof, see my book, *Value Investing in Real Estate* (Wiley, 2002).

Mortgage Secrets refutes both of these statements. Regardless of what the media reports, housing has always been the leading source of wealth for most Americans. Historically, however, the media have primarily focused on dire talk of housing peaks and bubbles. Take this quick review of headline stories and so-called expert advice from the past 50 years.

- The prices of houses seem to have reached a plateau, and there is reasonable expectancy that prices will decline. (*Time,* December 1, 1947)
- Houses cost too much for the mass market. Today's average price is around $8,000—out of reach for two-thirds of all buyers. (*Science Digest,* April 1948)
- If you have bought your house since the War . . . you have made your deal at the top of the market. . . . The days when you couldn't lose on a house purchase are no longer with us. (*House Beautiful,* November 1948)
- The goal of owning a home seems to be getting beyond the reach of more and more Americans. The typical new house today costs about $28,000. (*BusinessWeek,* September 4, 1969)
- Be suspicious of the "common wisdom" that tells you to "Buy now . . . . because continuing inflation will force home prices and rents higher and higher." (*NEA Journal,* December 1970)
- The median price of a home today is approaching $50,000. . . . Housing experts predict that in the future price rises won't be that great. (*Nation's Business,* June 1977)
- The era of easy profits in real estate may be drawing to a close. (*Money,* January 1981)
- In California . . . for example, it is not unusual to find families of average means buying $100,000 houses. . . . I'm confident prices have passed their peak. (John Wesley English and Gray Emerson Cardiff, *The Coming Real Estate Crash,* Warner Books 1980)
- The golden age of risk-free run-ups in home prices is gone. (*Money,* March 1985)
- If you're looking to buy, be careful. Rising home values are not a sure thing anymore. (*Miami Herald,* October 25, 1985)

- Most economists agree . . . [a home] will become little more than a roof and a tax deduction, certainly not the lucrative investment it was through much of the 1980s. (*Money,* April 1986)
- We're starting to go back to the time when you bought a home not for its potential money-making abilities, but rather as a nesting spot. (*Los Angeles Times,* January 31, 1993)
- Financial planners agree that houses will continue to be a poor investment. (*Kiplinger's Personal Financial Magazine,* November 1993)
- A home is where the bad investment is. (*San Francisco Examiner,* November 17, 1996).
- Your house is a roof over your head. It is not an investment. (*Everything You Know About Money Is Wrong,* Karen Ramsey, HarperCollins, 2000)

In the late 1940s, $8,000 to $10,000 seemed like an outrageous amount to pay for a house. In the late 1960s through the mid 1970s, $30,000 to $50,000 seemed well beyond anything reasonable. In the early 1980s, popular belief held that at $100,000, home prices in California could only go down. Today, similar comments about peaks and bubbles are being raised. But just as those past voices now sound foolish, so too will current opinion as we look back from the future.

Can some home prices soften or decline in the short run? Sure. They have done so before and will do so again. Local economies ebb and flow, but over periods of 5, 10, 20, or 30 years, well-selected properties will continue to register high-profit appreciation.[2]

Home Financing Magnifies Returns

Say a couple invests $10,000 in a $100,000 home. They finance their purchase with a 30-year, $90,000 mortgage at 7.75 percent. After eight years they will have paid down their mortgage balance to $81,585. With 4 percent a year appreciation for eight years, their home's value will have grown to $136,860. If we subtract the balance of $81,585 from the

2. Potential homebuyers: For more extensive discussion of this issue, see Chapter 3, "Home Ownership: How to Make It Your Best Investment," in my book, *The 106 Mistakes Homebuyers Make—and How to Avoid Them,* 3rd ed. (Wiley, 2002).

Table 10.1 **Low Appreciation Yields High Returns**

Today	
Home purchase price	$ 100,000
Original mortgage	90,000
Cash invested	10,000
Eight Years Later	
Market value @ 4% appreciation	$ 136,860
Mortgage balance	81,585
Home equity	55,275

Equity Growth Rate

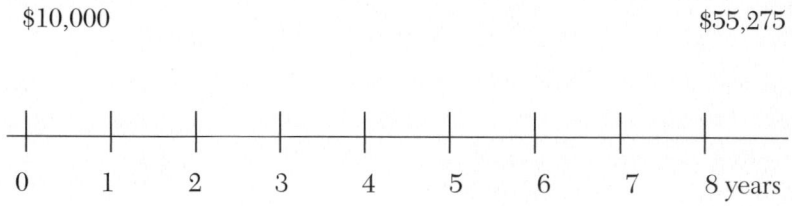

Annual growth rate of home equity = 24 percent. Of course, proportionately increasing the down payment and purchase price would still yield a 24 percent rate of return..

home's appreciated value of $136,860, we find that the couple's original $10,000 investment has increased more than fivefold to $55,275 of homeowners' equity. That result yields an after-tax annual rate of return of around 24 percent (see Table 10.1). Naturally, in recent years, lower rates of interest and high rates of appreciation have produced rates of return far in excess of 24 points.

Stocks Typically Yield Lower Results

In contrast, depending on whose numbers you use, stocks have yielded an average *pretax* return of between 9 and 12 percent a year over the longer run. On an *after-tax* basis, a 10 percent a year return on stocks is considered very good. In fact, over the long term, fewer than 2 percent of professional fund managers have been able to consistently earn after-tax returns on stocks of more than 10 to 15 percent a year.

Recall, for example, that at the end of 1965 the Dow Jones Industrial Average (DJIA) stood at 969.26. At the start of 1982, this index of blue-chip companies actually stood lower, at 884.36. During this entire 16-year period, the DJIA closed no higher than 1051.70, and it fell to as low as 577.60 in 1974.

Even if you compare stock gains during the *unprecedented* market boom that ran from 1993 (DJIA at 3,500) to early 2000 (DJIA at 11,700), you'll find home equity multiplying just as fast in many cities throughout the United States. For example, in the relatively slow growth town of Gainesville, Florida, a home bought in 1993 for $100,000 could have been sold in 2000 for $150,000. Assuming a $10,000 down payment, that $50,000 gain amounts to a fivefold increase in your investment—not counting mortgage paydown.

If instead, you had put $10,000 or $20,000 into, say, a home in boomtowns like Portland, Austin, Boston, Seattle, San Francisco, Park Cities, Denver, Boulder, Sarasota—or any one of dozens of other hot housing market cities—you would have enjoyed a tenfold (or greater) increase in your original down payment investment.

Summing Up

All things considered, an investment in a home can be expected to outperform the stock market. With a home you get the benefits of leverage. You invest a relatively small down payment, yet, you receive returns based on increases in the total value of your home. That's why even a lowly 4 percent annual rate of appreciation will nearly always outperform the price gains you might get from stocks. And not only is home ownership far less risky than stocks, but stocks won't keep you dry when it rains or warm when the weather is freezing cold.

Certainly, as you grow older, diversify your wealth into various types of investments. But don't substitute other investments for home ownership.

Future Uses of Home Equity

The financial planners derogate housing as an investment not only because they claim (erroneously) that you can earn better returns in stocks, but also because your home equity is illiquid. Wrong again. With home equity lines of credit (HELOC), refinances, and reverse annuity mortgages, you can easily extract tax-free money from your home.[3]

Moreover, as your housing needs change, you may choose to downsize. Sell the higher-priced family home and move into a lower-priced empty nester home. In doing so, you and your spouse could pocket up to a $500,000 tax-free gain. In contrast, the IRS will tax the money you withdraw from your 401(k) and other tax-deferred retirement accounts at your highest marginal ordinary income tax rates—even if a large part of those funds actually accrued through capital gains such as stock price appreciation.

Lack of Diversification

Today, with the exception of stocks for the long run, financial planners preach no gospel more loudly than that of diversification. "Never put all of your eggs into one basket," they say. No doubt, there's merit to this advice. But it doesn't apply to real estate in the way the stock enthusiasts think it does.

"Most experts argue—correctly, in my view"—writes Jonathan Clements of the *Wall Street Journal,* "that if you own your own home, you already have plenty of real estate exposure." And from *Barron's Guide to Making Investment Decisions,* the same Wall Street party line: "We will argue that one's own home [if that!] is probably enough exposure to the real estate market for the average individual investor. If you're thinking about buying [a home], please at least consider the alternatives."

Why this hostility to real estate? Well, according to this critique, real estate fails the test of diversity. If you maintain your job, your home, and your investments in the same community, you're placing too many eggs into one basket. If your employer, your industry, and your community slide into recession, your wealth portfolio could take a triple hit.

Unfortunately, this critique of homes as an investment confuses the short run with the longer run. It also mistakenly assumes that housing prices yo-yo up and down like the prices of stocks and bonds. Of course, that's hardly the case.

---

3. *Mortgage Secrets* discusses when and whether you should withdraw these monies later in this chapter.

The Short-Run Error

Unless you develop short-term ownership strategies such as fix and flip, view your home equity as long-term wealth, not wealth that you check three times a day by tuning into MSNBC. Sometimes local economies do sag. Job growth falters. Also, on occasion, home builders construct too many houses, condos, and apartments. Excess supply gluts the market.

Nevertheless, these localized downturns rarely last for more than a few years. In fact, severe downturns such as occurred in California in the early- to mid 1990s provide enormous opportunities to build home-equity wealth by trading up. I know California homebuyers who, in 1993, bit the bullet and took a mild loss on their $200,000 home. They then bought a $400,000 home that had sold three years earlier for $550,000. Today, their home is worth $800,000; they've accumulated around $500,000 in equity, and their monthly payments (due to refinancing) are only 15 percent higher than they were in 1990.

Volatility

If you own stocks, you must diversify your holdings even if you're investing for the long run. Stock prices and the profit performance of even the best of companies can plummet and remain down for decades. Name-brand highfliers of earlier eras can end up in bankruptcy. (To name just a few: Polaroid, Enron, United Airlines, WorldCom, U.S. Steel, Pan Am, and Pennsylvania Railroad.) Owning the stocks of just one or several companies can certainly expose you to financial ruin—*especially* when you plan to hold those stocks forever.

Homeowners confront no similar risk. Do you know of any decent homes that would sell today for less than they sold 5 or 10 years ago? Check the historical prices in so-called less-desirable neighborhoods. You will find that even these properties have appreciated. Certainly, individual owners can let properties run down, but I do not know of any urban, predominately owner-occupied neighborhoods in the United States where market values have declined from where they stood 10 years ago.

Plan to Build Home Equity Wealth

Most retirees today have gained greatly from the increased value of their home equity, but fortunately, most of these seniors haven't had to tap into it. Today's retirees still draw substantially from social security, company pensions, and, yes, the fantastic 1982–2002 eightfold increase in stock prices.

Tomorrow's retirees, though, can't count on the same degree of income support from social security, pensions, or stocks. No one predicts huge increases in future social security payments. (Indeed, approaching insolvency more often occupies the stage of debate.) Fewer and fewer companies offer guaranteed pensions. And who knows where stock prices might land 10, 20, or 30 years from now. Further, what will happen to those stock values when tens of millions of boomers try to liquidate their 401(k)s and IRAs?

In a world that presents great uncertainty, one constant remains: As long as the United States continues to grow its population and its economy, housing values and rent levels will continue to go up. Unless you know that you can safely and surely secure your financial future in other ways, don't leave your home equity gains to chance. Choose your home and your home financing with a *calculating* eye on the future.

SECRET # 99

Stay alert for opportunities to refinance.

With newspapers and magazines widely publicizing the refi boom of 2002, you might be surprised to learn that tens of millions of Americans still hold mortgages with interest rates above 7.5 percent. Even among the people who have recently refinanced, more than 50 percent held mortgages with interest rates greater than 8 percent. Amazing. People will drive across town to use a $3 coupon, but they consistently miss out on opportunities to save tens of thousands of dollars through refinancing.

Undoubtedly, the hassles of applying for a mortgage push people to procrastinate. A friend of mine who recently refinanced a 9 percent mortgage on an investment property had actually placed this task on his "to do" list three years earlier. During that period of procrastination, he could have profitably refinanced two or three times. His savings on interest and additional equity buildup would have totaled $15,000. That's a steep price to pay for procrastination.

Even filling out a mortgage application doesn't create enough pain to offset that kind of money. Should interest rates at some future time make refinancing profitable for you, work through the numbers. Don't procrastinate as do millions of property owners. Look closely at your cost savings and equity gains. Imagine how you might enjoy that money later. Measure the time required now against the gains to be realized. Translate that gain into a dollars-per-hour figure. You'll probably earn well in excess of $1,000 an hour. For most people, those are pretty good wages.

Lack of Awareness

Return to my friend Sue with her current 7.75 percent mortgage that was originated in 1993 (*Mortgage Secret* #97). She could have refinanced in 1994 at 6.5 percent and saved a vault load of cash. Why didn't she? Lack of awareness. She believed the 2 percent rule which says, "You can't profitably refi unless you lower your current rate by at least two points." Dear reader, you may be able to refi profitably even if your rate drops by just .50 percent. To answer the refi question, always calculate. Never rely on rules of thumb or back of the envelope guesstimates. Compound interest can easily play tricks with casual conclusions.

Equity Buildup, Not Merely Lower Payments

Let's return to that infamous no-cost loan (*Mortgage Secret* #97). Say your friendly loan rep calls with her "have I got a deal for you" pitch. "How would you like to drop your monthly payments by $200 a month—and it won't cost you a cent in fees or closing costs." Right now, about 25 percent of all refis are responding to this seemingly no-lose proposition.

Many borrowers fail to realize, though, that a good part of that $200 a month savings will result because the lender puts you back into a 30-year term. Assume you owe $200,000 at 7.5 percent with 21 years remaining on your mortgage. Your payments run around $1,578 per month. The loan rep says, "I can get you into a 7.0 percent loan that will drop your payments to $1,331. And it won't cost you any money out-of-pocket."

Who could turn this deal down? Seems like found money of $247 a month. But later on, this free lunch will cost you a large check—or to be precise—108 large checks. This refinance dramatically slows your equity buildup. Table 10.2 shows how the two loans compare after 10 years.

What you saved in monthly payments, you more than lost in equity buildup. Plus, your new loan runs for 30 more years, whereas the old loan would pay off in just 21 years. If you really wanted to use a no-cost loan, you could refinance profitably into a 7.0 percent (or maybe 6.75 percent) 20-year loan. Your equity would build even faster—after 10 years, you would owe $133,459.

Why do loan reps push the 30-year refi? Because the immediate monthly savings look so much better. With the 30-year loan at 7 percent, your payment drops by $247 per month. With a refinance into a 20-year loan, the payment slips just $28 to $1,550. Regrettably, most Americans think in terms of low monthly payments now. As a reader of *Mortgage Secrets*, you know better. Whether choosing home financing or refinancing, give as much regard to equity buildup as you do the amount of the monthly payments.

Table 10.2 **Equity Buildup Comparison**

	Interest Rate	*Current Remaining Term*	*Current Balance*	*Balance after 10 Years*
Old loan	7.5%	21 years	$200,000	$141,549
New loan	7.0%	30 years	$200,000	$171,675

The Equity Killer: No Cash Closings

As you saw with my friend Sue, many of these supposedly no-cost refis actually charge large amounts of fees at closing, but add them into the mortgage balance. When this add-on occurs along with a renewed 30-year term, equity buildup is set back years. Never sign up for such a loan. The money you lose will far exceed your apparent immediate gain. Get the loan rep to run amortization schedules for your various loan alternatives, or click on to any of the mortgage calculator Web sites and then compare the respective equity buildups. Make your loan decision with the facts in front of you. How much will that lower payment cost you in future equity?

SECRET # 100

Use refinancing to create other benefits.

Although most people refinance to lower their monthly payments, astute borrowers may use refinancing for other types of cash management and wealth-building purposes, such as:

- *Equity buildup.* About 20 percent of all refi borrowers are selecting shorter-term loans. Lenders are originating record numbers of 10-, 15-, and 20-year mortgages. As *Mortgage Secret #15* revealed, shorter-term loans build equity proportionately much faster than the more common 30-year amortization period. After 5 years, a 15-year loan will show a lower balance than will a 30-year loan after 10 years of payments.
- *Pay off credit cards.* Use lower-interest mortgage money to pay off higher-interest credit cards and installment accounts, but take this route only if you possess enough self-discipline to stymie your high-interest borrowing. Lenders are seeing increasing numbers of people who take out bill-payer refis and then run their bills right back up to where they were. They're still in debt, but now lack the cushion of home equity.

- *Eliminate mortgage insurance.* In certain circumstances, the law permits you to cancel your PMI (see *Mortgage Secret #103*). If your home has appreciated, however, or you've created value through improvements, you can accomplish the same savings with an 80 percent LTV refinance.
- *Switch an ARM to a fixed-rate mortgage (FRM).* If inflation appears to be heating up, you might go to the safety of a fixed-rate mortgage. Also, if you financed with a short-term horizon that now appears longer term, the FRM might prove the better choice—especially if FRM rates sit relatively low.
- *ARM to ARM.* This strategy can work well when ARM rates are hitting lows and you can refi into another AMR with lower caps, a slower moving index, a slimmer margin, or more liberal terms of assumption. Even if your current payment amount doesn't change, you win if the new ARM includes more favorable features.
- *FRM to ARM.* If you're just a few years away from selling your home, consider switching from an FRM to an ARM. Because your need for long-term interest rate protection has ended, save money with the ARM. Also, if your new ARM includes a good assumption clause, this feature could enhance the sales appeal of your house.
- *Streamline refi.* Here, *Mortgage Secrets* wants to remind readers that FHA and VA mortgages include a unique and desirable feature called streamlining. When rates fall, FHA/VA borrowers can refinance without an appraisal, credit check, income verification, or qualifying ratios. In the refi boom of the early- to mid 1990s, many Californians could not dump their high-rate mortgages from the 1980s because the value of their homes had dropped, thus leaving them upside down, or they were unemployed or underemployed and thus could not meet the qualifying standards. Thanks to streamlining, no FHA/VA borrower faced that frustrating dilemma.
- *The good life.* Although many homeowners do squander their home equity on new cars and trucks, boats, jet skis, European vacations, and junior's college expenses, regrettably *Mortgage Secrets* cannot abide such frivolities. You cannot build the wealth you

will need later if you dine on seed corn today. As to junior, tell him to get a job or take out a student loan.

In addition to the previously mentioned benefits, a refinance can serve at least one more important purpose: Generate funds for additional investment.

SECRET # 101

Refinance and safely invest the proceeds.

First, *Mortgage Secrets* would like to direct your attention to the word *invest.* In recent years, promoters of every type of cockeyed scheme and speculation have claimed to offer investment opportunities. Peddlers of financial products, purveyors of financial services, demagoguing politicians, and even new car dealers tell us to buy what they are selling because we would be making a good investment. Commodities, jewelry, condo timeshares, baseball cards, and old Mason jars all are marketed as worthy investments. Even items we used to call luxury goods or extravagances such as $5,000 wristwatches and $50,000 cars are now advertised as investments.

Wealth-Building Investments

If you're going to borrow against your home equity to invest, choose assets that will yield both a growing stream of income and a near certain increase in value. Naturally, *Mortgage Secrets* favors rental houses and apartments. In terms of cash flows, no other asset beats income properties. In terms of inflation protection, no other asset beats income properties. Yet, when inflation falls, interest rates fall. Property cash flows go up due to lower mortgage payments. Values go up because of increased consumer buying power. With rental properties, you win when inflation runs rampant; and you win as it declines.

In addition, rental properties give numerous tax advantages such as tax-free, cash-out refinances (to further pyramid your wealth), noncash tax deductions for depreciation, tax-free trade-up exchanges, and deferred taxes on capital gains through the use of installment sale contracts.[4]

Double Leverage

To pursue this investment strategy, you would use a cash-out refi (or a home equity line of credit) to raise, say, $25,000 or $50,000 (perhaps more). You would then apply that money as a down payment to acquire a rental property.

Your interest costs (at today's rates) should total less than 7 percent, but the rental income from your property should yield (after expenses) 8 to 11 percent. With this spread between borrowing costs and yield, your leveraged rate of return would skyrocket. Yet, if you chose your rental property according to sound investment principles (as explained in my books on real estate investing), you could achieve these very high returns with little risk. (*Mortgage Secrets* would never advise you to gamble your home equity with risky ventures.)

What about Stocks?

During the late bull run, numerous financial writers and advisors urged homeowners to cash out their home equity and invest it in the stock market. In his 1997 best-selling book, *The Strategy: A Homeowner's Guide to Wealth Creation* (Key Porter Books) Garth Turner painted a wealthy, risk-free future for homeowners.

> Imagine wealth virtually without risk. It's now possible thanks to the amazing convergence of low interest rates, solidly rising financial markets in the long run and an economic rebound in North America that will last well into the new millennium. . . . Today you can dip into your real estate equity and put that money into financial assets with confidence as long as you are a long-term investor.

Turner goes on to tell his readers, "The new rules of real estate: [a home] is now just shelter, not an investment. . . . What you ultimately want and need is wealth, not a house. . . . The future is in financial assets, not in real estate."

---

4. For more details, see my book, *Investing in Real Estate,* 4th ed., (Wiley, 2003).

Likewise, in his best-selling and highly influential book, *Stocks for the Long Run, 3rd ed.* (McGraw-Hill, 2002), esteemed Wharton professor Jeremy Siegel also enthuses over stocks as the salvation for all investors who will keep the faith.[5] "Buy and hold through the market's ups and downs," Siegel advises. You will become wealthy. Virtually guaranteed. Similar to Garth Turner, Siegel suggests (though not so emphatically) that homeowners leverage up their home financing and put the cash proceeds into the stock market.

The Reasoning

From a casual perspective, this idea seems to merit attention. Borrow mortgage money at a tax-deductible rate of 5 to 7 percent. Put that cash in a tax-sheltered, stock-based retirement plan. History shows that over the long run you can expect stocks to yield returns of 10 to 12 percent a year—albeit with bumps and jolts along the way. Hang on for the ride, and you will eventually end up with far more money. Why let that wonderful opportunity to borrow cheap and invest high go to waste?

Sounds pretty good, and it could work. If stocks for the long run do yield a near certain 10 to 12 percent annual return, this strategy will pay off big.

The Fallacy

Unfortunately, the 10 to 12 percent stock return figure doesn't hold up under close review. Stock market volatility creates far more uncertainty than the stock enthusiasts admit. If your retirement years coincide with a bear market, you could end up flipping burgers at McDonald's, or maybe greeting customers at Wal-Mart. Contrary to the stock enthusiasts' claims, financial assets do display considerable long-term risk. That's why *Mortgage Secrets* favors long-term investing in real estate rather than stocks: Not only do safely leveraged real estate returns outperform the stock market's supposed yield of 10 to 12 percent, but real estate (housing) experiences far less downside volatility yet gives near certain upside potential.

---

5. For a detailed critique of Siegel's analysis and conclusions, see my book, *Value Investing in Real Estate* (Wiley, 2002).

Less Risk with Real Estate

For proof positive that houses experience fewer and less severe price slides than stocks, try this experiment. Call several mortgage lenders. Ask them if you can borrow 80 percent of a home's purchase price for a period of 15 to 30 years at a fixed rate of interest. Of course you can. Now, ask those same lenders—or even your stock-touting brokerage firm—if they will make you a similar deal on a portfolio of stocks. "What? Are you crazy?" they'd respond. Or just as likely, they'd tell you to pay cash for your stocks with money borrowed with a *low-interest-rate home equity loan.*

This simple, commonsense approach to risk assessment speaks volumes. If stocks were less risky than real estate, why won't lenders grant stock portfolio loans for the same duration, terms, and cost that are widely available with mortgage loans? (Remember, too, property loans never include a margin call.)

More Income with Real Estate

Rental properties outperform stocks as an *investment* because they yield a dependable and growing flow of income. Over time, rents for well-kept homes and apartments consistently go up. In contrast, at current market valuation, most stocks pay dividends of only 1 to 3 percent a year. More than 125 companies in the S&P 500 pay no dividends at all; therefore, stocks include a large component of speculation. You buy stocks not for their income, but because you think you can later sell them for a higher price to someone else—and of course, your buyer feels the same. But when confidence in the "greater fool" theory wanes, the bear roars. Stock prices free-fall.

All true investments yield enough current income to justify their current price. If you're paying for hoped-to-be future outcomes, you're speculating, not investing.

Good Idea: You Choose

In briefly comparing the investment merits of stocks versus rental properties, *Mortgage Secrets* does not want you to lose sight of the basic theme of this chapter. As Garth Turner writes in *The Strategy* . . .

> The greatest threat facing North Americans is not having enough capital to finance decades in retirement. And one of the greatest assets you have for fighting that threat is your home. It can help save you, but only if you follow The Strategy.

Mortgage Secrets agrees that this threat is real and that you can profitably use 5 to 7 percent mortgage money to build wealth faster by *investing* in assets that pay considerably more. But you must choose for yourself whether this wealth management strategy is one you want to pursue. And if so, which investments will most likely help you reach your personal and financial destination.

SECRET # 102

Never buy biweekly baloney.

After closing a mortgage, some lenders go back to their borrowers to extract even more money. Preying on their borrowers' inability to perform compound interest calculations, these lenders promise to prepare a new early payoff system that will permit their borrowers to save thousands in interest—for a small fee of, say, just $395. Under these plans you pay half of your regular payment 26 times a year (biweekly) instead of the full payment 12 times a year.

Mortgage Secrets calls this type of scam biweekly baloney. Not because you can't profit by prepaying your mortgage. You can. Rather, it's because you need not pay your lender a fee to do so. Absent a prepayment penalty clause in your contract, you can prepay any time you want in any amount(s) you choose.

How to Achieve an Early Payoff

Your lender (or more precisely, your mortgage servicing company) wants you to believe that setting up a new payment schedule and processing all of those biweekly payments deserves an extra administrative fee. It doesn't. In fact, rather than give yourself more bills to pay, all you need to do each month is write a check for your scheduled payment; then write another check for $100 (or whatever amount you choose), and attach a note declaring that sum prepayment of principal.

Financial Tables, $19.95 Calculator, or Web Sites

Under the biweekly plan, you (in effect) pay one extra monthly payment per year. Typically, that prepay cuts the term of a 30-year fixed-rate mortgage down to about 22.5 years. Under the payment system proposed by *Mortgage Secrets,* you can create the same result by dividing your regular monthly payment by 12; then use that amount to supplement your monthly checks.

If you want to pay more or less than one-twelfth of your regular payment, you can easily calculate how quickly your loan will pay off and how much interest you will save. Nearly all major bookstores carry books that show compound interest tables. Simply multiply or divide the appropriate numbers, and you can evaluate the results of any proposed schedule of prepayments. (Note: Buy *compound interest tables* that show the interest rate factors, not precalculated mortgage payment books).

Although some people still rely on printed compound interest tables, most others use either a financial calculator (which you can buy at Wal-Mart or Office Depot for $19.95 or less) or the mortgage calculators available on a variety of Web sites such as www.hsh.com, www.bankrate.com, and www.mtgprofessor.com. If you do run through some prepay numbers, you will see that even modest prepay sums regularly made will save you years of mortgage payments and tens of thousands of dollars in interest.

Should You Prepay?

Lenders report that several million Americans with 30-year mortgages are now regularly prepaying their mortgages. Most of these people are making a costly mistake. Do you know why? You do if you recall *Mortgage Secret #15.* Rather than prepay their 30-year loans, these homeowners should refinance into a shorter-term mortgage. In addition to achieving early payoff, they could save big dollars in interest each year because 15-year loans carry a lower interest rate than 30-year loans. On a $200,000 loan the lower interest rate would save the borrowers at least $750 to $1,000 per year right off the top—unless interest rates have turned against you, such as the current refi interest rate for 15-year loans sits above the rate you're now paying for a 30-year loan.

Before you enter a regular system of prepay, first work through the numbers vis-à-vis a 15-year refi. In the present interest rate climate, the 15-year refi will yield much superior gains.

Qualifying and Flexibility. Many homeowners reflexively prefer a 30-year loan because they believe it's easier to qualify for a 30-year loan. Of course, that's true only if you borrow similar amounts. But as *Mortgage Secret #15* shows, when qualifying for a loan presents a problem, reduce the amount you are borrowing. Your smaller loan at 15 years will build equity faster than a larger loan at 30 years.

Homeowners also combine prepay with the 30-year loan because they like flexibility. "Yes, we're prepaying now, but if times get tough, we want the flexibility to cut back." This "tough times" problem can be dealt with more profitably, however, by maintaining a cash reserve or a home equity line of credit.

Loss of a Tax Deduction. Unbelievably, some advisers argue against prepayment and for 30-year loans as a way to keep the tax deduction for interest as high as possible. In responding to a published query, financial planner Marty David urges a homeowner couple (both aged 52) to dump their 15-year mortgage that's within 8 years of payoff in favor of a new 30-year loan. "I would recommend refinancing and getting a 30-year fixed mortgage," says David. This ensures that you will be paying mostly interest for the first 10 years, and get the largest tax benefits of mortgage interest. Think of it this way: The federal government has promised to pay you 30 percent of any interest payment you make (assuming you're in a 30 percent tax bracket). If you reduce your [total] interest payments, the checks from the government will stop coming sooner."

Folks, that's precisely the wrong way to think about it, yet I repeatedly see this misguided view. These people are 52 years old! They need to build as much wealth as possible now. To correctly address their dilemma, one need only calculate how much their net worth will differ in 10 years. Using the financial planner's approach, this couple will be far poorer than if they had stayed with a shorter-term mortgage.

Yes, they will have paid less in income taxes, but no one should try to minimize taxes *per se.* Tax-shelter promoters have lured many investors into financial ruin while baiting their hooks with that appealing promise. Rather than minimize taxes, you want to maximize after-tax wealth.[6] Regrettably, investors and financial advisers alike confuse these two very different—and often conflicting—objectives. Shorten the term of your mortgage through prepay if it enhances your net worth. Forget trying to minimize taxes as a goal separate from wealth building.

Alternative Investments. Ultimately, your decision to prepay turns on whether you can earn a higher risk adjusted rate of return on your investments. Throughout the 1990s, investment writers said, "Leverage the house to the hilt and put the cash into stocks." Take that mortgage prepay money and stick it into your tax-sheltered retirement account. Essentially, then, the prepay issue revisits the pros and cons discussed in *Mortgage Secret #86.* Fairly considered, stocks, bonds, and rental properties do typically offer a riskier use of home equity funds; however, between home equity, rental property, stock and bond alternatives, *Mortgage Secrets* recommends that wealth builders choose rental properties—as long as you still retain a comfortable cushion of home equity and cash reserves. For wealth preservers, that is for those people who have already accumulated the financial wealth and security they will need in life, *Mortgage Secrets* recommends mortgage prepay. As noted before, though, you must choose for yourself.

SECRET # 103

Cancel your PMI. Get a refund from FHA.

If you now or in the future pay mortgage insurance premiums (PMI, MIP/FHA), you're wasting money that could otherwise be slicing down your principal balance. You want to eliminate this expense as soon as possible.

6. The wealthiest 5 percent of all Americans pay 80 percent of total IRS collections. Obviously, these people have emphasized wealth building over tax reduction.

Although the rules for canceling PMI whip through some twists and turns that can confuse more than enlighten, these basics should put you on the right track.

Cancel Your PMI

For conventional loans (non-FHA) closed after July 29, 1999, upon your request lenders must cancel your PMI premium payments once your outstanding mortgage balance drops to 80 percent of your home's original purchase price. Should you fail to ask, the lender must automatically cancel when the balance hits 78 percent of your purchase price; however, because on a 30-year loan your paydown to 78 to 80 percent won't occur for more than 11 years, you need to look elsewhere for relief.

The Market Value Test

When your loan has been sold to Fannie Mae or Freddie Mac, the major players in the secondary mortgage market, you get a break. Fannie and Freddie apply a market value test:

1. *Two-year mark.* After your loan passes the two-year mark, you may cancel anytime as long as your loan balance totals no more than 75 percent of the *current* market value of the property.
2. *Five-year mark.* After your loan passes the five-year mark, you may cancel anytime as long as your loan balance does not exceed 80 percent of the property's *current* market value.
3. *Appraisal required.* To exercise either of these cancellation options, you must provide a market value appraisal that's acceptable to Fannie or Freddie as well as the originating lender. Acceptance cannot be arbitrarily denied.
4. *Credit.* Excellent payment record on your mortgage. No 30-day lates within the most recent 12 months. No 60-day lates within the past 24 months; however, the lender will not again run a full credit check.
5. *Second mortgage.* A home equity line of credit or second mortgage will mandate stricter review and lower LTV ratios.

6. *Rental property.* Stricter review and lower LTV ratios will also apply if you've moved out of your home and converted it into a rental.

Given the fact that PMI premiums typically cost anywhere from $75 to $200 a month (or more), figuring out ways to terminate this coverage can certainly pay off. Here are three ideas:

- *Improvements.* You don't need to wait for market appreciation to boost the value of your property. Improve it. Borrow, say, $7,500 to $10,000 to create value; then pay off the loan with the money saved by canceling the PMI premiums.
- *Prepayment.* If you lack ready cash, borrow money to pay down the mortgage balance. Execute an 80–10–10 plan retroactively. Pay off the loan with your mortgage interest and PMI savings.
- *Refinance.* On occasion, you might find it profitable to refi out of your mortgage insurance. Tom Warne, president of Majestic Mortgage, recently told how one of his customers refinanced at the same interest rate, yet by dropping his $168 per month PMI premium still managed to save money.

In other words, if it looks like you could get stuck paying PMI for four or five more years, see if you can figure a way to otherwise meet the cancellation rules. PMI savings represent free money. After you've closed your loan, you gain no benefit from PMI. Get rid of it.

Portfolio Lenders

If your lender holds on to your mortgage rather than selling to Fannie or Freddie, you're at the mercy of that lender. You can either wait out the time necessary to drop your loan balance down to 80 percent of your home's original purchase price, or accept whatever cancellation rules the lender makes.

Consequently, when first interviewing a lender about a mortgage (if your loan requires mortgage insurance), ask about its plans. Will it sell the loan to some firm other than Fannie or Freddie? Will the lender retain the loan in its own portfolio? Either way, try to pin down what hoops you must jump through to get the PMI cancelled as soon as possible.

FHA Benefits: Cancellations and Refunds

Year-by-year, FHA looks better and better. That's why this year nearly one million homebuyers will choose to originate an FHA home mortgage. Specifically with respect to mortgage insurance, FHA has cut its up-front premium from 2.5 percent to 1.5 percent. In addition, for loans originated after January 1, 2001, FHA will automatically terminate the monthly MIP premium when the loan balance drops to 78 percent of the property's purchase price. Not as good as the rules of Freddie or Fannie, but still an improvement—and FHA promises more to come as long as borrower defaults and foreclosures don't test fund solvency.

This past year, more than 200,000 borrowers who paid off their FHA loans through sale or refinancing also received a bonus from FHA of $700 (on average). Unlike PMI companies, FHA shares its mortgage insurance fund surpluses with borrowers whose long-term payment record (prior to payoff) has remained free of major blemishes.

SECRET # 104

Negotiate out of escrow.

Nearly all lenders require low-down-payment borrowers to pay their homeowners insurance premiums, HOA fees, and property tax payments into a lender-managed escrow fund. In addition, many high-equity borrowers also are required to fund escrow accounts. The balances in these accounts often total upward of $5,000, yet many lenders pay no (or only nominal) interest on these funds. Even worse, I've seen some lenders charge administrative fees to borrowers for the privilege of letting the bank keep their money for them. Contrary to what many lenders lead their borrowers to believe, however, no law or regulation requires these accounts. I recently saw an escrow statement with this heading:

Initial Escrow Account Statement
Required by Section 12(c)(1) of
Real Estate Settlement Procedures Act (RESPA)

RESPA requires the account statement; it does not require the escrow account. It is your loan agreement that imposes that disadvantage on borrowers. As such, it's fair game for negotiations. Naturally, borrowers with strong credit profiles and high down payments can press their cases hardest, but even when the lender won't set aside the escrow account, you could ask them to at least pay you a decent rate of interest. Alternatively, you could buy a certificate of deposit in an amount that exceeds all sums needed for the escrow account; then pledge that CD to the lender and pay your taxes, insurance, and HOA fees yourself.

As to complaints about escrow accounts, HUD receives piles of them. Here are the most important ones:

- *Escrow waiver fee.* Some lenders will try to charge you several hundred dollars to waive their escrow account rules. Don't pay it. It's pure garbage.
- *Overcollection.* HUD limits the amount that lenders can collect and hold in your escrow account. Generally, they're permitted a two-month cushion plus accrued pro rata (usually 1/12 per month) for all future disbursements that year. To precisely calculate your lender's maximums, go to the FAQ section on escrows at hud.gov. There you'll find an easy-to-use fill-in-the-blank worksheet.
- *Discounts and late fees.* Your insurer, property tax office, or HOA may offer discounts for early payment and assess late fees against tardy debtors. At present, no law requires lenders to pay your bills according to a time schedule that minimizes your costs. When the lender snoozes, you lose. Until pending federal legislation passes (the Mortgage Loan Consumer Protection Act), you must cajole and complain to make sure you don't pay more than necessary.
- *Return of escrow money.* No law or regulation currently requires lenders to return your money in a timely manner after you pay off your loan (refi, property sale). Often 30 to 90 days may pass before a clerk in mortgage servicing decides to cut you a check. This, too, may change with new laws. Until then, cajole and complain. Certainly, try to get your check at closing. But don't expect to see it unless your lender voluntarily agrees.

Within the context of your big-bucks mortgage, ill-managed escrow accounts and lost interest may seem like small potatoes. "Why worry over a few hundred dollars?" you might say to yourself. But would you complain to your grocer, dentist, and dry cleaners if they overcharged you "a few hundred dollars" a year? Sure you would. So, display the same moxie when dealing with your mortgage lender.

SECRET # 105

Just say no to home equity loans.

"Cash out your home equity while rates are low," "Use your home equity as a checkbook," "Take that vacation you've always wanted," "You've earned it, now use your home for the good things in life you couldn't enjoy before," "Pay down your credit card balances, buy a new car, consolidate loans—just 3.9 percent interest."

You've seen the ads. They're everywhere: radio, television, newspapers, and dinner-hour telephone calls. Lenders are pushing home equity loans with reckless abandon. Americans have encumbered themselves with more than $1 trillion in home equity debt. In fact, to call it home "equity" debt stretches the semantics because a growing number of Americans are now upside down with second, third, and sometimes fourth mortgages. Millions owe more than their home is worth. They're locked into debt for as far into the future as they can imagine.

The Wealth Destroyer

Just 25 years ago, most homeowners optimistically counted off the years and months that would pass before they were able to pay off their home loans. Take out a second mortgage (as home equity loans were then called)—unthinkable! Only dire emergencies could force such imprudent borrowing. That's why nearly all members of Tom Brokaw's the Greatest Generation crossed into retirement as homeowners free and clear.

From Fiscal Watchdogs to Selling Loan Products

Sometime in the mid to late 1970s, banks changed. Loans became products that banks wanted to sell. They reversed their long-established role as fiscal watchdogs. Rather than counsel people against the evils of needless borrowing, bankers blitzed the public. Banks mass-mailed unsolicited credit cards to people they had never seen or heard of.

"Spend, borrow; borrow, spend," the bankers urged. "No credit, slow credit, bad credit, no problem. If you own your own home, we've got a loan for you. No equity needed." No wonder that bankruptcies have climbed to levels 10 times higher than they were several decades ago. The loose-pocketed purveyors of credit are now reaping what they have sowed.

Weakness of Will and Financial Discipline

In adopting the sales approach, the bankers knew their marks. They knew that millions of people would jump at the chance to spend and borrow now, and then think about the destructive consequences later. You may have read news articles that talk about "the shrinking middle class." In its place we're seeing great growth in families and households with little or no positive net worth. Quite the opposite is true, too—great growth in the number of people who are prospering. And no, income differences don't primarily explain the wide disparities.

What does account for these discrepancies? Danko and Stanley (*The Millionaire Next Door*) coined the terms UAWs (under accumulators of wealth) and PAWs (prodigious accumulators of wealth). The critical distinction: patterns of spending, borrowing, saving, and investing. On a scale of 1–10, UAWs score 8–10 on spending and borrowing; 0–3 on saving and investing. PAWs reverse those scores: 8–10 on saving and investing; 3–6 on spending and borrowing.

Just Say No

Home equity borrowing vanquishes your capacity to build wealth. If you do use it, use it only for productive investment that offers low risk for good returns, as mentioned earlier in this chapter. Never dine on seed corn. In contrast, the data on home equity loans overwhelmingly show that borrowers most frequently put these funds into consumption, including *ill-considered* home improvements.

What about bill consolidation, or paying off high-interest-rate credit card balances? Again, prudence says no.

Rather than paying less interest, this approach often leads to even larger amounts going to interest and higher amounts of debt. Why? Because borrowers who wrap their credit card balances and other bills into home equity loans (or refinances) temporarily minimize the pain of debt. Yet, with a longer term and lower payments, the debt generates higher long-term costs. Even worse, many borrowers run their credit card balances climb right back up to where they were previously. "Uh-oh, better up the home equity limit or refi again. Thank goodness the home went up $10,000 in value last year." Wealth destruction continues.

What to Look for in Home Equity Loans

If after careful review of the numbers you still decide to load up your home with debt, at least closely examine the terms of your home equity loan (lump sum borrowing) or home equity line of credit (spend your equity directly through the checks or credit card the bank gives you). Borrow with the same savvy you would apply to any other home finance agreement that you would enter into, as discussed throughout *Mortgage Secrets.* After all, no matter what cute marketing terms the lender coins, a home equity loan carries the same types of terms, conditions, obligations, and rights of foreclosure as does any other mortgage.

No, let me revise that statement. Don't merely borrow with savvy; borrow with magnifying-glass scrutiny. Lender hype and fine-print gotchas multiply with home equity loans.

Most people pursue purchase mortgages or refinancing out of need. These loans are bought as much as they are sold. Not true with home equity loans. Ninety percent of the time, lenders *sell* these loans. Relative to their dollar volume, lenders spend far more to promote and market home equity loans. Also, predatory lenders stalk the jungles of home equity lending in fierce competition with other members of their species.

Specifically, here are several of the more important terms and conditions to watch out for:

- *ARMs.* Adjustable-rate mortgages account for most home equity loans. Scrutinize caps, adjustment periods, and margins.
- *Teaser rates.* Nearly two-thirds of home equity loans start with teaser rates. How long will it last? How high can it jump?
- *Prepayment penalties.* Great teaser rates often come with prepayment penalties. Lenders don't want you to grab a below-market rate for three or six months and then bail out before they've extracted their pound of flesh.
- *Balloon payments.* When does the loan fall due? Is it callable prior to that date? If you want to renew, must you requalify? Must the lender order a new appraisal?
- *Garbage fees.* Usually not as bad as with purchase/refi mortgages, but some lenders will sting you if you're not swatting as necessary.
- *Maintenance and inactivity fees.* Some borrowers set up home equity lines of credit only to be used in emergencies. The lender may require you to either borrow some stated minimum amount, or pay a fee for the privilege of refraining.

Note also that an open line of home equity credit—whether used or not—could reduce your credit score. If you plan to refinance or buy another property anytime soon, weigh this borrowing within the context of your total credit profile. Might the credit scoring program judge you to be extending yourself too far?

SECRET # 106

Trouble, trouble, what to do?

Given the high tide of delinquencies, foreclosures, and bankruptcies rolling over the country, mortgage lenders have decided to approach troubled borrowers with a velvet glove and an olive branch rather than the iron fist of lawyers and legal process. Within the past year or so, the *Mortgage Banker* has published a variety of articles with titles such as, "Compassionate Servicing," "Rescuing Latepayers," "The Delinquency

Story," and "Wells Fargo Implements [Freddie Mac's] Early Resolution System."

Borrowers Won't Listen

As it turns out, though, borrowers all too often rebuff their lender's peaceful problem solving. Why? Because they won't open their mail or answer their telephone. They turn tail against anything or anyone that looks like or sounds like a collection effort.

To move past this avoidance mentality, First Nationwide Mortgage has even tried to disguise its "please come in and talk with us" letters. Instead of those offensive pink past-due notices, First Nationwide has placed its pleas for loan workout in envelopes that look like wedding invitations or greeting cards.

Yet, even that effort gained only a 13 percent reply rate. Yes, that creative collection effort clearly beat the ordinary response rate of 2 percent, but 13 percent still leaves the majority of troubled borrowers in hot water with temperature rising.

What to Do

When you suspect that you might encounter financial difficulties, call your mortgage servicer. Better to put on a life jacket before you need it than wait until your lungs are half-filled and you're going down for the third time.

"If you know you're going to have heart surgery, we can suspend your payments until you recover," says Paula Edwards, a workout and loss mitigation official with Countrywide Home Loans. "But we can't do anything if we don't know. I've helped all sorts of people—mechanics, doctors, judges, professors. But only when they call."

Although early beats late, late beats never. Amazingly, among all of the borrowers who do eventually seek peaceful resolution, 85 percent are almost in sight of the courthouse steps. By then, their legal costs, past-due payments, late fees, and escrow shortages can amount to a staggering sum. To succeed in workout, a borrower need bring only two things: a willingness to eventually pay, and some foreseeable and provable steady source of income. (For a look at major workout alternatives, please read through Figure 10.1.)

Before a lender enters into a mortgage workout, it will first try to learn the real cause of the problem. It will then judge whether the borrower stands a good chance of financial recovery. With this assessment in view, the lender can choose from one of the following workout alternatives:

- *Forbearance.* This alternative can succeed when the borrower suffers a temporary setback. Normally, the lender will agree to reduce or suspend payments for 6 to 24 months; then when the borrower can afford it, a new payment amount is figured that will eventually get the borrower caught up.
- *Modification.* When good faith borrowers suffer a permanent setback, senders may sometimes rewrite the loan to extend the terms, lower the interest rate, or both. This loan modification will hopefully result in a payment amount that the borrower can pay without difficulty.
- *Advances.* When a borrower has missed fewer than 12 payments on an FHA/VA loan, the lender may bring the loan current by advancing funds to the investor on the borrower's behalf. In return, the borrower signs a note promising to pay back the advance—but without interest.
- *Deed in lieu of foreclosure.* Rather than suffer the stigma, costs, and stress of foreclosure, some deep-in-debt borrowers maybe be able to just give the property to their lender. If the lender accepts this offer, it then releases the borrower from all personal liability under their mortgage and promissory note.

  In some cases, the FHA will even pay the borrowers $500 to $1,000 to move out of their home and deed their property to FHA.
- *Short sale (short payoff).* Sometimes in times of economic distress, borrowers want to sell their home, but they owe more than the property is worth. To facilitate the sale, lenders may accept a loan payoff that's less than the outstanding balance on the mortgage.

(Continues on next page)

Figure 10.1 Alternatives for Workouts

- *VA refunding*. The Department of Veterans Affairs (VA) sometimes buys delinquent VA loans from lenders and takes over the servicing. The VA then tries to structure a loan plan that the veteran borrower can handle safely.

  In any workout situation, the lender will weigh many factors. "We don't want to set you up to fail," a Los Angeles family was told by John Plaisted, a workout specialist with Countrywide.

  But to achieve a workout of any sort, loan counselors must assess the real reasons for the delinquency, and they must judge whether the borrowers truly want to keep their home. Most importantly, counselors must be able to find and talk to the borrowers. Lenders are the enemy only if they are forced to be. To start the workout rolling, borrowers must not hide from their problems. They must sit down for candid conversation.

Figure 10.1 (continued)

For years, lenders have tried their best to bury people in debt. So in the future, should your mortgage payments ever weigh more than you can bear, act smart. Give your lenders the chance to help you dig out.

CONCLUSION:

You Can Live on the House

Financial planners and the personal finance magazines routinely tell Americans to load up with stocks for retirement. "The U.S. stock market," says *Smart Money* (September 2002) is still the best place for the long-term investor." As to homes, buy one, if you must, but only as a comfortable place to live. Certainly don't think of it as a bank account with a white picket fence. Apart from the supposedly *low* appreciation of just 3 to 5 percent a year, "There's no liquidity in property. You can't take that unused bedroom to the supermarket to buy groceries," says *BusinessWeek* in quoting financial planner, Thomas Grzymala.

The New Rule of Personal Financial Management

Absurdly, the previously cited historical, clichéd advice still passes for wisdom among the financial cognoscenti. Yet, it completely ignores these six critical facts about homes as investments:

- *High returns through leverage.* Widely available techniques of home finance enable homeowners (and property investors) to magnify seemingly low rates of home appreciation into high returns with no significant long-term chance of loss.
- *Home equity wealth exceeds all other assets.* Even at the top of the late, great bull run in stocks, the overwhelming majority of homeowning Americans had built more wealth in their home equity than they owned in stocks. Contrary to Wall Street hype, homes

remain—and will continue to remain—the largest asset for most households.

- *Cost of financing.* Closing costs, interest expense, and mortgage balances remain the largest drain on household incomes and net worth.
- *Tax advantaged.* The tax advantages of home ownership far surpass those of any other asset. Tax deductibility of interest and closing costs; tax-free, cash-out refis; and tax-free capital gains provide huge tax advantages for homes over stocks. Remember, the IRS will eventually tax all of those 401(k) and IRA capital gains at ordinary (high) rates of taxation.
- *Boosting home equity gains.* When you own stocks, the fate of our hoped-for appreciation rests on the competent and trustworthy performance of CEOs and their acolytes. With homes, you can create value through productive property improvements and neighborhood upgrade.[1]
- *Bedrooms will buy groceries (and many other things).* After achieved, home equity wealth does not and need not remain idle (or "dead," as the stock enthusiasts like to say). You will be able to use it to increase your standard of living and quality of life in future years.

As you come to realize through the previous facts, you can see that the value of your home and the costs and amounts of your home financing will dramatically affect your future net worth. Accordingly, Americans must develop and practice the new rule of personal financial management. No longer can Americans depend exclusively on social security, company pensions, or so-called financial assets. They now must explicitly consider their homes as an investment account to be prudently and opportunistically managed just as any other investment. Your accumulated home equity will contribute significantly to your well-being in future years.

---

1. I thoroughly discuss these topics in my books on real estate investing. Also see my forthcoming book (Wiley, July 2003) which is tentatively titled *Make Money with Fixers, Rehabs, and Renovations.* Of course, not all home remodeling adds commensurate value to a property. My books, though, do focus on productive, value-creating improvements.

Living in and on the House

Let us count the ways that home equity can add to your well-being as we look into the future: live rent free; live rent free and collect an income for life; downsize tax free and invest the difference to supplement your income; create an accessory apartment; and operate a share-a-home or bed and breakfast.

Live Rent Free

When the financial press tells you not to count your home as an investment, they omit the number one reason to own a home free and clear—or even with a mortgage. Homeowners will never see another increase in rents. Read any news story about the plight of seniors who do not own their own homes. Nearly every one of these articles laments the financial trials these seniors must navigate to contend with the (denounced) greed of landlords.

In contrast, owners who accumulate large amounts of equity are, in effect, investing early to avoid future rent payments that will continue to go up. Even better, a relatively new type of mortgage called a reverse annuity mortgage (RAM) allows homeowners to not only live in their homes, but also to live on the house.

The Reverse Annuity Mortgage (RAM)

Nikki Wendt, a retired window, is a member of the house-rich generation. "I wanted to travel more, and I wanted to help my kids," says Mrs. Wendt, "but I couldn't do it. I had all this equity tied up in my house, but I couldn't do anything with it. It was like having a pile of money in the bank, but not being able to touch it."

Then Mrs. Wendt learned about a new type of home financing called the reverse annuity mortgage. The RAM differs from other types of refinancings because it doesn't need to be repaid until the borrowers die or eventually sell their homes.

Like Mrs. Wendt, many homeowning parents may be reluctant to borrow against their paid-off homes because they don't want the burden of making monthly payments again. The reverse annuity mortgage solves that problem. Under the RAM financing plan selected by Mrs.

Wendt, her lender agreed to pay her $900 per month for as long as she lives. From this $900 Mrs. Wendt gives $400 a month to her son, and she uses the other $500 a month to enjoy her life more. The extra $400 a month has helped Mrs. Wendt's son, his wife, and their two children to own their first home. With the extra $500 a month Mrs. Wendt spends on herself, she has taken a trip to Hawaii, paid for some surgery to improve her hearing, and remodeled her kitchen. "Everything is just wonderful now," reports Mrs. Wendt. "I'm not just getting by anymore—my reverse mortgage is providing me a new life. And it's given my son and grandchildren a new home."

A good source of information on reverse annuity mortgages is the booklet *Home-Made Money,* put out by the American Association of Retired Persons (AARP). To obtain a copy of this booklet, go to www.aarp.org/revmort/. Also, the FHA has begun to sponsor a variety of reverse annuity mortgage plans. Many older parents believe a RAM provides the best of two worlds: It permits parents to remain in their long-term home and improve their living standards, and it allows parents the opportunity to help their children buy a home now rather than wait for money they would otherwise inherit later.

Downsize Tax Free, Invest the Difference

As *Mortgage Secrets* has noted elsewhere, married homeowners now can realize up to $500,000 tax free when they sell their homes. Future homeowners who choose this alternative will be able to pay cash to right-size their housing and invest the net proceeds in an income-producing asset such as rental property, annuity, high-dividend-paying stocks, bonds, and so on.

Create an Accessory Apartment

Seniors who want to remain in their current home can generate income by creating an accessory apartment or a mother-in-law suite. Homeowners can use excess space to buy groceries. Of course, this possibility doesn't apply just to seniors. You can also use this technique to help build equity faster during the years that you're paying down the mortgage balance. A good variety of publications (cited earlier in this book) explain how to execute this income-generating idea.

Share-a-Home or Bed and Breakfast

Do you remember the Golden Girls television show? These senior women shared a home. Traditionally viewed as an affordability tactic of the young, housesharing actually cuts across all age groups. A firm in Florida called Tropical Village is now designing and building six-bedroom houses that are marketed specifically as senior share-a-homes. These houses are selling out and renting up almost as fast as the company can construct them.

Because we've broached the subject of television shows, do you also recall the Bob Newhart show where he had abandoned the rat race to open and operate a country inn? This, too, reflects an emerging trend, and you don't even need to move to the country. *The New York Times* reports:

> Increasingly, New York homes, from hi-tech lofts in Soho to Victorian brownstones in Brooklyn to prewar apartments in Queens, are being opened to travelers. Visitors are offered comfortable surroundings, continental breakfasts, and a whole new way to see New York: as paying houseguests of real New Yorkers, rather than simply as tourists.

Valerie Griffith, a freelance writer and consultant, has enjoyed her creative source of income. "It's been really wonderful," she says, "It's almost never empty. . . . We were cautious in the beginning, but in more than three years, we've never had a problem."

Or if a country inn/bed and breakfast (B&B) doesn't appeal to you, how about converting some excess space for use as a rental office or studio. Consider this ad that ran in a Berkeley, CA, newspaper:

> Beautifully converted large garage. Very quiet. Large skylights. Windows looking out to a Japanese garden. Excellent workspace for writer or artist. $650 per month. Call 765–4321.

I telephoned the day after this ad first appeared. The owner had already rented the space.

Home Financing: A Means to an End

Most homebuyers believe that home financing exists to help them buy a home. In coming to this conclusion, they're only right by half. When used productively, home financing actually helps you achieve another important goal: accumulating a higher net worth through home equity. Yes, buy and finance a home to obtain that "comfortable place to live," but keep in mind, too, the home(s) you buy, the mortgage type(s) and amount(s) you choose, and the costs and interest you pay throughout your life can add (or subtract) hundreds of thousands of dollars to (from) your future financial well-being.

I truly hope that *Mortgage Secrets* has provided you with insights and knowledge that will help you achieve and enjoy a more prosperous life.

Index

Accessory apartment, 44–45, 266–267
Adjustable rate mortgages, 79–104
Affordability, 4–6, 18
Appraised value, 205–210
Appreciation, 234–235
APR, 101–103, 197
ARM caps, 99–100
ARM hybrids, 56–59
ARM index, 94–97
ARM margin, 98–99
Assumable loan, 60–65, 85–88, 203–205

Bait and switch, 215–216
Balloon mortgage, 161–162
Bankruptcy, 124–125
Bi-weekly baloney, 248–249
Bruss, Robert, 39, 78, 153, 166
Builder incentives, 71–72
Buydowns, 70–71

Capacity, 108–109
Capital gain exclusion, 17–18, 266
Character, 107–108
Closing costs, 197–198
Co-borrower, 36–38
Collateral, 109–110
Community lending, 139–140
Compensating factors, 31–33
Contract rates, 93–94
Contract shock, 93–94
Contract-for-deed, 162–165
Convertible ARMs, 100–101
Co-owner, 36–38
Cosigner, 36–38
Credit blemishes, 212–213
Credit counseling, 121–124
Credit profile, 105–106
Credit repairs, 121–122
Credit reports, 114, 118
Credit scores, 30, 111–122

Debt, 29–30
Debt management, 123–124
Dialing for dollars, 47, 211
Discrimination, 214
Diversification, 237–238
Double counting, 126–127
Down payment assistance, 144–145
Due diligence, 171–174
Due on sale, 62–63

Employer assistance, 67–68
Equity build-up, 7, 41, 50–51, 240–243

Equity sharing, 38
Escrow accounts, 254–255

FHA loans, 130–137
FICO score, 114–118
Foreclosures, 177–185
Foreclosure workout, 174–175, 260–261

Garbage fees, 194–195, 228
Good faith estimate, 195–197
Graduated payment loan, 82–83

Habitat for Humanity, 142
Home equity, 236–237
Home equity loans, 256–259
Home equity wealth, 263–264
Housemates, 42–43
Housing "bubble," 231–233
Housing cost ratio, 22–23
HUD homes, 155, 179–180

Income tax break, 17–18, 266
Income tax deductions, 75–78
Inflation, 88–90
Installment sale, 162–165

Jumbo loans, 72–73

Land contract, 162–165
Lease option, 165–168
Lease purchase, 167–170
Loan application, 35–36
Loan status, 46–47

"Market rate," 221–222
Market value, 205–210
Money management, 11–13
Mortgage bonds, 57–58
Mortgage credit certificate, 66–67
Mortgage index, 94–97
Mortgage insurance, 146–148, 152
Mortgage insurance refunds, 251–253
Mortgage points, 69–71
Mortgage referrals, x

No-cost mortgage, 198–200
Nominal interest rates, 89
Nothing down, 129–130

Owner will carry, 153–154

Payment shock, 82, 90
Pledged collateral, 149–150
Portfolio lender, 20
Possibility thinking, 6
Preapproval, 1–3
Predatory lending, 192–193
Prepayment, 200–202, 213–214, 249
Prequalification, 1–3

Qualifying income, 25–27
Qualifying ratios, 22–25

Rate lock, 216–218
Rate quotes, 47–48, 215

Rate sheet, 199
Real interest rates, 88–90
Refi blend, 159
Refinance, 239–240, 242–244
Rental properties, 39–40, 74–75, 244–245
REOs, 186
Reverse annuity mortgage, 265–266
Risk (real estate), 247
Risk-based pricing, 105–106, 146–148

Second mortgage, 148–149
Self-talk, 10–11
Seller financing, 153–154
Seller second, 160
Speculation, 210
Stock market, 231, 235–236, 245–247
Stop Renting Now!, xiii, 38
Streamline refi, 243–244
Subject to, 63–65
Sub-prime mortgage, 192

Teaser rates, 91–93
Total debt ratio, 24–25
Trailing spouse, 26
Tricks of the trade, 225–226

Upfront mortgage broker, 222–223

VA loans, 137–138
Verifications, 34
Volatility, 238–239

Wealth building, 6–8
Wraparound, 170–171

Yield-spread premium, 211–212